The White House in Mourning

The White House in Mourning

Deaths and Funerals of Presidents in Office

MARTIN S. NOWAK

McFarland & Company, Inc., Publishers
Jefferson, North Carolina, and London

LIBRARY OF CONGRESS CATALOGUING-IN-PUBLICATION DATA

Nowak, Martin S., 1951–
 The White House in mourning : deaths and funerals of presidents in office / Martin S. Nowak.
     p.   cm.
 Includes bibliographical references and index.

 ISBN 978-0-7864-4775-6
 softcover : 50# alkaline paper ∞

 1. Presidents—United States—Death. 2. Presidents—United States—Biography. 3. White House (Washington, D.C.)—History. 4. Funeral rites and ceremonies—United States—History. 5. United States—Social life and customs. I. Title.
 E176.1.N78   2010
 973.09'9—dc22   2010012885

British Library cataloguing data are available

©2010 Martin S. Nowak. All rights reserved

No part of this book may be reproduced or transmitted in any form or by any means, electronic or mechanical, including photocopying or recording, or by any information storage and retrieval system, without permission in writing from the publisher.

On the cover: The caisson bearing the flag-draped casket of assassinated president John F. Kennedy pauses in front of the U.S. Capitol in Washington, D.C., en route to the grave site at Arlington National Cemetery on Nov. 25, 1963. (AP Photo)

Manufactured in the United States of America

McFarland & Company, Inc., Publishers
 Box 611, Jefferson, North Carolina 28640
  www.mcfarlandpub.com

To my parents,
John and Emily Nowak

Acknowledgments

First of all, I want to thank my parents, John and Emily Nowak, without whom I would be nothing.

Of course, many organizations and institutions assisted me, and I am grateful to their librarians, archivists and staff. They include: Buffalo and Erie County Historical Society, Buffalo and Erie County Public Library system, State University of New York at Buffalo libraries, E.H. Butler Library at the State University College at Buffalo, Dallas County Historical Commission, Sixth Floor Museum in Dallas, Dallas Public Library, University of Texas at Arlington Library, Southern Methodist University Library, Texas Christian University Library, and the John F. Kennedy and Franklin D. Roosevelt presidential libraries.

For IT help in taming the computer monster, I am indebted to Daniel Blachaniec and Raymond Grabowski. Also, many thanks to Mark Kohan of the *Polish American Journal* and John Conlin of Western New York Heritage Press for their faith in me as a beginning writer. Everyone needs a teacher, and I am particularly grateful to three of them who have made an impact on my life: my sixth grade teacher, Ruth McRobert; my high school American history teacher, Dr. Charles W. Stein; and my Polish language teacher, Pani Lucyna Dziedzic.

For inspiration, tea and sympathy, I wish to thank the following: the late Michael Drabik, Linda Grabowski, Carol Grohmann, Kevin Kaczmarek, Charles T. Kowal, James J. Kilpatrick, Linda Nelson, David and Lynne Nowak, David Ruda, Kyle Paschen, John I. Riggs, Christine (Bunny) and Edward Wells, and Nancy Wujek. Also, the Pietrzak family, the Ruhland crew, and the boys at Tuesday night basketball.

And most of all, I would like to thank the most important person in my life for the past thirty years, my partner and special friend Lawrence Grabowski, who served as my research assistant and sometime chauffeur, and had the patience to tolerate my many long hours of research and writing.

Contents

Acknowledgments	vii
Preface	1
Introduction	3
1 — Keeping the President Safe	15
2 — William Henry Harrison	29
3 — Zachary Taylor	46
4 — Abraham Lincoln	58
5 — James Abram Garfield	95
6 — William McKinley	122
7 — Warren Gamaliel Harding	149
8 — Franklin Delano Roosevelt	169
9 — John Fitzgerald Kennedy	189
Appendix — Laws and Regulations	213
Notes	229
Bibliography	237
Index	243

Preface

My parents gave me my first book about the presidents when I was a mere eight years old, and I became fascinated with their lives and times. The first president I ever saw in person was John F. Kennedy at the Pulaski Day parade in Buffalo when I was eleven. After his assassination I became interested in the other presidents who had died in office and the national pageants of grief that followed.

This work took decades to make the journey from conception to reality. It is the result of painstaking reading and research. It draws primarily from period newspapers and magazines.

Biographies about the eight U.S. presidents who have died in office usually contain an account of their deaths and funerals, but, understandably, only as a sort of brief addendum or afterthought, a tidy finish to the man's life and presidency. To be sure, entire books have been written about, or relate to, the deaths of our four assassinated presidents, especially those of Abraham Lincoln and John F. Kennedy. Likewise, whole books have been authored about the funerals of Lincoln and Kennedy. What has not existed is one work that covers the deaths and funerals of all eight presidents who have died in office. *The White House in Mourning* fills that void on the history shelves.

This work, out of necessity, does not contain each and every detail of the events. Such a work would encompass thousands of pages. For those who want more exhaustive treatments of individual presidents' deaths and funerals, I point them to the bibliography, which lists many excellent sources for further study.

Some of the facts presented here can be challenged as to accuracy and debated due to differing versions of the same event. Eyewitness and earwitness accounts regarding a traumatic event, such as the death of a president, can be unreliable. Often, each witness recalls the facts differently, or they are heard or interpreted in another way. In cases where the facts presented by different sources varied, I used my judgment, deductive reasoning and consideration of the source. The conclusions I reached and any outright mistakes of fact are solely my own.

The deaths of all eight of these men are among the saddest and most emotional events to have occurred in the history of America. May they never be repeated.

Introduction

Throughout history the leaders of society have elicited extremes of emotion: respect and contempt, praise and ridicule, love and hate. They attract our constant attention and serve as lightning rods for us. When things go wrong they get the blame. When things go right they receive the credit. Unfortunately, some who disagree with our leaders attempt to remove those persons from their positions not through legal or peaceful means, but through violence. In American history, four of the persons who have served as president of the United States have been removed from office by an assassin's bullet. Despite the realization that our presidents need to be safeguarded from those people bent on physically harming them, protection of the president has at times been inadequate; and even when adequate, such protection can only go so far in a free society. Politicians, including our presidents, want the opportunity to meet and mingle with the people, if for no other reason than to curry an image that they are one of us, that they are not shut behind the proverbial castle wall, out of touch with their constituents, and that they will meet with and listen to the citizenry. Our presidents cannot be sealed off from the people. Neither they nor we want that. Like anything else, protection of and access to the president is a delicate balancing act.

Disease and injury are also dangers to the well-being of the president. Four of the eight presidents who died in office succumbed to illness—from pneumonia, gastroenteritis, heart disease and stroke.

Our early presidents were not, for the most part, provided round-the-clock medical care at the expense of the federal government. Things were much more democratic then. As any citizen, he was expected to pay for his own medical care and seek help on his own when needed. Granted, our presidents were able to secure the best care available, but it must be remembered that medicine in the late eighteenth and throughout most of the nineteenth century was still in the relative dark ages. Rapid progress in the field really began about the turn of the twentieth century. Before then, the presence or absence of medical professionals usually made little difference in curing an illness or extending life. In some cases the medically established practices made the situation worse for the patient. Before we criticize the medical care that our early presidents received, we must temper such criticisms by remembering the type of care available at the time these men lived and died. A hundred years from now, people will look back at today's medical practices quite incredulously and wonder how we ever survived with these primitive ideas.

It has been speculated that three of the presidents who died of natural causes — William Henry Harrison (of pneumonia in 1841), Zachary Taylor (of gastroenteritis in 1850), and Warren G. Harding (of heart disease in 1923) — were murdered and died quite unnatural deaths.

Harrison died in office on April 4, 1841, just one month after taking the oath as ninth president. Death was attributed to pneumonia contracted after the 67-year-old gave a long inaugural speech in the cold rain. But soon after his death, rumors began circulating that he was murdered, poisoned by his political enemies. When his coffin was opened one last time before being deposited in its crypt in Ohio, witnesses reportedly told of Harrison's face being swollen and black. Supposedly, only poison would have brought about such a result.[1] Southerners in Washington were the alleged culprits. The impetus? President Harrison was from the North, the non-slave state of Indiana, and could not be trusted to respect Southern interests. He was succeeded in office by John Tyler, a slave-holding Southerner who believed in preserving the "peculiar institution" of slavery.

After Zachary Taylor's death in 1850, stories began making the rounds that he, too, had been poisoned. His death was attributed to cholera morbus, but most likely was due to gastroenteritis, possibly the result of contaminated food or drink. Skeptics pointed out that the rugged president, a career soldier known as "Old Rough and Ready," who was in apparent good health, was not likely to become deathly ill after merely eating and drinking — unless something toxic had deliberately been added to the food or drink.[2] Again, conspiracists pointed to President Taylor's Southern political enemies. Though a Southerner and slaveholder himself, Taylor was opposed to the extension of slavery. This raised the ire of the pro-slavery factions, it was said, resulting in the successful plot to poison the president.

Those who believed in this scenario pointed out that Taylor's successor, Millard Fillmore of upstate New York, turned out to be more favorable to slave-holding interests by signing into law the Compromise of 1850. This series of laws was seen as largely pro-slavery. However, in 1991, at the urging of an author who had written a book supporting the poisoning theory, and with the acquiescence of Zachary Taylor's descendants, the president's body was exhumed from its resting place in Zachary Taylor National Cemetery in Kentucky. The remains were taken to a laboratory, where hair and fingernail samples were tested. The results showed that the president had *not* been poisoned.

Warren G. Harding died in San Francisco on August 3, 1923, after a grueling tour of the western states and Alaska. He had a history of habits that promoted heart disease and died in his hotel room. The official cause of death was listed as "stroke of apoplexy," but rumors began not long afterwards. His wife, Florence, was implicated in the death by these scandalmongers. It was said that she had poisoned her husband in order to spare him the agony of facing the serious scandals in his administration that were coming to light at the time. Another good reason she had to poison him, it was said, was his womanizing. Some even claimed that he had fathered a child by another woman and had had affairs while president. The fact that Harding died while he was alone with Mrs. Harding, and that she refused to allow an autopsy to be performed, added fuel to the fire. Some even claimed that she murdered one of the president's attending physicians who later discovered the supposed truth.[3]

As for Franklin D. Roosevelt, only the Soviet dictator Josef Stalin thought that he had been poisoned. He intimated that he thought Winston Churchill had murdered the president. These were obviously the unfounded assertions of a paranoid, homicidal dictator.

None of the poisoning allegations about any of the presidents have been proven true.

Four of the eight presidents who died in office were murdered by the use of firearms—Abraham Lincoln, James A. Garfield, William McKinley and John F. Kennedy. Only Garfield's death failed to spawn conspiracy theories. President Garfield was shot by a deranged gunman, Charles J. Guiteau, in July 1881 as he walked through a Washington train station. He died two and a half months later of his wounds.

After Abraham Lincoln was shot in Ford's Theatre in Washington in April 1865, conspiracy was immediately suspected. Lincoln had been shot by the actor John Wilkes Booth, a Confederate sympathizer, just a few days after General Robert E. Lee had surrendered to Union forces, essentially ending the Civil War. All Southern forces had not yet capitulated, and pockets of resistance still existed. The Union government was wary of a resurgence in hostilities. After Booth killed Lincoln it was generally believed that the gunman had acted as an agent of the Confederate government, and that the murder of the president would serve as a catalyst for a renewed fight by the South against the government in Washington. That did not happen, for Southerners were defeated and war-weary, with no inclination to resume the fight. In fact, most Southerners condemned Booth's action.

A conspiracy had indeed existed against the president, but it did not involve the Confederacy. At first there was a plan put together by Booth to kidnap Lincoln. But Booth changed his plans to kill Lincoln instead, and only two fellow plotters were aware of this change. The idea that a Confederate government conspiracy was responsible for the assassination was never proved, although it was believed by the highest authorities in the federal government.

Another prominent conspiracy theory in the death of Abraham Lincoln involved Secretary of War Edwin Stanton. Suspicion fell upon him because Booth's assassination plot also involved plans to kill Vice President Andrew Johnson and Secretary of State William Seward. Johnson's assigned assailant never followed through, and Secretary Seward survived a vicious knife attack. No one has ever been able to tie Stanton to the murder of President Lincoln, but if Johnson and Seward had died, Stanton would have been president under the laws of succession to the presidency in force at the time.

President William McKinley was shot to death in 1901 in Buffalo by a mentally disturbed young man. Leon Czolgosz fancied himself an anarchist. The anarchist movement at the turn of the twentieth century was akin to communism in the mid-twentieth century or terrorism in the twenty-first century. It was the scourge of western civilization. Anarchists believed that governments were evil and those who ran them were enemies of the common people. Many believed that heads of state should be removed from their positions of power through violent means. Before McKinley was killed, anarchists had been responsible for other assassinations of national leaders around the world. Between 1894 and 1900, anarchists murdered the president of France, the premier of Spain, the empress of Austria, and the king of Italy.[4]

Czolgosz attended some anarchist meetings and read their literature. But even the anarchists could see that something was strange about him. Many of them believed that he was a government infiltrator and did not trust him at all.

After McKinley was shot, Czolgosz's connection to anarchism was uncovered, and several prominent anarchists were arrested and interrogated. But while the assassin's confused mind may have been influenced by them, no anarchist conspiracy, or any kind of conspiracy, was ever discovered.

The tragic death of John F. Kennedy in Dallas on November 22, 1963, stunned the nation. A suspect was arrested for the president's murder that same day. Lee Harvey Oswald was a young man with a strange background. He was a U.S. Marine veteran who, apparently disenchanted with America, moved to the communist USSR after he was discharged, married a Russian girl and started a family there. Disillusioned by life under Soviet communism, he returned to the United States. He was an apparent supporter of Fidel Castro's Cuba.

While he was in police custody for Kennedy's murder, he himself was shot to death by a nightclub owner with underworld crime connections. Conspiracy theories in this case began the day of the crime, when Oswald's Russian-Cuban connection was revealed. Was he working as an agent of the communist Soviet or Cuban governments? After he was killed, it was widely believed that he was murdered to shut him up. Thus, a conspiracy theory involving mob bosses was born. The Warren Commission Report, the government's official investigation into the assassination of President Kennedy, found that Oswald, acting alone, killed the president, and that no conspiracy existed.[5]

But the Warren Report was questioned from the start as a flawed, hurried and incomplete investigation. Allegations of a government cover-up arose. Conspiracy theorists' new ideas now involved the Central Intelligence Agency, Federal Bureau of Investigation, Dallas police and others. Over the years, hundreds of conspiracy theories have been put forth concerning the Kennedy assassination. None has ever been proved. But neither has the idea that Oswald acted alone been proved. A House of Representatives investigation in the late 1970s threw further doubt on the Warren Commission's findings and came to its own muddled conclusion that Oswald probably shot the president but did not act alone, and that an unknown conspiracy existed. In the end, the truth about the Kennedy assassination, and who was and was not involved, may never be known. It will forever be the subject of controversy and skepticism. Kennedy's death remains the most puzzling of any of the eight presidential deaths, and the only one that could have possibly involved a major conspiracy.

The eight presidential successions that took place upon the death of the incumbent occurred rather seamlessly and orderly, once a precedent was established. That precedent fell upon John Tyler, the first man to succeed to the presidency upon the death of his predecessor, William Henry Harrison in 1841.

When he received word that Harrison had died, Vice President Tyler hurried to Washington from his Virginia home, took the presidential oath of office and became the tenth president of the United States. Despite many protestations over many weeks, Tyler insisted that he had indeed become president to complete Harrison's term, with the full powers of the office, and was not merely acting president until a new president could be chosen.

The wording of the Constitution was not clear on that point, and there were no survivors of the Constitutional Convention debates to consult on the matter. As it turned out, it was the intent of the framers that he should have been merely an acting president. This was revealed when James Madison's notes on the Constitution were made public years later. But in 1841, because Tyler had the courage to insist that he had assumed the office of president and not merely its duties temporarily, we have inherited his legacy, which has since been clarified by Constitutional Amendment.[6] John Tyler is often reviled as a slaveholder, supporter of slavery, and Confederate officeholder. Yet it can be said that our history and the functioning of our government would be quite different today had he acquiesced to his critics and accepted the idea that he was only a temporary, caretaker chief executive.

When in 1850 President Zachary Taylor died in office, the succession to President Millard Fillmore came wholly without dispute. The Harrison-Tyler precedent of nine years earlier was followed. And so it went each time a president died in office. The presidency has changed hands those eight times in an orderly manner, established by precedent and backed by rule of law.

These transitions of power usually brought forth statements from the new president that he would continue the policies of his predecessor. In reality, few did so. Each successor was not a carbon copy of the man he succeeded. Each had his own personality and his own political ideas and biases, even if from the same political party. Nothing bound him to the policies and practices of his predecessor if not enshrined in law.

Spurred by the formation of political parties in the early United Sates, the Twelfth Amendment to the Constitution all but assured that members of the same party would be elected as president and vice president. This seemingly removed an incentive to remove the president from office in order to drastically change policies, whether by impeachment, forced resignation, or murder, because the vice president who would succeed him would most likely be from the same party.

Before the Twelfth Amendment, the person receiving the greatest number of electoral votes in a presidential election became president. The second highest vote-getter became vice president. The new Amendment ordered that the president and vice president were to be elected separately. In theory, the president and vice president might still be from different political parties, but states began linking the two candidates on their ballots; and even in states that allowed separate votes for president and vice president, voters were likely to vote for the candidates from the same party.

Reality has a way of intruding upon theory. When William Henry Harrison and John Tyler were elected to the presidency and vice presidency, respectively, in 1841, both were members of the Whig Party. But Tyler was a lifelong Democrat who had a falling out with party leader Andrew Jackson and so had accepted the Whig nomination for vice president when that party sought a Southerner who would appeal to Democrats and balance the ticket. The Whigs expected Tyler to languish harmlessly in the vice presidency for four years as they went about running the country in their own fashion. Only in their wildest nightmares did they foresee their president dying in office and being succeeded by Tyler.

When that event did occur, the Whigs were devastated. President Tyler began running his office as a Democrat, appointing Democrats to office and adopting Democratic policies. The Whigs disowned him, and the Democrats distrusted him for abandoning their party.

Nine years later, when Millard Fillmore became president upon Zachary Taylor's death, both men were true Whigs. Yet Fillmore signed into law the Compromise of 1850, something that Taylor would not have done. Taylor was that strange breed of slave owner who was opposed to its extension. He hoped that during his administration he could once and for all solve the North-South division. Fillmore, on the other hand, was a Northerner who favored the Compromise in the hope that it would prevent civil war over the slavery issue.

When Lincoln was assassinated he was succeeded by Andrew Johnson. Lincoln was a Republican from the North, and Johnson a Democrat from Tennessee who had remained loyal to the Union. Lincoln and the Republican Party, hoping for a display of unity late in the Civil War years, chose Democrat Johnson as the vice presidential candidate in 1864 and temporarily renamed the ticket the National Union Party. As in 1841, Johnson, a lifelong Democrat, succeeded to the presidency upon the death of an incumbent from a different political party. Though the transition of power went smoothly at first, Johnson was disrespected and even hated by Lincoln administration officials. He pledged to carry out Lincoln's post-war policies but was opposed at every turn by the Republicans in his administration and in Congress.

Finally, in 1868 he was impeached by the radical Republican-controlled House of Representatives. In dramatic fashion, he retained his presidency by one vote in the Senate, which acted as jury in his impeachment trial. The whole impeachment matter had been a politically motivated exercise from the start, for President Johnson had committed no impeachable offense. He went on to serve out Lincoln's second term at a most critical time in our nation's history. He had become president before the Civil War had been fully brought to a conclusion and when Reconstruction policies had to be put into place. The stamp of the Executive Branch was put forth not by Abraham Lincoln, as had been expected, but by Andrew Johnson.

In 1881 the assassination of President James A. Garfield resulted in the accession to office of Chester A. Arthur. Though both men were Republicans, they came from different wings of the party. Arthur was a conservative who favored the status quo, warts and all, and had a reputation for being a "good old boy" politician. He had flirted with scandal, was favored by big money interests and was considered dishonest. Many feared a corrupt presidency. But to everyone's surprise, President Arthur turned out to be honest and incorruptible, and, in fact, became a reformer, championing changes in the spoils system and implementing legislation which was the beginning of the modern civil service system. Garfield had been murdered by a man seeking appointment to a federal position.

When Theodore Roosevelt succeeded President William McKinley in 1901, he promptly promised to carry out the policies of his predecessor. That was a very hollow promise. As in the 1881 transition, McKinley and Roosevelt were from different factions of the Republican Party. McKinley was the conservative and Roosevelt a progressive liberal. The young new president was an activist reformer who pushed through significant changes in the federal government, championing reform that favored the little man. He could not have been more different than staid old McKinley in either politics or personality. While the changes that occurred during the Roosevelt presidency were inevitable, they probably came about at least a decade earlier than if he had not become president when he did.

The death of President Harding in 1923 may have saved him from being impeached, and at the very least from being thoroughly disgraced and discredited as a politician and president. At the time of his death the scandals occurring in his administration were just beginning to come to light. The cronies he had appointed to some of the highest offices in the federal government were being discovered to be thieves and liars using their positions to defraud the United States.

Harding's successor, Calvin Coolidge, was untouched by the scandals. "Silent Cal" was a quiet, unassuming man who trusted the country to run itself without government interference. And America trusted Calvin Coolidge. He was very popular, and the stench of scandal was soon left behind.

On April 12, 1945, World War II was nearing its end in Europe. In the Pacific, Japan was still far from being defeated. On that day, Harry S Truman took the oath of office as thirty-third president of the United States. President Franklin D. Roosevelt had just died.

Not only was the war not over, the shape of the post-war world was nowhere near settled. At this uncertain, extremely critical time, Truman inherited a huge burden. What's more, as vice president, Truman had been kept in the dark on all the issues. He never attended any meetings, never received position papers or policy briefings from the president. He had no idea what specific policies Roosevelt was pursuing or proposing until briefed by administration officials when he became president. He did not even know that the United States possessed an atomic bomb. Truman had to be a quick study, and thankfully he was. It did not hurt that politicians of both major political parties, as well as the American people, fell solidly behind him. A skilled, no-nonsense negotiator, the new president brought the war to a successful conclusion and followed up with a solid post-war recovery plan. Politically, he and Roosevelt were not much different from each other; had Roosevelt lived, he may have acted much the same as Truman did.

John F. Kennedy also died in office at a very crucial time in American history. The Cold War between the democratic Western world and the communist East was at its height. Just a year before he died in 1963, Kennedy had faced down Soviet premier Nikita Khrushchev in the Cuban missile crisis. The world had come close to the brink of nuclear war, and tensions still ran high when the president was murdered.

Immediately after Kennedy was shot, no one knew for sure what was happening. Was it the communists? Was it a domestic coup d'etat? When the alleged assassin was apprehended a few hours later, his pro-communist background seemed to point to Russian-Cuban involvement.

Fortunately, the reins of government had been secured in a confident, self-assured manner by Vice President Lyndon B. Johnson. Johnson was probably the most well-informed vice president in our nation's history up to that time. President Kennedy had made him privy to administration debate and functions. The new president's strong demeanor and leadership qualities, forged through thirty years in the political arena, began to put the nation at ease.

President Johnson was able to successfully push legislation through Congress that Kennedy had proposed. But Johnson, who had resented Kennedy's popularity, made one of the biggest blunders in American political history when he needlessly involved the United States in the Viet Nam War under false pretenses. His popularity plummeted as he committed more and more young Americans to service in Viet Nam, 58,000 of whom would ultimately not return alive. American cities broke out in racial conflict. One can only wonder what would have happened had Kennedy not been assassinated.

The funerals of each of the presidents who have died in office have been national pageants. The deaths of these men have elicited feelings of shock and sadness. The funeral of President Harrison set the tone in both private and public mourning. In keeping with the tenor of the times and the circumstances, the ceremonies varied somewhat in style, intensity and length.

Early on, the vice president was officially notified by the president's cabinet of his death. Orders to the military were sent, usually by the secretaries of War and Navy, informing them of the death and the fact that they now had a new Commander-in-Chief, and instructing them to observe traditional military mourning procedures. Flags were lowered to half-staff, continuing a mourning custom first recorded in 1612 in Britain, but which probably dates from medieval times in Europe. The White House and many other buildings in Washington, both public and private, were draped in black mourning cloth. Plans were made by officials in consultation with the family of the deceased president. Government offices, as well as private businesses, were often closed on the day of the death, as well as the day of the funeral. An official day of mourning was declared by the new president, most often designated as the day of the burial ceremony. Obsequies were held in many cities and towns throughout the U.S.

Each of the men who died in office has had a Christian religious ceremony performed at his funeral, but only two—McKinley and Kennedy—had their bodies taken to a church. All except Garfield had their bodies laid out in the East Room of the White House. Five of the eight lay in state in the Capitol Rotunda. Only Harrison, Taylor and Roosevelt did not. Public viewing of the coffin varied. It was allowed in each case except Roosevelt's. For Harrison, it was in a White House entrance hallway. The public was allowed into the East Room to view the Taylor and Lincoln caskets, and into the Rotunda for the five who lay there. In addition, there was a public viewing of Garfield's remains at the house in which he died in New Jersey, as well as in the main square in downtown Cleveland.

McKinley's body was laid out in Buffalo City Hall and the Canton Courthouse, and Harding's in a Marion, Ohio, house. Lincoln's body was displayed not only in the East Room and the Capitol Rotunda, but in twelve other cities as his funeral train made its way from Washington to its burial site in Springfield, Illinois.

Open coffin viewing by the public was allowed in each case except Roosevelt's and Kennedy's, though Harrison's, Taylor's and Harding's were through a glass covering.

Seven of the eight who died in office were interred in or near their home towns. John F. Kennedy, who was from Massachusetts, was buried in Arlington National Cemetery in Virginia. The bodies of all except Roosevelt were eventually reinterred in new locations, most near their original resting places. Abraham Lincoln was moved many times, and one attempt was made to steal his body.

Today they all rest in grandiose tombs befitting a president of the United States—except for FDR, whose grave in the rose garden near his home is marked only by a large granite block. The grave of Warren G. Harding is probably the most aesthetically appealing of *any* president's, whether they died in office or not.

It is a fact that every man chosen to be president in the general election in years evenly divisible by twenty, from 1840 to 1960, has died in office. Over the course of the years, this strange coincidence came to be known as the Curse of Tippecanoe, Tecumseh's Curse, the Twenty Year Curse, the Zero Year Curse, or the Presidential Curse. The origin or origins of the curse stories are unclear, although it would not have taken long for people to notice the coincidence of the deaths. It reportedly first surfaced in print in a Ripley's Believe It or Not book published in 1934, with no mention of a curse.[7]

The curse stories probably originated as folk tales to explain the seemingly unexplainable. The usual story is that the Shawnee Indian Chief Tecumseh, or his half-brother Tenskwatawa, known as the Prophet, leveled the curse. Supposedly, after general and future president William Henry Harrison defeated the Shawnees at the Battle of Tippecanoe, Indiana, in 1811, Tecumseh proclaimed that if Harrison should be chosen as the "Great White Chief" he would die in office. The other version has Tenskwatawa uttering the curse in revenge for his brother's death at the hands of the white man in 1813. No first-hand evidence of either man having pronounced the curse has ever been found.[8]

Some astrologers contend that the conjunction of the planets Jupiter and Saturn foretold the demise of the eight presidents who have died in office.[9]

But did the curse finally end after Ronald Reagan was elected in 1980 and survived his two terms in office? And was the end of it reaffirmed after George W. Bush, elected in 2000, outlived his time in the White House? The mysteries of astrology supposedly can explain these exceptions. And proponents of the Curse of Tippecanoe claim that the hex is merely asleep. Reagan survived an assassination attempt, they point out, that would have killed him except for modern medicine. As for Bush, well, they say he was not actually chosen president in the 2000 general election; Albert Gore received the most popular votes nationwide. But the electoral college officially elected George W. Bush president when that body met in 2001. So is it over? Stay tuned to the election of 2020 and that president's tenure in office.

For more than a century the demise of a sitting president was a regular, common occurrence in America. Looking back, one wonders how this country survived it all, but survive it did. It even thrived. The eight presidential deaths happened from 1841 to 1963, a period of 123 years. Almost one of every three chief executives died in office during that period, at a rate of one every fifteen years.

As an example, let us take someone who was born on January 1, 1830. In 1841, at the age of 11, he would have been fully aware of the death of President Harrison, and even somewhat conscious of its consequences. In 1850 he would have been a young man of 20 when Zachary Taylor died in office, and 35 when President Lincoln was killed. The assassination of James A. Garfield in 1881 occurred during his middle age, and that of William McKinley when he was 71. And if by chance he was lucky enough to live into his 93rd year, he would have received news of the death of President Harding.

Most Americans alive today cannot remember the death of a sitting President of the United States during their lifetimes. The baby boom generation, as children, lived through the gut-wrenching experience of the assassination of President Kennedy, which ushered in two decades of violence that they would witness and that would profoundly affect their lives. In 1965, Malcolm X, revered by many African Americans, was brutally murdered. In 1968 it was Martin Luther King, Jr. Then two months later Senator Robert F. Kennedy, younger brother of JFK, was gunned down while running for his party's nomination for president. These occurred against the backdrop of American involvement in the Viet Nam War and racial strife in our cities. In 1972, George Wallace, Democratic candidate for his party's presidential nomination, was seriously wounded by a gunman. Three years later, President Gerald R. Ford survived two assassination attempts. In 1978 the mayor of San Francisco and a city councilman were shot and killed by a political rival. In 1980, entertainer and political activist John Lennon was shot to death. The 1981 shooting of President Reagan seemed to bring an end to the mad orgy of violence in this country, but St. John Paul the Great, the Roman Catholic pope and spiritual leader of millions of Americans, was shot in an attempt on his life less than two months later in Vatican City.

CHAPTER 1

Keeping the President Safe

In the early years of the American republic, not much attention was paid to the safety and well-being of the president of the United States. To be sure, the drafters of the Constitution in 1787 were well aware of the possibility that a president could die in office. Hence the final version of that document included in Article II, Section 1 a short provision to cover that dire circumstance and provide for a peaceful and orderly transfer of power:

> In the case of the removal of the president from office, or of his death, resignation, or inability to discharge the powers and duties of the said office, the same shall devolve on the vice-president, and the Congress may provide for the case of removal, death, resignation or inability, both of the president and vice-president, declaring what officer shall then act as president, and such officer shall act accordingly, until the disability be removed, or a president be elected.

There was to be no royal family or pseudo-monarchy in America, no right of the eldest son to succeed his father as head of state and government, no army to step in and usurp authority.

In 1792, Congress resolved the issue of who should follow in line to the presidency after the vice president by passing the first Presidential Succession Act. It specified that the president pro tempore of the U.S. Senate would be next, followed by the speaker of the House of Representatives. This law remained in effect until the Presidential Succession Act of 1886. It provided that, following the vice president, the order of succession would be the cabinet officers in order of the creation of their respective departments: state, treasury, war, attorney general, postmaster general and interior. The old law was changed out of concern for the fact that when Congress was not in session, the positions of president pro tem and speaker were vacant, and there would technically be no one under the law to succeed to the presidency should something happen to both the president and vice president.

In 1947 a new Presidential Succession Act was signed into law by President Harry S Truman, who favored an elected member of Congress be next in line of succession after the vice president, because that person was democratically elected. It specified that the speaker of the House would follow, then the president pro tem of the Senate, then the cabinet officers.

Though a line of succession was established, for almost two centuries no real plan existed in the executive branch as to what protocol should be followed if the worst should happen. If the president dies, what then? What legalities had to be followed? Who needed to be informed and by whom? What about funeral plans and obsequies for the deceased chief executive? Who does what first? Each of the eight times a death occurred, officials groped for answers, trying to follow precedents established in previous tragedies — if they could find them.

After President Reagan was shot in March 1981, administration officials realized that they were not really prepared for such a crisis situation. But Reagan's legal team had already been preparing an emergency book, which was eventually completed, that covered every possible scenario involving the president's health and well-being, including his possible death, with a step-by-step guide detailing exactly what is to be done and by whom. The book was designed to be passed from president to president as administrations changed, and as far as is known, that has been done. The book exists today, with a copy in possession of key government officials in the White House.[1]

In the opening decades of our constitutional government, the greater danger to the safety of our presidents came not from assaults on their persons by others wishing to do them harm, but from disease. Medicine was still in the relative dark ages, and comparatively little was known then about the causes of disease, how to prevent their spread, and how to effectively treat the victims. Sanitation was rudimentary, and antiseptic procedures were unknown.

Concerning protection of the president from assault, in the early days of the nation there was remarkably little concern over the safety of presidents, and few measures were taken to protect them. They were at times the objects of abuse and the recipients of threats, as has always been the case, but they did not take the threats seriously and moved about freely without protection.[2]

In the history of the United States, four presidents have been assassinated—from 1865 to 1963. Attempts were also made on the lives of six other presidents, one president-elect and one former president running for president in the general election. In addition, one person campaigning for a major political party's presidential nomination was murdered, and another grievously wounded in an assassination attempt. Over the years, numerous plots to attack the president, president-elect, ex-presidents and presidential candidates have been uncovered and stopped by authorities.

Attempts have been made on the lives of one of every four incumbent American presidents, and one of every eleven has been killed. Six of the eleven presidents from Harry S Truman to George W. Bush had attempts made on their lives.

It was only after President William McKinley was shot in 1901 that systematic and continuous protection of the president was begun. Protection before then was sporadic at best. The problem had existed from the days of the early presidency, but no action was taken until McKinley's murder, the third killing of a U.S. president in little more than thirty-six years.

A prime example of the absence of security for presidents is the case of Thomas Jefferson, who, on his inauguration day in 1801, walked unescorted from his Washington boarding house to the Capitol to take the presidential oath of office. There was no police force in the city until 1805, when the mayor appointed a constable and forty deputies.

John Quincy Adams was on one occasion threatened in person at the White House by a court-martialed army sergeant. Despite the incident, he requested no protection and continued to take solitary walks around the city, as well as lone early morning swims in the Potomac River.

Adams' successor, Andrew Jackson, received many threatening letters that he would contemptuously endorse and send to a Washington newspaper for publication. In May 1833 he was assaulted by a former navy lieutenant, Robert B. Randolph, but refused to press charges against him. This was not an assassination attempt, since Randolph apparently did not intend serious injury.

On January 10, 1835, Jackson was accosted as he emerged from the east entrance of the Capitol by Richard Lawrence, an English house painter. Lawrence pulled a pistol on the president, but it misfired. He drew another, which also misfired. He was taken into custody, tried and found not guilty by reason of insanity. He was confined to mental institutions for the rest of his life.

This was the first assassination attempt against an American president, but it did not prompt any action to provide protection for the chief executive. Following the attack, Jackson's vice president, Martin Van Buren, regularly carried two pistols with him.[3] When he became president, Van Buren often walked or went horseback riding alone in the woods near the White House.

In August of 1842, an intoxicated man threw rocks at President John Tyler, who was walking on the grounds south of the White House. Following this incident, Congress passed an act to establish an auxiliary watch for the protection of public property in Washington, consisting of a captain and fifteen men. This apparently was done more to protect the White House, which had been defaced on occasion, than to protect the person of the president.

But the possibility of violence against the president was less worrisome for him than the ever-present threat of serious illness, especially in the malaria-ridden swampland that was then Washington, D.C. When the president gets sick or is injured, it has always been important to the country that he receives appropriate medical attention. Four of the eight presidents who died in office expired from natural causes: William Henry Harrison from pneumonia in 1841, Zachary Taylor from gastroenteritis in 1850, Warren G. Harding from heart disease in 1923, and Franklin D. Roosevelt in 1945 from a stroke.

The lives of Harrison and Taylor may well have been saved with modern medicine, and maybe even Harding's. But Roosevelt's case is a little more complicated. Once he had his massive stroke in Warm Springs, Georgia, his recovery was probably impossible. But in the year or so prior to his death, FDR was seriously ill with vascular disease. He chose not to seek treatment for it, and his doctor took little or no action to impose treatment, despite ominous signs and test readings.

Besides these four fatal cases, other incumbent presidents came close to death, mainly in the early years of the republic. Only a year into his presidency in May 1790, George Washington contracted a severe case of pneumonia. He was so sick that those near him feared for his life. He completely recovered.[4]

Our fourth president, James Madison, suffered an acute attack of malaria in June 1813 that left him bedridden for three weeks and near death.[5] His wife Dolley nursed and cared for him day and night during the illness until finally his fever subsided and he began to recover.

Madison's successor, James Monroe, suffered an attack of severe cramps and convulsions that resulted in a loss of consciousness in August 1823. This lasted for two hours, and it was feared he would die. But Monroe made a complete recovery, with no aftereffects. This mysterious bout may have been a vascular spasm involving an artery to the brain.[6]

Before Zachary Taylor's fatal gastroenteritis in July 1850, he became very ill during a trip to the northern states the previous summer. In Erie, Pennsylvania, he experienced a case of severe diarrhea, accompanied by high fever, and his doctor was concerned for the president's life. Taylor did, however, recover.[7]

Five presidents have been the victims of gunshot wounds. Four proved fatal. In the cases of Abraham Lincoln and John F. Kennedy, they sustained grievous wounds to the head, and no amount of medical attention would have saved their lives, even today. The cases of James A. Garfield and William McKinley are more problematic. Their wounds were not immediately lethal. Death occurred much later. The treatment these two men received from their attending physicians was later criticized as either inadequate or botched. Both would probably have survived in today's world of medicine.

The treatment Ronald Reagan received after the assassination attempt on him was state-of-the-art for 1981 and roundly praised. He made a complete recovery from a serious bullet wound to the chest, becoming the only president to have survived a gunshot wound.

Besides these five instances of presidents being attacked, no others have been seriously injured in accidents while in office.

Even before he took office, Abraham Lincoln was thought to be the object of plots to kidnap or kill him. Certain elements apparently considered violent measures to prevent his inauguration, including one plot to attack him while he passed through Baltimore on his way to Washington by rail in March 1861. A detective assigned to protect the president-elect learned of the plot, and no harm came to Lincoln.

At the time of the inauguration, tension prevailed in the nation's capital, with civil war looming. The army took precautions that were unprecedented up to that time, and probably more elaborate than any taken before the latter part of the twentieth century. Soldiers occupied strategic points throughout Washington, along the procession route and at the Capitol, while armed plainclothesmen moved among the crowds. Lincoln was surrounded by dense masses of soldiers that obscured him from the view of the people.

Lincoln's life seemed to be in danger during all his years in office. The volume of threatening letters he received was high, but little attention was paid to them. He was reluctant to surround himself with guards, and often rejected protection or sought to slip away from it. This has been characteristic of most American presidents. They have regarded protection as a necessary nuisance and contrary to a politician's natural instinct for freedom to meet the people. Presidents also value their privacy. Lincoln regularly scoffed at attempts to safeguard him.

Protection of the president varied during the Civil War. Military guards were often assigned to guard the White House and accompany the president as he moved about. Once while Lincoln rode on horseback through the city unaccompanied, a shot was fired at the president. The marshal of the District of Columbia provided guards for the protection of the president, but Lincoln would not cooperate. Finally, in November 1864, four District policemen were assigned to the White House as bodyguards to the president, and Lincoln reluctantly tolerated them — as long as they remained inconspicuous. At times during the war, federal troops camped out on the White House lawn, and even in the East Room, but these men were not specifically assigned to protect either the president or the Executive Mansion.

Near the end of the war, the Confederate sympathizer John Wilkes Booth plotted with others for months to kidnap President Lincoln. This eventually changed to plans to kill him. Booth carried out the deed on the night of April 14, 1865, when he shot Lincoln at Ford's Theatre in Washington. A bodyguard named John F. Parker, of the Washington police, was supposed to remain on guard in the corridor outside the president's box in the playhouse, but he wandered off to watch the play, then left the building to have a drink at a nearby saloon. This left the president unprotected and made Booth's task much easier. After being shot in the head, Lincoln died the next morning. No charges were ever filed against Parker for leaving his post.

Americans in 1865 could accept death from natural causes. It was a part of life. The child mortality rate was extremely high, and there were a myriad of diseases to which adults could succumb. But even in the wake of the deadliest war in American history, the taking of the president's life was truly shocking.

Lincoln's assassination brought to the fore the inadequacy of presidential protection. A Congressional committee looked into the matter, but, with traditional reluctance, called for no action to provide better protection. Nor did requests for increased protection come from the president or other government departments. This lack of concern may have derived from the tendency to regard Lincoln's murder as part of a unique crisis—the Civil War—that was not likely to occur again.

For a short time after the war, soldiers assigned by the War Department continued to guard the White House. Washington city police assisted on special occasions to maintain order and prevent unruly crowds. The permanent police guard in place since 1864 was reduced to three and assigned entirely to provide protection at the White House. There was no special group of trained officers to protect the president. Our chief executives continued to move about in Washington virtually unattended. Their main line of defense at the White House was the doormen, who were not especially trained to protect the president. The White House grounds were open and unfenced, and anyone could walk in the front door and request a meeting with the president.

This lack of personal protection for the president came again to the fore with the shooting of President Garfield on July 2, 1881. An obviously mentally unbalanced Charles J. Guiteau mortally wounded Garfield in a Washington railroad depot. He had acted alone and had stalked the president. Guiteau testified at his murder trial that he had three opportunities to attack Garfield prior to the day he shot him. On all of these occasions, within a period of three weeks, the president was completely unguarded.

The *New York Tribune* predicted that the assault on Garfield would lead to the president becoming "the slave of his office, the prisoner of forms and restrictions," in contrast to the simple, unfettered life he had been able to live before. But this did not yet come to pass. Though the nation had once again been shocked by the killing of a president, no steps were taken to provide the president with personal protection besides the three officers assigned to him at the White House. There seemed to be no public outcry for an increased guard.

The president continued to move about, sometimes completely alone, and travel without special protection. Chester A. Arthur, Garfield's successor, once hailed a public taxi in front of the White House in order to attend an event at the Washington Navy Yard. But during his term of office in the early 1880s, Arthur's biggest threat came from an illness for which he was diagnosed — the progressively serious, and ultimately fatal, kidney ailment known as Bright's Disease. He was never in any danger of dying while president, however, and he and his physician hid the truth from the public.

President Arthur was not the only chief executive diagnosed with a deadly disease. Soon after Grover Cleveland was inaugurated for his second term as president, he secretly had a cancerous growth on the roof of his mouth removed during two procedures in the summer of 1893. The operations were completely successful. The president's life was apparently in no immediate danger from the malignancy, and it is not known whether he could have survived his term of office if the surgery had not been performed or been unsuccessful.

Some presidents have entered office in frail health, most notably Madison, Andrew Jackson and Franklin Pierce. John F. Kennedy, despite appearances, was not a completely well man. Dwight Eisenhower suffered a heart attack and a mild stroke, and underwent intestinal surgery during his presidency, and Ronald Reagan underwent surgery for colon cancer. These conditions were not immediately life-threatening. Other presidents have been treated for various ailments and undergone surgeries during their terms.

During Cleveland's second presidency, from 1893 to 1897, the number of threatening letters received by the president increased markedly, and Mrs. Cleveland convinced her husband to seek an increase in the number of White House policemen. This resulted in upping the guards from three to twenty-seven. These men were still provided by the Washington police department. It wasn't until 1894 that the Secret Service began to provide protection, and then only on an informal basis.

The United States Secret Service had been established on July 5, 1865, just two-and-a-half months after the assassination of President Lincoln. But it was organized as a division of the Treasury Department to suppress counterfeiting. Protection of the president or anyone else was not part of its function.

It began protecting the chief executive in response to a need for a trained organization with investigative capabilities to perform the task. It started in an indirect way. In 1894, as part of its mission to stop fiscal crimes against the United States, the Secret Service had been investigating a plot by a group of gamblers to assassinate President Cleveland. As part of this investigation, the Secret Service assigned a small detail of agents to the White House to help protect him. This is how the organization became involved in the role of presidential protection.[8]

Secret Service men accompanied President Cleveland on trips around Washington, as well as outside the city. For a time, two agents rode in a buggy behind Cleveland's carriage, but after much criticism, the president insisted that the practice be stopped.[9]

During the Spanish American War in 1898, a Secret Service detail was stationed at the White House to protect President William McKinley. Though this vigilance was somewhat relaxed after the war, Secret Service guards were on duty at the Executive Mansion at least part of the time. Because of fear of the anarchist movement, which had murdered four heads of European countries between 1894 and 1900, the number of Secret Service guards at the White House increased, and men were assigned to accompany McKinley on trips outside of Washington.

On September 6, 1901, President McKinley was attending the Pan American Exposition in Buffalo. He was shaking hands with members of the public when he was shot by a professed anarchist, Leon F. Czolgosz. McKinley died eight days later. This occurred despite the fact that McKinley was being guarded by three Secret Service agents, four Buffalo police detectives and at least four soldiers. Czolgosz had no accomplices and was not part of any conspiracy. Like the assassin Guiteau, he was obviously mentally disturbed.

Once again the people of the United States were shocked and outraged at the murder of a president. Though Congress passed no legislation concerning the protection of the president, it informally requested it. And on its own initiative, the Secret Service assumed full-time responsibility for the safety of the president in 1902. Two full-time operatives were assigned to a White House detail, and additional men were provided whenever the president traveled. As newspapers and journals examined and opined on the state of an American society that could continually produce these assassins, they reflected the public's feeling that the time had come for enhanced, permanent, round-the-clock security for the president.

It was Theodore Roosevelt, McKinley's successor, who first experienced this more extensive system of protection. Roosevelt called the Secret Service "a very small but necessary thorn in the flesh." He felt they would be useless in preventing an assault on his life, but realized they were valuable in separating him from office seekers, cranks and the just-plain-curious who would otherwise interrupt his routine.[10] It was also during Roosevelt's administration that a fence was erected around the White House grounds.

Full-time protection of the president by the Secret Service was not sanctioned by Congress, nor were funds provided for it, until 1907. After the election of William Howard Taft in 1908, the Secret Service began providing protection for the president-elect, and this practice was enshrined in law in 1913. The same year, Congress authorized permanent protection of the president, but this authority had to be renewed annually until 1951.

There was no protection for former presidents until 1961, nor for presidential candidates until 1968. Former president Theodore Roosevelt had been wounded in an assassination attempt while running for president in 1912, but not until Senator Robert F. Kennedy, the late President Kennedy's brother, was murdered fifty-six years later while seeking his party's nomination for president did Congress authorize Secret Service protection for major presidential candidates. But this did not prevent an attack upon Alabama governor George C. Wallace in 1972 while he sought the presidential nomination. He was seriously wounded by gunfire as he campaigned in Maryland.

In 1917 a law was passed making it a federal crime to threaten the president, and legislation for protection of the president's immediate family by the Secret Service was also passed. That same year the police force guarding the White House increased to thirty-four, then ballooned shortly after that to fifty-four. After the United States entered World War I in April of 1917, armed soldiers guarded the gates of the White House complex for the duration of the conflict.

In 1922, at President Warren G. Harding's request, Congress passed legislation creating a White House police force that replaced the Metropolitan Washington Police force. Though composed largely of the same men from the Washington Police, the new force was wholly federal and under the control of the president. This new unit became part of the Secret Service in 1930, making that organization responsible for all aspects of White House and presidential protection from that point forward.[11]

In 1933, at an outdoor political rally in Miami, a gunman fired five shots in the direction of President-Elect Franklin D. Roosevelt. He somehow was not hit, but Chicago mayor Anton Cermak, who was with Roosevelt, was fatally wounded. In the following years, and especially during World War II, the number of Secret Service agents, as well as the number of White House police, grew exponentially as their roles expanded. An investigative section was added to the Secret Service to analyze threats against the president. The vice president came under Secret Service protection in January 1945. During the war, military sentries patrolled the White House fence, and machine-gun-toting soldiers were stationed on the White House roof. A tunnel was built from the White House to the Treasury Building as a means of escape for the president.

In 1950, two Puerto Rican nationalists attempted to shoot their way into Blair House across from the White House in order to attack President Harry S Truman. The president had been staying there while the White House was being renovated. One of the assailants was killed in the ensuing gun battle with White House policemen, as was one of the police officers, but Truman was unharmed.

The year after this attack, legislation was passed to permanently authorize the Secret Service to protect the president, his immediate family, the president-elect and the vice president. No longer would the authority have to be renewed on a yearly basis. Also, the number of White House policemen was increased again. In 1961 Congress authorized protection of former presidents, and the next year, protection for the vice president or next officer in line to succeed the president, as well as the vice president-elect.

After the tragic assassination of President John F. Kennedy in Dallas in 1963, some criticized the Secret Service, saying it had become complacent about protecting the president. Following that event, the Secret Service began protection of former presidents' spouses or widows, and minor children up to age sixteen.

In September 1975, President Gerald R. Ford was the target of two assassination attempts within a few days of each other. In the first instance, a Secret Service agent wrestled the gun from the female assailant's hand before a shot was fired. In the second, a bystander pushed the arm of a woman as she fired at the president, diverting the bullet. President Ford reportedly wore a bulletproof vest in public after these attacks, and presidents since then have occasionally worn them.[12]

On March 30, 1981, as President Ronald Reagan emerged from a Washington hotel, he was fired upon by a gunman. A bullet struck him in the chest, barely missing his heart. His press secretary and a Secret Service bodyguard were also wounded in the attack. The president survived, and the Secret Service was praised for its lifesaving actions. During Reagan's term, barriers were erected around the White House complex perimeter to prevent any vehicle from crashing through the surrounding fence.

On October 29, 1994, a gunman opened fire with a semiautomatic rifle through the White House gate at the north front of the mansion along Pennsylvania Avenue. At least twenty-nine shots were fired, and eleven rounds struck the White House facade. One bullet penetrated a window in the west wing. Miraculously, no one in a tour group in front of the White House was hit. The gunman thought that one member of the group was President William J. Clinton, his intended target. The assailant ran along the fence, firing, and was tackled by three bystanders. Uniformed Secret Service officers responded within seconds and were praised for their actions. President Clinton was in the White House residence at the time and was not injured. Though the assault was carried out on foot, it resulted in the permanent closure of Pennsylvania Avenue to vehicular traffic in front of the Executive Mansion.

On May 10, 2005, President George W. Bush was speaking to a crowd from a platform in Tbilisi, Republic of Georgia. An unknown man, later identified as a Georgian citizen, threw a live hand grenade toward the president. It struck a girl, landed sixty-one feet from President Bush and failed to detonate. Cooperation between the U.S. Secret Service and Georgian authorities led to the capture and conviction of the assailant for the attempted murder of President Bush. This was the only instance of an assassination attempt upon an American president outside of the United States.

In 1994 legislation was passed limiting Secret Service protection of former presidents, their spouses, widows and minor children to ten years after the president leaves office. This applies to any president first elected to office after January 1, 1997.

Currently there are about 1,200 members of the Uniformed Division of the Secret Service and around eight hundred plainclothes agents. The role of the Secret Service has expanded greatly over the past century, beyond protection of just the president. In 2003 the Secret Service was transferred from the Treasury Department to the newly created Department of Homeland Security. The Federal Bureau of Investigation also investigates threats against the president in coordination with the Secret Service, though the FBI takes no active role in the protection of the president or the White House. The U.S. Park Police and the Metropolitan Police Department of the District of Columbia are responsible for security in the immediate vicinity of the White House. A no-fly zone has existed over the area of the White House for decades, though intrusions occasionally occur, most notably a 1994 incident in which the pilot crashed his airplane into the south lawn of the White House, striking the building's southwest corner.

The poisoning of the king has a long and fabled history in both fact and fiction, but the president has no food taster. His meals are prepared, and food supplies procured, in a controlled environment.[13]

Medical care of the presidents has changed and evolved from the early days of the country to the present time. Of course, health care for all persons has improved over the centuries as medical science has advanced. The medical practices of two hundred years ago seem primitive and even barbaric today.

From the start, presidents have received, or at least had available, the best medical care, either as a result of their social or financial status, or simply because they held the important office of the nation's chief executive. In this area, as in so many others, George Washington set the precedent. There was no doctor exclusively assigned to care for him. There was no established position of presidential physician, and presidents received no regular medical checkups. They were free to call upon a doctor of their choice if they desired treatment. The federal government did not provide health care, and the president, like any other citizen, was expected to handle his own medical affairs and treatments, and to pay for them out of his own pocket. Washington made no objection to this.

Twice, President Washington was sick enough to be attended by a physician. His regular family doctor having remained with his practice in Virginia, the first president called on a pre-eminent New York physician to administer to him when that city was the nation's capital. When Philadelphia became the capital, Philadelphia physicians assumed the role of Washington family doctor. Very few of our presidents have chosen their regular family doctor to be their White House physician once they became chief executive.

In the early years, the President's doctor was almost always a civilian. In addition to the president's regular doctor, one Washington physician, Thomas Miller, was often on call to service the White House from the administrations of Martin Van Buren through James Buchanan.[14] But occasionally a military doctor provided services, free of charge. The president was, after all, commander-in-chief of the armed forces, and military doctors his subordinates. James Monroe was the first president to regularly use a military physician, probably due to the doctor's availability. By the second half of the nineteenth century, the president's physician was always a military man, and this continued through the end of Eisenhower's administration in 1961. Convenience, control and availability have been cited as reasons that the armed forces were favored.[15] In some cases, the fact that the care, which extended to the president's family, was free of charge was also a factor.

This free medical care caused anger in the ranks of the Washington, D.C., civilian medical establishment, which considered such gratis care to civilians a threat to the economic interests of civilian practitioners. But eventually the offended doctors conceded that the free care was a benefit of the presidency.[16]

At first, no doctor accompanied the president on trips outside the capital, but by 1900 the practice had become standard. At that time, Dr. Presley M. Rixey of the navy became William McKinley's White House physician. He was the first doctor whose primary responsibility was to care for the president and first family, and the first to have a treatment room in the White House, a converted linen closet.[17] In 1928 and 1930 the first laws came into effect that acknowledged the existence of a Physician to the White House, and clarified the rank, responsibilities and privileges of military physicians assigned to the White House.[18]

Herbert Hoover's doctor, naval officer Joel T. Boone, was the first to have an assistant. Boone was given a larger office in the White House, and his responsibilities were expanded from care of the first family to looking after the health of political appointees, staff members, and even visitors.

Over the ensuing years the White House physician's staff was expanded, with the addition of more doctors, nurses and administrators. By the latter half of the twentieth century the position of White House physician had become more of a prestige appointment, more bureaucratic and occasionally somewhat political. Day to day care of the president was often left to subordinate doctors on staff, even when the president traveled.

Today, the doctor's office in the Executive Mansion is officially called the White House Medical Unit (WHMU), and is under the command of the White House Military Office. The doctor with the longest tenure is called the Senior White House Physician, and is supervisor of an ever-expanding group of medical personnel. More then a dozen people now staff the office, with a doctor or nurse present in the White House twenty-four hours a day. The Physician to the President, which may or may not be the senior doctor, is the president's personal physician, and can be a civilian or a military officer, at the president's discretion. Sometimes it is a doctor with whom the president is familiar, sometimes not. He is completely free to choose anyone he wants.

The WHMU's responsibilities extend to the care of the vice president and his family, and it is available to White House staffers and the two thousand workers of the Executive Office Building on the White House grounds. The unit occupies a suite on the ground floor of the White House. It coordinates emergency care with the Secret Service, staffs a medical area on Air Force One, checks out the level of care existing in foreign countries the president visits, and sometimes assures the off-shore presence of a ship with medical facilities if the country's care level is considered inadequate.

The staff of the WHMU is paid by the federal government. Special doctors, surgeons, or consultants used by the president are billed to him or his insurance company. At times of serious illness, injury or in emergency situations, specialists and consultants are necessarily called in for their expertise. This has been true since Washington's time.

Treatment of the president has often been controversial, not only in the cases of Garfield and McKinley, but of Grover Cleveland, Franklin D. Roosevelt and John F. Kennedy, among others. Doctor-patient confidentiality can be a problem, since it must be balanced in today's world with the public's desire — some may say right — to know the status of the president's health. For political considerations, the truth about a president's illness or condition has often been withheld from the public, with the full knowledge and complicity of the president's physician.

Today, the president of the United States is undoubtedly the most well protected person in the world. Secret Service security is top notch. Still, as has often been said, any person who is willing to give up his or her life to take the life of the president could possibly be successful. Agents must be forever vigilant to prevent such an occurrence.

As for health care, as President Barack Obama was fond of saying, "I have the best health care in the world. I have a doctor following me around all the time." And the president does indeed have the best medical care in the world, with an attendant medical staff ready to spring into action in any emergency, twenty-four hours a day.

In today's world, the people of the United States would have it no other way. The safety and well-being of the president is paramount to avoid the trauma, sadness and uncertainty that has occurred eight times in our history.

CHAPTER 2

William Henry Harrison

9TH PRESIDENT OF THE UNITED STATES
TERM OF OFFICE: MARCH 4, 1841, TO APRIL 4, 1841
BORN: FEBRUARY 9, 1773; DIED: APRIL 4, 1841
AGE AT DEATH: 68 YEARS, 54 DAYS
PLACE OF DEATH: WASHINGTON, D.C.
CAUSE OF DEATH: PNEUMONIA
BURIAL PLACE: NORTH BEND, OHIO

On April 16, 1841, Congressman John Quincy Adams wrote in his diary, "I paid a visit this morning to Mr. Tyler, who styles himself President of the United States, and not Vice-President acting as President, which would be the correct style. But it is a construction in direct violation both of the grammar and context of the Constitution, which confers upon the Vice-President, on the decease of the President, not the office, but the powers and duties of said office."[1]

Mr. Adams was referring to the status of John Tyler upon the death of William Henry Harrison, the first American president to die in office. A controversy had arisen over the proper role of the vice president when the president dies. Article II, Section I, Clause 5 of the U.S. Constitution reads, "In Case of the Removal of the President from Office, or of his Death, Resignation, or Inability to discharge the Powers and Duties of said Office, the Same shall devolve on the Vice President, and the Congress may by Law provide for the Case of Removal, Death, Resignation or Inability, both of the President and Vice President, declaring what Officer shall then act as President, and such Officer shall act accordingly, until the Disability be removed, or a President shall be elected."

The problem was, to what were the framers of the Constitution referring with the word "same"? Was it the duties of the office or the office itself? Did the vice president automatically become president, or was he still vice president, acting as president?

More than fifty-three years after the Constitution was written, all the men who were privy to the secret deliberations over that document had passed away. James Madison's journals of the Constitutional Convention, the only detailed account of the debates, had not yet been made public. Almost no one knew of their existence. When the writings were made known, years after President Harrison's death, it became clear that the intent of the framers was that only the powers and duties of the presidency should devolve upon the vice president, and that he should be acting president until a new election was held. The vice president was not empowered to fill out the remainder of the deceased president's term, for apparently a new election could be held before the expiration of that term.

The Constitution gave Congress the power to call a special election but did not require it to do so. When Harrison died, Congress could have called for a new election for a new four-year term, or a new election to fill the remainder of the unexpired term of the dead president; or it could have chosen to have the vice president fill out the remainder of the term, which, in effect, it wound up doing.

But in April 1841 the intent of the Constitution was not clear. It was open to different interpretations. Vice President Tyler, from the very start, assumed the full title, office, and powers of the presidency, in his mind, for the remainder of Harrison's four-year term of office. He was backed up in this assertion by the cabinet. Others in and out of government took opposing stands on the issue. But by June 1, 1841, both houses of Congress had passed resolutions recognizing Tyler as president of the United States and made no effort to call a special election.

No one again mounted a sufficient challenge to Tyler's assumption, and one of the most important precedents in American history was set. And once the Tyler precedent was established, it was never altered or broken. It became the Constitutional norm. On all eight occasions when a president has died in office, the vice president has automatically become president for the remainder of the deceased president's term.

It was not until 1967, when the Twenty-fifth Amendment to the Constitution was adopted, that all doubt was erased. That Amendment reads, in Section 1, "In case of the removal of the President from office or of his death or resignation, the Vice President shall become President." However, it could have been made much more clear if the following words had been added to the sentence: "...for the remainder of the four-year term of office."

William Henry Harrison was a member of one of the leading political families of eighteenth and nineteenth century America, perhaps second only to the Adamses. His father was a signer of the Declaration of Independence as well as a congressman and governor of Virginia; his brother was a congressman; his son John Scott Harrison was also a congressman and the father of Benjamin Harrison, twenty-third president of the United States.

As a young man William attended medical school but dropped out and joined the army. His venue of action was mainly the Northwest Territories, where he fought Indians. He distinguished himself well enough to be appointed secretary of the territories in 1798, and also held the post of territorial delegate to the U.S. House of Representatives. In 1801 he was appointed governor of the Indiana Territory, a position he held for twelve years. Toward the Indians he was protective so long as they submitted to the white man's rule. He secured huge chunks of land from them and was always ready to crush any protest.[2] In 1811 he defeated an uprising of Indians near Tippecanoe Creek in Indiana — hence his nickname, the Hero of Tippecanoe.

In the War of 1812 Harrison was commissioned a general and fought the British and their Indian allies as leader of the Army of the Northwest. After the war he tried and failed to make a living on his Ohio farm. Needing income, he sought political office. In between his frequent failures to secure such an office, he was a congressman for two and a half years, served a term in the Ohio legislature, then three years in the U.S. Senate. He was also minister to Colombia, then for seven years a county court clerk in Ohio.

Always on a quest for political office, he was accused of seeking those positions only because he considered them an easy way to make a living.[3] Harrison made convincing arguments in his favor during his bids for appointment or election. He was amicable, had a good manner about him, and had a certain popular appeal, being a military hero.

In 1836 he had enough nerve to seek the new Whig Party's nomination for president, a large step upward from a court clerkship. He was considered but not chosen. Four years later he was the nominee, selected because he was thought of as a safe, well-liked candidate with no clear past record on divisive issues of the day. His supporters concocted a rousing "log cabin" campaign for "Tippecanoe and Tyler, Too," and Harrison easily defeated the incumbent Martin Van Buren in the midst of an economic depression. He became the oldest man to enter the presidency at age 68, a distinction he would hold for 140 years.

As far as is known, Harrison did not suffer from a plethora of illnesses either as an adult or child. He apparently had malaria, for there are two instances at about age 60 when he had serious attacks of "ague and fever." And he did have a chronic stomach and intestinal disorder. Since his diet consisted mainly of dairy products and meat, it is assumed that the problem was an ulcer. This diet resulted in chronic constipation, for which he took strong laxatives, resulting in an irritable colon. He avoided alcohol, probably because his sensitive stomach would not tolerate it.[4]

Upon taking office, the ninth president was in relatively good physical condition. Harrison rode on horseback to his outdoor inauguration at the Capitol building on a windy, cold, and, some reports say, rainy day. Despite the raw weather, he wore neither a hat nor an overcoat. He delivered the longest inaugural address in history, lasting almost two hours, still hatless and coatless in the inclement weather. Perhaps it was to play the role of the brave soldier, or maybe to assure everyone of his good health, despite his age, but the President's decision not to protect himself from the elements on that day only served to weaken his system. He had already been taxed physically by the campaign and a flood of office seekers who besieged him day and night for appointments to federal positions. Harrison caught a cold at the inauguration, and some say he never fully recovered.

The new president continued to be hounded by office seekers. During his month as chief executive he did little more than appoint his cabinet and a few other officials.

In late March, he supposedly had his hair cut and exposed himself to the cold air afterward. Then, during one of his morning walks, he was overtaken by a rain shower and thoroughly soaked. And once again ignoring the elements, he walked through slush to offer a diplomatic post to John Taylor, who lived in Octagon House, a short distance from the White House.[5]

By March 25 the president was quite ill, and the following day he summoned a doctor, something he was generally loathe to do. Harrison told the physician, Thomas Miller, that he had been sick for a few days and attributed it to fatigue and anxiety. The doctor simply ordered him to stay indoors.[6]

On the morning of the twenty-seventh, Harrison took his usual walk to the market, and those who saw him there daily thought he looked careworn. Later he complained of a headache, and then he was seized with a chill and fever, for which he took to his bed.[7] That afternoon, Dr. Miller was

At age 68, William Henry Harrison was the oldest person to become president until Ronald Reagan in 1981. Harrison took sick shortly after his inauguration and died after one month in office, on April 4, 1841. (ImageEnvision)

again called. He prescribed warm drinks, heat to the arms and legs, and more bedclothes to keep the patient warm.

The next day Dr. Miller made the diagnosis of pneumonia of the right lung and congestion of the lower lobe of the right lung, and congestion of the liver. During the next few days he called in three other doctors for assistance: Fred May, N.W. Worthington and J.C. Hall.

In 1841 the practice of medicine had not advanced very far from the days of Washington, and President Harrison was accorded similar treatment. Bleeding was tried and stopped due to the patient's age and weakness. The doctors used ointments to cause blisters and cupping to try to draw the illness out of the body. In cupping, a cup was heated over a lighted candle, then applied to the skin, which was drawn into a lump under the cup.

The president was given cathartics like calomel, castor oil and rhubarb, which gave him a severe diarrhea. He was given ipecac to make him vomit, and laudanum, camphor, wine whey and brandy to ease his pain, plus pills of different kinds. After seeing no improvement, the doctors even tried the Indian remedies of Virginia snake weed and crude petroleum.[8]

The intake of all these poisons caused jaundice, and the purging of body fluids severely depleted Harrison's strength. The doctors thought the condition of the lungs and liver had improved, but acknowledged the stomach and intestines had not. Indeed, the intestinal problems were largely brought about by the doctors' severe "remedies." Surprisingly, it is said that the president actually felt better for a short time on Saturday, April 3, and asked for a reading from the Bible. But also on that day he seemed to sense the finality of his illness and confided to a female attendant, "Ah, Fanny, I am ill, very ill, much more so than they think me."[9]

News of the president's illness apparently did not get out to the public until April 2. This brought callers to the White House who numbered in the thousands. They were told by the porter that the president was better. Those who spoke to Harrison's longtime friends Colonel C.S. Todd and General John Chambers were told there was no change in his serious condition.

On April 3 at three in the afternoon a profuse diarrhea came on. The patient sank rapidly. Dr. Ashton Alexander of Baltimore was called in, and Dr. Chapman of Philadelphia was sent for. At 6 P.M. the four attending physicians pronounced President Harrison beyond recovery. He sank into a stupor and spoke in broken phrases: "These applications, will they never cease?... I cannot bear this.... Don't trouble me." It was as if he were addressing the office seekers who had pestered him for weeks, the office seekers who now speculated over their chances with Harrison's successor.

Religious services were performed by the Rev. William Hawley of the church that Harrison attended. He had been in constant attendance at the bedside.

The last words of the president, as heard by Dr. Worthington, were spoken at about 9 P.M.: "Sir, I wish you to understand the true principles of the government. I wish them carried out. I ask nothing more." Worthington immediately wrote them down. The doctor said that the words were spoken in a strong voice.[10] Another witness, J.G. Bennett, said the words were barely audible and were as follows: "I wish you to understand, and remember, the principles which govern me, and carry them out. I ask no more."[11] In delirium, Harrison may have been addressing the words to his successor, John Tyler, who was not present but at his home in Virginia, completely unaware of the situation.

After this the president slept as his breathing became less and less and his pulse more faint. His skin became cold and clammy. At 11 P.M. he raised his head and coughed.

Downstairs, throngs of callers inquired about the sick man's condition. In the second floor room where he lay were five physicians, personal attendants and the Reverend Hawley. In the adjoining apartment were several of the president's close friends, associates and relatives, and in the room adjoining that were five of the six cabinet officers: Secretary of State Daniel Webster, Secretary of the Treasury Thomas Ewing, Secretary of War John Bell, Attorney General John J. Crittenden, and Postmaster General Francis Granger.

At 12:30 A.M. on Palm Sunday, April 4, 1841, William Henry Harrison breathed his last. He passed away sleeping, without a struggle. There was a slightly audible respiration at the instant he died. Family and friends vented their sorrow, and many wept. The only family members present in the mansion were the president's nephew D.O. Coupeland, his niece Mrs. Taylor, grandson Findlay Harrison, and his late son's widow Jane Harrison and her adoptive mother. The president's wife Anna was at the family farm in North Bend, Ohio, not yet having made the trip to Washington to join her husband.

The five cabinet members at the White House immediately drew up and signed the following statement, which went out to newspapers and government officials with the morning mail:

> An all-wise Providence having suddenly removed from this life William Henry Harrison, late president of the United States, we have thought it our duty, in the recess of Congress, and in the absence of the Vice President from the seat of government, to make this afflicting bereavement known to the country, by this declaration, under our hands.
> He died at the president's house, in this city, this fourth day of April, Anno Domini, 1841, at thirty minutes before one o'clock in the morning.
> The people of the United States, overwhelmed, like ourselves, by an event so unexpected and so melancholy, will derive consolation from knowing that his death was calm and resigned, as his life has been patriotic, useful and distinguished: and that the last utterance of his lips expressed a fervent desire for the perpetuity of the constitution and the preservation of its true principles. In death, as in life, the happiness of his country was uppermost in his thoughts.

The cabinet also made out a letter for the State Department files, signed by several of those present at the White House, attesting to the death of the president. They addressed a personal message to Vice President Tyler and dispatched Fletcher Webster, chief clerk of the State Department and son of the secretary of state, to deliver it.[12] Accompanied by Senate assistant doorkeeper Robert Beale, young Webster journeyed by train, boat and horseback to Tyler's home near Charles City, Virginia, and delivered the news to him in the early morning of April 5. Tyler ate breakfast, talked to his family and decided to leave for Washington immediately. Stories that he was playing marbles with his sons when he received the message, or that he burst into tears, or had to borrow money for the trip, are simply not true. Myths tend to grow up around such momentous events in history.[13]

The deathbed of President Harrison. From left to right: Treasury Secretary Thomas Ewing, Secretary of State Daniel Webster, Dr. N.W. Worthington, the Rev. William Hawley, President Harrison, his niece, his nephew, and Postmaster General Francis Granger in the doorway. (ImageEnvision)

It was a gloomy, rainy day as word of Harrison's death spread throughout Washington, then slowly from city to city. Where railroads were in operation, the message went by train, otherwise by horseback. The telegraph was still a rather new invention, and no network existed to disseminate the news by that method. The news reached Baltimore and Philadelphia on Sunday, the day of the death, and also New York City just before midnight, but did not get to Boston till Tuesday. The sad intelligence took longer to reach smaller, more isolated cities and towns, and eventually reached the new widow, Mrs. Harrison, in Ohio. Everywhere the news was received with sorrow and dismay. People were stunned that the man who had assumed the chief magistracy of the land just one month earlier was gone in so short a time. Some compared the event to the passing of Washington, and indeed it may have seemed so under the circumstances. It was unprecedented. No other president had died in office.

Political foes of Harrison joined in the mourning and gave tributes to him, although even at such a time there were isolated cases of continued partisan animosity. One such example were the comments of the *New York Evening Post*, regretting the president's death only because he died before he could prove his incompetence.[14] And the vitriolic ex-president Andrew Jackson in Tennessee privately expressed his happiness at the Whig Harrison's passing, because he believed that the ex–Democrat and Southerner Tyler was closer to his political beliefs.[15]

As communication of the death was disseminated, flags were lowered to half-staff, and many buildings, both public and private, were decorated in black mourning crepe. City and state governments passed resolutions of mourning and urged citizens to wear mourning badges and attend memorial services and ceremonies.

In yet another signed statement, the five cabinet members on April 4 issued general plans for the funeral in Washington. On Tuesday, April 6, more detailed arrangements were made public. After consulting with the late president's family and personal friends, it was decided that the obsequies would take place on Wednesday the seventh. Religious services would be conducted by the Episcopal Church in the White House, followed by a procession to the Congressional Burial Ground. It would be a military and civic ceremony, and everyone was invited to attend. Former president and now congressman John Quincy Adams was specifically invited by name.

Orders were issued to the army and navy to take appropriate measures to mourn the loss of their commander-in-chief. These included, upon receipt of the orders, the day-long firing of minute guns at army posts, and twenty-six minute guns by navy yards and vessels; the wearing of badges of mourning; and the lowering of flags to half-staff. Flag standards and regiment colors were ordered "put in mourning" by the display of black streamers on them.

On Monday, the day following the death, all government offices in Washington were closed and would remain so until Thursday. Civil and military leaders met to make plans for the Wednesday funeral. In cities and towns throughout America, many offices and businesses, especially places of amusement, were closed.

In the White House a post-mortem examination of the body of President Harrison was conducted. Dr. John Williams shaved and dressed the body, and supplied a winding sheet and coffins and cases. Eleven other merchants, led by Alexander Hunter, supplied various goods and services for the ceremonies. It was Hunter who was responsible for many of the funeral decorations used.[16] The total of all the funeral bills would cost the government $3,088.09.[17]

The body was laid out in a coffin and placed on a table in the middle of the entrance hall of the Executive Mansion. The room was hung with black crepe around the windows and draped on the chandeliers. A large crowd had congregated in front of the house as early as 11 A.M., but it was two hours later that the public was admitted to pay their respects.

The remains were enclosed in a lead coffin with a roofed lid and a glass over the face. The lead coffin was inside a black velvet–covered, gold lace–trimmed mahogany one, hermetically sealed with zinc sheets, also roofed, with a glass window, then covered with a fringed, black velvet pall trimmed with gold lace. On top of all this rested two wrought swords. There was no plaque or inscription on the coffin.

Thousands of people passed through the hall all day long to look upon the president's face, which wore a natural and peaceful expression. Many of the ladies laid flowers upon the bier, and quite a few mourners broke into tears. Among those paying their respects were Mr. and Mrs. John Quincy Adams.

On Tuesday the sixth the White House was closed. Troops from the surrounding areas began arriving in the capital for the funeral, and the arrangements for the ceremonies were outlined in the day's newspaper.

John Tyler arrived in Washington at five o'clock that morning, having traveled the 230 miles from his home on horseback, by boat and finally by special train from Richmond to Washington. He took a room at Brown's Indian Queen Hotel and got a few hours rest. At noon the five cabinet officers (the sixth, Navy Secretary George E. Badger, was still out of town) called on him at the hotel. Daniel Webster carried a rolled document with him, presumably the official account of the death of President Harrison. Tyler asked the cabinet to remain in office and expressed confidence that they would help him with the heavy responsibilities thrown upon him at so grievous a time.

After a consultation, the gentlemen sent for the chief justice of the U.S. circuit court of the District of Columbia, William Cranch, who administered the presidential oath of office to Tyler in the hotel. U.S. Chief Justice Roger Taney was originally asked to come in from his home in Baltimore to deliver the oath, but he refused because he had not been properly invited.[18] The following affidavit, signed by Judge Cranch on April 6, divulges the views of the new president regarding the oath taking:

> I, William Cranch, chief judge of the circuit court of the District of Columbia, certify that the above named John Tyler personally appeared before me this day, and, although he deems himself qualified to perform the duties and exercise the powers and office of president on the death of William Henry Harrison, late President of the United States, without any other oath than that which he has taken as vice president, yet, as doubts may arise, and for greater caution, took and subscribed the foregoing oath before me.[19]

Tyler was probably correct in his assumption that no oath was required of him, although the Constitution does not specify what, if any, oath should be taken by a vice president. That was instituted by law. Additionally, there is no doubt that the vice president must assume the duties of the president immediately upon the president's death. There is no such thing as an interregnum under the Constitution, no tense moments when the country is leaderless awaiting someone to be sworn in as president.

At 2 P.M. the new president visited the White House and expressed his condolences, in deep sorrow, to the relatives of the late President Harrison. The body had been moved to the East Room in preparation for the next day's funeral services. Mr. Tyler paid his respects and looked upon the face of his predecessor.

Wednesday, April 7, dawned cool and overcast. At sunrise the sound of booming cannons could be heard from the several military stations in and around the nation's capital. Minute guns began firing during the morning. They were joined by the tolling of bells throughout the city. Almost every house along Pennsylvania Avenue and its contiguous streets was hung with black festoons, streamers and mourning emblems. All businesses in the city were closed. Railroad cars arriving in Washington were packed, even though their number had been doubled. People also arrived by steamboat and horseback and carriage from the surrounding countryside.

The northern portico of the White House was hung with long, black banners extending from column to column. Carriages of the guests invited to attend East Room ceremonies were admitted through the front gate. Soon there were several coaches parked on the front lawn of the mansion, as tens of thousands of people began to gather around the house and along Pennsylvania Avenue. The military companies also began arriving for the procession, forming on New York Avenue, north of the White House. An elaborate funeral car pulled up in front of the mansion shortly before noon.

As the official guests entered the White House, dressings of black cloth confronted them on every side, hanging from the lofty ceilings to the floor. In the East Room, the furniture, windows, huge mirrors, and great chandeliers were all hung in black. In the center of the room was the table upon which reposed the coffin, head toward the entrance, covered by the pall, on top of which rested the two elegant swords. A profusion of flowers was strewn on and about the coffin, imparting a sweet scent to the room. Next to and crosswise of the coffin's table was another table upon which rested a Bible and a prayer book.

In a circle surrounding the coffin were seated, beginning at the left side entering the door, President Tyler with Secretaries Webster and Bell on one side, and Granger, Ewing and Crittenden on the other. Next to the secretaries was former president John Quincy Adams, then four members of the previous cabinet. Completing the seated circle were about forty clergymen of every denomination, and close friends and relatives of the late president. Immediately behind President Tyler sat a large group of foreign ministers in splendid dress of stars, epaulettes and insignias. Standing up around the seated circle were senators and congressmen who were in the city (Congress was not in session), the twenty-six honorary pallbearers in white sashes, the physicians who had attended the late president, judges, many officers of the government, and various ladies and guests, including members of the bar.

At noon, the Reverend Hawley stood before the tables and began the reading of the Episcopal funeral service, and the seated guests rose to their feet. He gave no eulogy, but pointed out that one of the first acts of the late president, upon moving into the White House, was to purchase the prayer book and Bible displayed on the table, and that he read daily from that Bible. He further revealed that it had been President Harrison's intention to fully join the Episcopal Church on the following Sunday, which was Easter Day.

After the conclusion of the short service, the Clerk of the Supreme Court, who had organized the ceremonies in the East Room, called out the names of the mayors of Washington, Georgetown and Alexandria, then the clergymen and the physicians. Then eight Marines entered the room and carried away the coffin. It was followed by the twenty-six pallbearers, one for each state in the Union. The other guests in the room trailed after them.

As the coffin emerged from the White House, a detachment of musicians in front of the portico struck up a hymn, and the body was placed on the immense funeral car. The car was in the shape of an oblong platform with a raised dais for placement of the coffin, all covered in black velvet. From the platform was draped more black velvet, almost down to the ground, covering the wheels. From the corners a black crepe festoon was formed and looped in the center by a funeral wreath over the whole. Placed on the coffin were the swords, a scroll of the Constitution, and a funeral wreath of yew and cypress. This vehicle was drawn by six white horses draped in black, with black plumes upon their heads. At the head of each horse was a Negro groom dressed in white, with white turban and sash.

The procession formed and, upon the firing of a signal gun, moved forward down Pennsylvania Avenue toward the Capitol. Minute guns started firing near the White House, and at the City Hall and the Capitol as the column reached those points. Bells tolled throughout the city. The muffled drums of the military beat out a slow march, and the martial bands played mournful tunes.

The order of the procession began with the military escort, led by two mounted generals, followed by fifteen companies of artillery, infantry, cavalry, Marines and militia of several states and the District of Columbia, all in full dress uniform. Next came Harrison's horse, Old Whitey, walking saddled and riderless. In coaches came the marshall of the District of Columbia, who had arranged the civic part of the procession; the clerk of the Supreme Court; the mayors of Washington, Georgetown and Alexandria; the forty clergymen; the physicians; the hearse, led by the grooms, with the pallbearers walking alongside; and relatives and friends of the deceased. Then came the coaches containing President Tyler and Daniel Webster; other cabinet members and department officials; former president John Quincy Adams; supreme court justices and other federal judges; U.S. senators; foreign diplomats; members of the House of Representatives; state governors and legislators; judges of the D.C. circuit court, members of the bar and state judges; and U.S. Treasury officials and other officers of the federal government. On foot came the War of 1812 veterans who had served under General Harrison; societies and associations, preceded by their banners; and the fire companies of Washington in cloaks and hats, with accoutrements. Bringing up the rear were thousands of ordinary citizens.

The entire line stretched for more than two miles and consisted of about ten thousand people and ninety-seven carriages. They moved down Pennsylvania Avenue, a corridor lined by tens of thousands of solemn and silent spectators against the backdrop of black-shrouded buildings.

The procession moved around the south end of the Capitol, with minute guns firing from the west portico, and then eastward another mile and a half to the Congressional Burial Ground. The columns halted in front of the cemetery, and the troops were formed into a line across the road. The funeral car was then pulled up to the entrance as the soldiers presented arms. A dirge was played, and the coffin was taken form the hearse by the bearers. The clergymen came forward, and the Reverend Hawley began reciting the Episcopal liturgy as the coffin was carried down the cemetery lane. The procession of mourners followed till all reached the receiving vault at the far end of the burial ground.

Sentries had kept open a square around the vault. The coffin was taken down into it, a spacious, arched structure that had been hung with festoons of black crepe. There were eight other coffins already inside the vault. In the center was a walnut shell into which the coffin was placed, and the lid was put on the shell. It was then placed in the tomb. President Tyler and the cabinet officers entered the vault to take a last look at the coffin and re-emerged. A salute was fired by the military companies, firing from left to right and continuing three times up the line. The military returned to the center of the city in formation and were dismissed, while the civilians dispersed from the cemetery and returned home.

The days following, memorial services or elaborate public funeral pageants were held in many cities and towns. Particularly noteworthy were observances in Baltimore, Philadelphia, Boston and New York.[20] New York City's ceremony on April 10 was especially impressive, with a mock funeral carriage and huge procession featuring former president Martin Van Buren as its chief mourner.[21] In Lancaster, Pennsylvania, senator and future president James Buchanan delivered the eulogy at that city's memorial meeting. On April 13, President Tyler issued a proclamation recommending a national day of fasting and prayer for May 14 in memory of President Harrison.

Congress had not been meeting at the time of President Harrison's death and funeral, but convened on May 31 in a special session that had been called by the late president before his death. On June 4 Congress passed resolutions in connection with Harrison's death. One directed that the chairs of the speaker of the house and president of the Senate be shrouded in black for the remainder of the session, and that all members of both houses wear a badge of mourning for thirty days. Another expressed the condolences of Congress to the late president's widow, and yet another requested the president transmit the resolutions of condolence to Mrs. Harrison. Tyler complied with the request, adding his own personal message.

Congress also considered a bill to grant $25,000 to Mrs. Harrison and give her the postal franking privilege for life. In the early days of the republic there was much opposition to the granting of pensions and gratuities to privileged persons, but in a few days Congress approved the bill and the president signed it into law, thus making the first payment ever to a president's widow.[22]

In May, William Henry Harrison's old comrade Colonel Todd called on the widow Harrison at her home at North Bend, Ohio. While there he consulted with her and her only surviving son, John Scott Harrison, as to the final disposition of the remains of the late president. It was decided to remove the body to North Bend immediately, to be buried at a site overlooking the Ohio River.[23]

The city of Cincinnati formed a committee and received permission from the family to petition the federal government for removal of the body from Washington. This committee for the removal traveled to the nation's capital in June and formally notified President Tyler of its wishes. Tyler, without objection, transmitted the request to Congress, which readily assented. There had been hope among a few people that President Tyler would order permanent burial of President Harrison under the Capitol Rotunda in the vault that had been originally constructed for the body of George Washington.

The House formed a twenty-four man committee and selected Saturday, June 26, as the date for the removal. The Senate also formed a committee, and representatives of these groups and the Cincinnati committee worked out details of ceremonies to accompany the removal.

On the twenty-sixth, at 9 A.M., the members of the three committees met at the Capitol and proceeded in carriages to the Congressional Burial Ground. Also attending was John Scott Harrison and, under order of President Tyler, eight Marines under the charge of a colonel. The *Baltimore Clipper* newspaper gave the following interesting description:

> The body is enclosed first in a leaden coffin, which is placed in a mahogany one, and then in one of zinc, hermetically sealed. This is enclosed in a coffin of walnut, with chloride of lime filled in between it and the zinc, which is very sub-

stantially made, and air-tight.... When the body was exposed to the Committee at Washington a short time previous to its removal, it had undergone little change. The features appeared as at his death, except that the face was a little swollen.

The casket, which weighed about a thousand pounds altogether, was drawn from the vault by the Marines and placed upon a hearse. According to John Quincy Adams, a House committee member, the hearse "was then followed in a somewhat irregular procession to the railway depot at the foot of Capitol Hill."[24]

At the depot were President Tyler and his cabinet, and a great crowd of people, who were orderly and showed no emotion. The Marines lifted the casket onto the special train, whose locomotive and cars were decorated in black. At noon it departed for Baltimore with the committee from Cincinnati and the Marine detachment, which would accompany the body all the way to North Bend.

Arriving a little later at Baltimore, the body was conveyed to the City Hotel. Since the arrival was not announced in advance, very few citizens witnessed the small group of men following the coffin from the railway station to the hotel. There it lay in state under a military guard until Monday morning, when it was taken to a special train. The directors of the railroad company accompanied the body to the end of the line at Columbia, Maryland. From there the committee from Cincinnati and the Marines continued overland to the Ohio River, where the coffin was placed onboard the steamboat *Raritan*.

The steamer docked in Cincinnati on July 5 at 3 A.M. Five hours later a huge crowd witnessed the transfer of the coffin , followed by the committee and a group of the late president's old friends, to the home of Colonel William Henry Harrison Taylor, Harrison's son-in-law. On Thursday morning, July 7, the body was taken from the home in a large procession to the *Raritan*. Several military companies, from as far away as Louisville, marched in the parade, with bands playing dirges. Also in the procession were relatives and close friends of the deceased, the committee which had accompanied the remains from Washington, the Cincinnati city council and various local government officials, members of the bar, civic organizations, firemen, private citizens, and a group of thirty or forty old veterans who had served under General Harrison in the War of 1812. An estimated 15,000 to 20,000 spectators watched from windows and lined the streets.

When the wharf at the foot of Main Street was reached, the coffin was carried onto the *Raritan* and placed in the center of the cabin. At about 1 P.M. the boat left for North Bend, fifteen miles downriver. Aboard were the committee, the Marine detachment and relatives.

It had been the intention to have the services at the tomb restricted to the family, but that was impossible. Three steamboats left Cincinnati, following the *Raritan*. Also, at the burial site thousands of people from the neighboring countryside had gathered. The widow Harrison did not attend.

At 3 P.M. the *Raritan* arrived at North Bend, and the Marines carried the coffin to the stone vault in an informal little procession, through a phalanx of mourners gathered in the falling rain. This tomb was located on a knoll about 200 feet above a bend in the Ohio River and could be seen from a great distance in either direction as one passed by on the water below. It was on the Harrison farm overlooking the president's home, and the site was said to have been selected by him.[25] The services at the grave were jointly performed by the Rev. John T. Brooke (Episcopal) and the Rev. Joshua L. Wilson (Presbyterian). Afterward, the iron door of the vault was closed, and the crowd slowly dispersed.

The late president's widow, Anna Tuthill Symmes Harrison, survived her husband by twenty-three years and died on February 25, 1864, at age 88. A short time later her body was placed in the tomb next to that of her husband. Over the years the tomb fell into disrepair. Vandals removed the door, the stucco walls crumbled, and weeds grew everywhere. In the summer of 1897, William Henry Harrison's grandson, former twenty-third president Benjamin Harrison, had the tomb restored.[26] Today, a 60-foot-high obelisk towers over the site.

The cause of death of William Henry Harrison was laid to bilious pleurisy, known today as pneumonia. Shortly after the president's death the attending doctors issued a statement in which they blamed the immediate cause of death on diarrhea, complicated by congestion of the liver and pneumonia.

In reality, the immediate cause was diarrhea and bodily exhaustion brought on by the purging effects of the administered drugs and remedies. The primary causes of death were pneumonia and hepatitis that was caused by the harsh medications. The doctors were criticized by a few men for their treatment of Harrison, but by and large they had followed the standard medical practices of the day. As in George Washington's case, this treatment made the patient weaker and unable to fight his disease. Whether President Harrison could have survived had he not been given the harsh cathartics and emetics is a matter of speculation, for the pneumonia may have carried him off anyway; but there is little doubt that the doctors at least hastened his death.

There were stories going around at the time of Harrison's death that he was the victim of foul play, that he had been poisoned by pro-slavery elements who wanted the Southerner Tyler to become president. John S. Dye published such a theory in 1866, saying the poisoning was done under the direction of the great Southern statesman John C. Calhoun.[27] And a Philadelphia

The tomb of William Henry Harrison in North Bend, Ohio, on the banks of the Ohio River near Cincinnati. (M. Nowak)

hotelier wrote a letter to Abraham Lincoln in 1860, warning him of the possibility of such a fate. The letter stated that Harrison's sarcophagus had been opened and the body examined prior to its permanent burial by the committee from Congress that had accompanied it from North Bend. The head and chest of the corpse were swollen, and the face and breast were black as though bruised. Supposedly, a doctor who was there said that only poison could produce such a result and suggested an investigation. But Senator Thomas Ewing of Ohio ordered the sarcophagus closed and deposited in its final resting place, out of fear that if poisoning was found to be the cause of death, it could cause a civil war.[28]

There is no evidence to back up these contentions. In the case of the hotelman's story, it is not true that the congressional committee accompanied the body to North Bend. The body was examined by the committee at Washington, but there is no evidence that the body they saw had turned black. Even if it had, it should be remembered that Harrison's doctors had administered strong medicines and poisons to him as part of their accepted treatment.

Harrison's death started one of the strangest coincidences in American history. Every person elected president in the general election in a year ending in zero, from 1840 to 1960, died in office. The only president to die in office who was not elected in a zero year, Zachary Taylor, died in a zero year. In the 1980s this zero year coincidence came to be popularly known as the Curse of Tecumseh, the Indian Chief who died in a battle against the white man in 1813. Ronald Reagan broke this "tradition" by surviving an assassination attempt and serving eight years in office — despite being elected in 1980.

William Henry Harrison left a will that did not legally conform to Ohio law. It was not witnessed and did not dispose of all his property, dealing only with pieces of real estate. It is not known if this caused any problems for his family, to whom he left most of the real estate. Harrison died in debt and directed some land be sold to pay off those obligations. He left his home in North Bend to his widow, and she inherited his personal property as well.[29]

CHAPTER 3

Zachary Taylor

12TH PRESIDENT OF THE UNITED STATES
TERM OF OFFICE: MARCH 4, 1849, TO JULY 9, 1850
BORN: NOVEMBER 24, 1784; DIED: JULY 9, 1850
AGE AT DEATH: 65 YEARS, 227 DAYS
PLACE OF DEATH: WASHINGTON, D.C.
CAUSE OF DEATH: GASTROENTERITIS
BURIAL PLACE: LOUISVILLE, KENTUCKY

Zachary Taylor was a career soldier who never even voted until age 62. As a young army officer he lived through bouts of yellow fever, severe dysentery and malaria as he served in mosquito-infested, swampy camps around the country.[1] He also survived the War of 1812, Indian battles and the Mexican War, during which he suffered only a grazed arm, and earned the status of military hero for his triumphs and exploits. He was called "Old Rough and Ready" by his troops because of his gruff, rather unsoldierly appearance, weatherworn face and sloppy manner of dress. His typical "uniform" consisted of a pair of ill-fitting, baggy pants, a worn jacket with no military insignia, and an old farmer's hat.

At the end of the Mexican War, the Whig Party, eager to recapture the White House from the Democrats, eyed the immensely popular General Taylor for its presidential nominee in 1848. At first dismissing such talk as nonsense, Taylor wound up accepting the Whig nomination and went on to win the presidency. History had repeated itself by putting a Whig general in the White House, as had been the case eight years earlier with William Henry Harrison. Unfortunately, the dark side of history would also repeat itself, as President Taylor would become the second president to die in office. Only two Whigs were elected president, and they both died in office.

It was July 4, 1850, sixteen months to the day from his inauguration as twelfth president of the United States, that Zachary Taylor attended ceremonies at the site of the Washington Monument. The program was connected to the laying of the cornerstone of the huge obelisk, and the president listened to patriotic speeches and music for more than two hours under a hot afternoon sun and in oppressive heat. He drank plenty of water. Once the ceremonies were over, he took a walk near the Potomac River, even though he had complained of dizziness and a headache before leaving his carriage at the start of the festivities.[2] In fact, he had complained the day before about feeling very fatigued.

When he returned to the White House later, the president was tired and very hungry. He consumed a large quantity of raw fruits and/or vegetables, and washed them down with ice cold drinks. Legend has it that he ate cherries and drank ice milk, but what exactly was ingested is not clear. Accounts vary: cherries, wild berries, cucumbers, cabbage, mush, milk, water, and various combinations of these.[3]

"Old Rough and Ready," Zachary Taylor, survived a career serving in swampy, diseased military camps, but as president he succumbed to gastroenteritis after ingesting tainted food or drink in July 1850. (ImageEnvision)

At dinner, Taylor once again partook of raw fruit, reportedly cherries, against the advice of military White House physician Dr. Alexander S. Wotherspoon, who was with the president at the meal. Within an hour, Taylor was seized with severe intestinal cramps. Wotherspoon prescribed medicine, but the president refused to take it.[4]

Asiatic cholera was in the country, but there was no evidence that it had reached Washington that summer. However, many people in the capital were suffering from gastrointestinal pain and diarrhea, then called cholera morbus and not related to the deadly Asiatic type. Dr. Wotherspoon diagnosed the president's ailment as cholera morbus.[5]

Toward midnight the attack worsened, but apparently Taylor felt a little bit better the next day, at least well enough to transact a little paperwork. Yet one report said that his condition did not really improve at all.

The next afternoon, Saturday the sixth, the president's family became worried about him and sent for Dr. Wotherspoon. He administered the laxative calomel, also called mercurous chloride, and opium. These seemed to bring some relief to the bedridden patient. However, his condition worsened steadily during the weekend, and army physician Richard H. Coolidge and Dr. James C. Hall of Washington were called in to help. On Monday, Dr. Robert C. Wood of Baltimore arrived. More medicine was given, and a fever developed. Taylor ate ice constantly, but his stomach would not tolerate anything.

This illness seemed to be much like the one the president had endured during a trip to Pennsylvania and New York a year earlier. During August and September of 1849, Taylor traveled by rail across the Keystone State to the city of Erie. Just a few days into the journey, he felt sick. Though better after a few days, he took a turn for the worse at Erie. He was severely ill with diarrhea and a burning fever. Doctors thought it to be cholera morbus and for a time feared for his life. But once again he rallied, and on September 1 he continued the trip by lake steamer to Niagara Falls, New York. Because he was still weak, as a precaution a planned continuation of the sojourn to Buffalo then New England was cancelled, and the president returned to Washington after only a couple of brief stops in New York. He seemed to have completely recovered by the time he returned to the White House.[6]

Now ten months later, in the Executive Mansion, Taylor became despondent of his life. His dysentery stopped, but vomiting ensued. The president's family gathered in an anteroom. They included his wife Margaret, his brother Joseph and family, his two daughters and their spouses, and Jefferson Davis, husband of Taylor's late daughter Sarah. Only the doctors were allowed in the actual sick room.

At 11 P.M. on Monday the public was first informed of the president's condition, although there had been rumors going around that he was ill. The doctors issued a bulletin stating that "the President is laboring under a bilious remittent fever, following an attack of serious cholera morbus; and is considered by his physicians seriously ill."

Bulletins were then issued hourly stating the progress of the patient. As Tuesday dawned, thousands of curious and concerned citizens began to gather around the White House to quietly await the reports on Taylor's condition. A messenger was posted at a door to answer questions. The news was disseminated throughout the country by telegraph, and it was at times confusing. One bulletin stated that he had rallied; the next proclaimed him "dangerously ill." A rumor circulated at 1 P.M. that the president was dead, but a 3:30 bulletin claimed that he was out of immediate danger, and the crowd rejoiced. Then at 7 P.M. it was announced that he was dying.

Both the Senate and the House of Representatives were in session and were informed early Tuesday afternoon that the president was not expected to survive the day. Both houses immediately adjourned. Department heads, diplomats and military officers called at the White House during the day to pay their respects. Vice President Millard Fillmore and the cabinet appeared.

Shortly after 10 P.M. a minister, the Rev. Smith Pyne, was called to the bedside to pray. Then the dying man asked for his family. His final words were "I am about to die. I expect the summons soon. I have endeavored to discharge all my official duties faithfully. I regret nothing, but am sorry that I am about to leave my friends."[7]

He attempted to speak once more, to his wife who was kneeling beside him, but could not. Dr. Wotherspoon then administered a stimulant, which had no effect. President Taylor died without a struggle at 10:35 P.M. on Tuesday, July 9, 1850. In addition to the family, also present were Vice President Fillmore, the cabinet, the doctors, a few senators, congressmen and diplomats, and a few intimate friends.[8] Mrs. Taylor was inconsolable and had to be carried from the bedside. Death was ascribed to cholera morbus, but it was most likely gastroenteritis, which includes food poisoning as well as other serious ailments of the digestive tract.

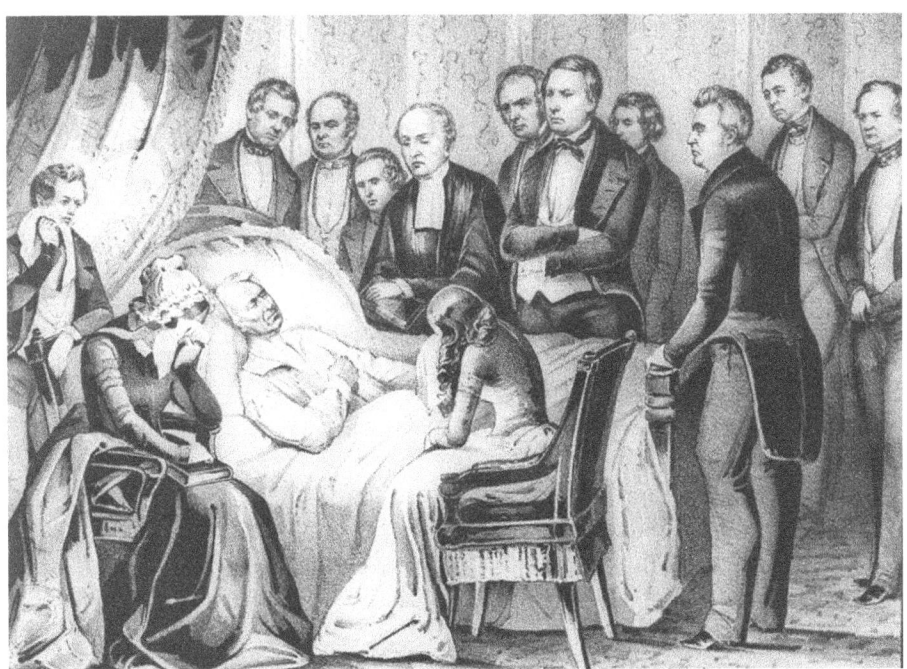

Deathbed scene of President Taylor. In the foreground are the president's son Richard, wife Margaret and daughter Mary. The Rev. Smith Pyne stands over Mr. Taylor, surrounded by administration officials, including Vice President Fillmore, standing with arms crossed. (ImageEnvision)

Shortly after Taylor's passing, the cabinet sent an official letter to Millard Fillmore, formally advising him of the president's death: "The melancholy and most painful duty devolves on us to announce to you that Zachary Taylor, late President of the United States, is no more. He died at the President's mansion this evening at half-past 10 o'clock."

Mr. Fillmore sent a brief reply saying he would appoint a time for his oath-taking as thirteenth president of the United States. He officially communicated news of Taylor's death to both houses of Congress in a letter on the morning of July 10, which also set forth his proposal to take the oath of office at noon that day in the hall of the House of Representatives. Resolutions were adopted by both houses to attend the ceremony, and this was done. The oath was administered to Fillmore by William Cranch, chief justice of the U.S. circuit for the District of Columbia. This was the same man who nine years earlier had sworn in John Tyler as tenth president upon the death of William Henry Harrison.

The spectator galleries were packed. The new president gave no speech, but sent another message to both houses urging them to take proper steps to honor Mr. Taylor and asking for their help in the discharge of his duties.[9] Both House and Senate then reassembled in their respective chambers, and appropriate eulogies were read, most notably by Senator Daniel Webster and Representative Abraham Lincoln.

The news of President Taylor's death was disseminated within a few minutes of the event. It was telegraphed around the country and was received with sadness everywhere. From prominent citizens and political entities came expressions of sympathy. Memorial services were scheduled in most cities and towns, and newspapers throughout the land printed solemn eulogies. Many pointed out the unfortunate time at which the death of the president took place. Zachary Taylor was looked upon as a man who could have been the savior of the country. Being well respected and a Southern slave holder who was opposed to the extension of slavery, he was in a unique position to find a solution to the tension between North and South, and may well have succeeded. Had he lived, the Civil War may never have happened, or military actions may have been considerably less.

In Washington, D.C., flags were lowered to half staff, and many buildings, including public offices, were hung with black cloth. The White House itself was heavily draped in black. All government offices were closed, and every kind of business was suspended. Groups gathered on street corners to converse, wearing expressions of concern and sadness on their faces. City bells, which began sounding as soon as the president's death was announced late on July 9, tolled throughout that night and all the next day.

Shortly after Taylor died, undertaker Samuel Kirby and his assistants were called in. The body was encased in ice, and Mrs. Taylor would not allow it to be embalmed. An Italian artist was sent for to sketch Taylor's face, but no cast was taken for a death mask so that the skin would not be disfigured. Three times during the next two days the ice was removed from the body and it was laid out for the widow to view.[10] It was not until July 12 that the remains would be displayed for public viewing. Mrs. Taylor was very grief stricken. She was not well to begin with, and now she could not sit or stand without support. A "committee of ladies" called at the White House to help console her and the family. Congress sent a message to President Fillmore asking him to transmit its condolences to Mrs. Taylor.

In the meantime, plans were made for a grand funeral. On July 10, both houses of Congress appointed a joint committee of several members to formulate, coordinate and carry out a state funeral in the nation's capital in consultation with the family. The next day, congressional resolutions fixed Saturday, July 13, as the date of burial, temporary interment to be at the Congressional Burial Ground in Washington. The overall plan would be that adopted at President Harrison's funeral in 1841.[11] It was expected that the body would be removed to a permanent burial site in the following weeks.

On July 11, orders went out to the army from Secretary of War George W. Crawford, directing all officers to wear crepe on the left arm and sword hilts for six months, and to fly flags at half staff during that period. The day after receipt of the orders at all army bases, the troops were to be assembled and read the official announcement of President Taylor's death, and all work would be suspended for the day. A salute of thirteen guns was to start the day, with a single gun fired every half hour till sunset, when there would be a salute of thirty guns. Similar orders went out to all navy yards and facilities from Secretary of the Navy William B. Preston.

On Friday, July 12, the undertaker readied the body for public viewing. It was placed in a lead coffin, which was placed in one of mahogany covered with black cloth and ornamented with eight silver eagles. The interior was lined with white satin. The exterior had a plate fixed to the top with the name and dates of birth and death. The closed coffin was partially covered with a pall of black cloth with silver fringe. The face and breast of the late President were visible through a large pane on the top. The facial features were described as being perfectly preserved, looking full and firm, but the body itself was greatly emaciated. It was covered with a shroud, with a white cravat about the neck.[12]

The coffin was placed on a catafalque opposite the most southerly door of the East Room of the Executive Mansion. The room's brilliant chandeliers and huge mirrors were shrouded in black. The casket rested about four feet above the floor. In front of it was a set of steps carpeted in black velvet, which the viewing public would ascend to look upon the remains. Over the whole was an arched canopy curtained with silks of black and white. A large collection of flowers was placed around the room.

In the afternoon the public was admitted. There was some shoving and pushing, but the mourners were generally well behaved. Thousands queued up and passed through during the few hours the room was open, some taking a small leaf or flower from the bier as a souvenir.

On Thursday and Friday, out-of-towners and military troops began arriving in Washington for the Saturday funeral. The schedule and arrangements were made public and published in prominent newspapers throughout the country. The arrivals continued on Saturday morning, and soon all the hotels were full.

On that day, businesses and government offices were closed. Early in the morning people began lining up along the announced route of the procession and around the White House. At sunrise, artillery cannons began firing periodically from positions in the vicinity of the nation's capital. Bells in the city began to toll mournfully. At an early hour religious services took place in the East Room for the family. At 9 A.M. certain dignitaries were allowed into the White House to view the body. House and Senate members assembled in their chambers during the 10 o'clock hour, and then proceeded in carriages to the White House for noon services. President Fillmore, the cabinet and other dignitaries began arriving. At 11 A.M. the military began forming on the streets nearby, as well as the various civic groups which would march.

By noon, an impressive array of dignitaries, both friend and foe of the late president, had taken their places in the East Room. At the foot of the coffin sat President Fillmore and the cabinet; at its head was the Rev. Smith Pyne of St. John's Episcopal Church, where President Taylor had attended services in Washington. Next to him was the Rev. Dr. C.B. Butler, the Senate chaplain, who would assist in the ceremony. Nearby sat commander of the army General Winfield Scott and various other military officers, the foreign diplomats, the honorary pallbearers, including Daniel Webster and Henry Clay, and family members, including Jefferson Davis. Mrs. Taylor was not present.

A little after noon the hour-long services began with a choir singing a hymn. The Reverend Pyne read a passage from the Bible, then delivered a eulogy that closed with an appeal to have George Washington's Mount Vernon purchased by the federal government, and to have the bodies of all the U.S. presidents buried there. Following the benediction, a dirge was sung, with the accompaniment of a seraphine, by two young girls who had been favorite singers of President Taylor. During the song, the coffin was carried outside by a group of Marines into the bright sunshine.

An impressive funeral car stood near the doors. It measured twelve feet long by six feet wide, was covered in black broadcloth hanging to the ground, and sported a raised dais in the center upon which the coffin was placed. An arched canopy of black cloth extended over it, and this was topped with a gold eagle swathed in black crepe. At each corner of the canopy top were gold urns, also shrouded in black. From the canopy hung curtains of black and white tied back with rosettes, fringes and tassels. On top of the coffin was placed the departed soldier's sword and formal army uniform, as well as many floral arrangements.[13]

It was a little past 2 P.M. when the huge wooden wheels of the hearse began moving. The car was drawn by eight white horses caparisoned in black, each led by a Negro groom dressed in white, with white turban and a black sash around the waist.

The order was given, and down Pennsylvania Avenue toward the Capitol the procession moved, past buildings heavily draped in mourning cloth. Church bells were tolling, and the artillery began firing minute guns from three points along the route. The military bands filled the air with dirges and marches. The way was lined heavily with spectators, not only along the street, but occupying every window of every building; some hearty souls were even in the trees. Rough estimates of the crowd ranged from 50,000 to 100,000.

The long line of marchers began with columns of soldiers, sailors, Marines and militiamen from various locations around the east coast. Naval officers marched on foot, but the army officers were on horseback. General Scott on his stallion, wearing a high plume of yellow on his helmet, brought up the rear of the troops. The various colorful military uniforms were quite an impressive sight. The civic part of the procession began with the U.S. marshal of the District of Columbia, followed by the mayors of Washington and Georgetown, the joint congressional funeral committee, the clergymen, the attending physicians, and then the funeral car, with the twenty honorary pallbearers, many of whom were members of Congress, walking close by.

Next came Old Whitey, his saddle empty and his master's boots reversed in his stirrups. This was President Taylor's horse, which had carried him for years through Indian Wars and the recent Mexican War. He was led by an army veteran who had fought with Taylor in the Seminole Wars. Everyone's attention seemed riveted on the famed, restive steed. In carriages followed the late president's family, President Fillmore and the department heads. Then marched the senators, congressmen, supreme court justices, governors, legislators and a large number of local, state and federal officials, military veterans, students and professors of various area institutions, and members of societies and fraternities. The entire line stretched for one and a half miles and was made up of more than 15,000 participants.

The procession marched past the Capitol building and on to the Congressional Burial Ground. Upon arriving at the north entrance of the cemetery, the military took up positions just outside. The burial ground itself was densely occupied by mourners, having been assembled there for several hours. While sentries kept the crowd back, the coffin, led by the clergy and accompanied by the pallbearers, was carried from the funeral car by soldiers down the gravel pathway to the receiving vault. A brief benediction was read by a minister, the coffin was placed in the vault, which had previously held the remains of President Harrison and former president John Quincy Adams, and three volleys were fired by both infantry and artillery. The crowd slowly dispersed and headed back to the city, and the military units returned to their home bases shortly thereafter.

President Fillmore offered to allow Mrs. Taylor to remain in the White House until it was convenient for her to move, but she left for the residence of a friend the evening of the funeral.

In other cities and towns throughout the country, worship services, public meetings and funeral ceremonies were held. Appropriate resolutions of sympathy and eulogies were pronounced and read by various government bodies. In New York, in late July, a five-mile-long funeral procession was witnessed by a quarter of a million people.[14]

The family had to decide where the body should be permanently buried. Though Taylor had been born in Virginia, had lived all over the country, and had resided in Louisiana when elected president, Mrs. Taylor chose to have

Mock funeral pageant for the late President Zachary Taylor held in New York City on July 23, 1850. (ImageEnvision)

her husband interred in the Taylor family cemetery near Louisville, Kentucky. There he had lived as a boy and young man, and it was there that he met his wife. The city of Frankfort, the capital of Kentucky, requested that Taylor be buried there, but this was rejected.[15]

On October 25, 1850, the body was removed from the Congressional Burial Ground in the presence of District of Columbia officials, brother Colonel Joseph Taylor, and son-in-law Colonel William W. Bliss. The coffin was put aboard a special railroad car and, accompanied by the two men, was taken through Baltimore, Harrisburg and Pittsburgh. There, on October 28, it was transferred to the steamboat *Navigator*, which headed down the Ohio River to Cincinnati where proper respects were paid to President Taylor. On the morning of November 1 the steamer docked at Louisville. It was met by a large group of citizens that had marched from the courthouse to the wharf. It was composed of military and fire companies, the mayor and other government officials, as well as many city residents. Native son and U.S. Attorney General John J. Crittenden, who had been in Louisville, made a few remarks, voicing the pride that Kentuckians felt that the state had been chosen for the final resting place of such a great man.[16]

The coffin was carried to a waiting hearse and covered with the American flag. A military contingent led the procession to the cemetery seven miles to the east, followed by the horse-drawn hearse carrying the remains, the city authorities, and firemen and citizens on horseback and in carriages. There, in the small graveyard still owned by the heirs of his uncle, Zachary Taylor was laid to rest in a newly built modest limestone vault, not far from his boyhood home.[17]

The late president's wife, Margaret "Peggy" Mackall Smith Taylor, died on August 18, 1852, at age 64 of unknown causes in Mississippi. She was eventually interred in the crypt next to her husband.

There were proposals to move the bodies to Frankfort in 1878, and to Washington, D.C., in 1911, but these were not acted upon.[18] In 1883 the state of Kentucky erected a 50-foot granite shaft near the burial vault, topped by a life-size statue of the twelfth president.[19]

On May 6, 1926, the bodies of President and Mrs. Taylor were moved to a new, grander mausoleum several yards away, constructed of limestone with a marble interior. The transfer was attended by Frederick Jouett, grandnephew of the late president, his wife, and Colonel R.R. Hannay, who represented the federal government. The coffins were in good shape, practically intact. On May 31 the new tomb was dedicated under the auspices of Louisville's Outdoor Arts League. The 10:30 A.M. ceremony was open to the public, and the dedicatory speech was delivered by U.S. Representative Maurice H. Thatcher of Louisville.[20]

At the time, plans sponsored by Mr. Thatcher were already underway

Tomb of President Zachary Taylor in Zachary Taylor National Cemetery, Louisville, Kentucky. To the left is an obelisk topped with a statue of Taylor. To the right is his mausoleum crypt. (M. Nowak)

for the small burial ground to be converted into a national cemetery, provided the land adjoining it could be purchased for additional acreage. Ownership of the cemetery was passed to the federal government in 1928 and was named the Zachary Taylor National Cemetery. Veterans of several wars lie there.

As was the case with the death of President William Henry Harrison, rumors circulated that President Taylor had been poisoned by Southern political enemies. Though Taylor was a Southerner and slave holder, he vehemently opposed its extension and was against compromise in the matter. Vice President Fillmore favored compromise; so, the story went, pro-slavery Southerners conspired to poison Taylor, thereby making Fillmore president. Some even believed that Fillmore was involved in the alleged murder plot. Indeed, as president, Fillmore signed into law the Compromise of 1850, which included pro-slavery provisions.[21]

Almost 141 years after Taylor's death, Clara Rising, an author of historical novels, convinced the president's descendants that the poisoning theory might be true. They sought and received permission from the U.S. Department of Veterans Affairs, which has jurisdiction over the cemetery, to have the body exhumed and tested for signs of poison. At 9 A.M. on the morning of June 17, 1991, a team of several specialists and family members arrived at the cemetery. About twenty reporters and photographers, and about two hundred onlookers, were kept twenty yards away by four uniformed VA guards. Those allowed in and near the mausoleum included Miss Rising, Dr. Richard Greathouse, the Jefferson County coroner, who agreed to test the remains, an undertaker from the same firm that had placed the body there in 1926, Anne LeBourgeois and Helen Ruffy, great-great-great-great granddaughters of the former president, and Helen Taylor, a collateral descendant.

For about an hour workers, pathologists and the family members milled about and walked in and out of the crypt. A green curtain hung across the double-doored glass-paneled entrance. The experts had planned to remove only small samples of hair, bone and fingernails to be tested, but once the heavy marble lid of the sarcophagus was lifted off, the coffin was too badly deteriorated to take samples on site. It still bore remnants of the cloth that had covered it. It was lifted out and placed in a protective pouch, wrapped in an American flag and put on a gurney, then wheeled to a black hearse.[22]

The samples were taken at the county coroner's office. A power saw was used to open the coffin and reveal the mostly skeletal remains. It was said that the skull looked recognizable as Zachary Taylor. The procedure was photographed and videotaped and witnessed by about a dozen people, including the three relatives. It lasted about four hours, after which the remains were returned to the tomb, at about 4:30 P.M. Once again a crowd had gathered to watch as the flag-draped coffin was carried back inside the mausoleum while a military color guard stood nearby. The flag was presented to the family afterward.[23]

Nine days later Kentucky's chief medical examiner, Dr. George Nichols, held a news conference and announced that Zachary Taylor had not been poisoned and had died of natural causes, though the exact cause of death could not be determined. Tests on the samples had been conducted independently at three different locations — in Louisville, Frankfort, and at the nuclear reactor at Oak Ridge, Tennessee. Only naturally occurring traces of arsenic were detected, though the final report stated that the symptoms and manner of death were consistent with arsenic poisoning, as well as other illnesses.[24] The hair and nail samples removed from the body were deposited with the Filson Historical Society of Louisville.[25]

Zachary Taylor's estate was worth about $150,000, most of it in land in Louisiana, Mississippi and Kentucky, and warehouses in Louisville, but also a considerable amount in slaves, stocks, cash and a home in Baton Rouge. He had prepared a will that was legally flawed, but his family carried out his wishes. His property was divided among his wife and three surviving children more or less equally.[26]

CHAPTER 4

Abraham Lincoln

16TH PRESIDENT OF THE UNITES STATES
TERM OF OFFICE: MARCH 4, 1861, TO APRIL 15, 1865
BORN: FEBRUARY 12, 1809; DIED: APRIL 15, 1865
AGE AT DEATH: 56 YEARS, 62 DAYS
CAUSE OF DEATH: GUNSHOT WOUND TO THE HEAD
BURIAL PLACE: SPRINGFIELD, ILLINOIS

By the year 1865 the United States had survived the deaths of two of its presidents in office. Both William Henry Harrison and Zachary Taylor had died of natural causes, although rumors of poisoning by political enemies circulated. These stories were never proved. An unsuccessful attempt had been made to assassinate President Andrew Jackson in 1835 on the steps of the Capitol. A plot to kill President-Elect Abraham Lincoln was squelched in early 1861, and a shot or shots were fired at him in 1864. But in 1865, after four bloody years of civil war that tore the nation apart, a traumatic event would top off those years of violence. President Lincoln would be shot and killed a few weeks into his second term of office, becoming the first president to be assassinated.

Abraham Lincoln was born in Hodgenville, Kentucky, in 1809. His family moved to Knob's Creek, then Spencerport, Indiana. Like most frontier boys, Lincoln worked at farm chores. At seventeen he operated a ferry boat, then a flat boat on the Mississippi River. Finally, at twenty-one he became independent of his parents. Lincoln's family was dirt poor, and he had only one year of formal education; but through reading he had educated himself.

As a young boy he almost drowned in Knob's Creek, and as a youth he was kicked in the head by a horse and knocked unconscious. He was tall and gangly, yet physically strong, and grew to a height of six feet four inches. Because of the features of his body, including long legs and arms, and big hands, feet and ears, many historians believe that he suffered from Marfan Syndrome, an abnormality of the body's connective tissue. Lincoln also suffered from bouts of severe depression, especially after the deaths of his mother, his fiancée, and his son Willie.[1]

As a young adult, Lincoln worked in a general store, volunteered for service in the Black Hawk Indian War (though he saw no action), was partner in a general store that failed, and was postmaster of New Salem, Illinois, for three years.

Politics first attracted Lincoln at the age of twenty-three, when he lost an election for the Illinois State Legislature. Two years later he was successful and served in the statehouse for six years, until 1842. During this time he studied law, and was admitted to the bar in 1837. He moved to the capital of Springfield and practiced law in partnership with two men.

In 1846 he was elected to a single term in the U.S. House of Representatives as a Whig, and campaigned for the party's presidential nominees. In 1854 he again served in the state legislature, and joined the new Republican Party.

Despite his brief stints in public office, Lincoln had gained a favorable reputation among the party leaders. Some wanted him to be the Republican nominee for vice president in 1856. In 1858 he was the Republican candidate for U.S. senator, but was not chosen. But in 1860 he was nominated for president by the party. In a fractious, sectional election, Lincoln managed to win enough electoral votes to become the sixteenth president of the United States.

Knowing the anti-slavery stance of Mr. Lincoln and the anti–Southern bias of the Republican Party, Southern states began to secede from the Union even before the new president took office. Lincoln would not change his principles and refused to compromise with the South. When the militia of South Carolina moved to take over Fort Sumter, President Lincoln defended the installation. What was perceived as a small rebellion mushroomed into a bloody civil war.

After four years of the deadliest war ever fought by Americans, Lee surrendered to Grant on April 9, 1865, four weeks after President Lincoln began his second term of office. Five days later, on Good Friday, the president was scheduled to attend a play at Ford's Theatre in Washington, along with Mrs. Lincoln and General and Mrs. Ulysses S. Grant. The general turned down the invitation, and Secretary of War Edwin M. Stanton and his wife declined to take their places, so Mrs. Lincoln invited Major Henry R. Rathbone and his fiancée, Clara Harris, the daughter of Senator Ira Harris of New York. The couple accepted.

Lincoln did not feel like attending the theater that night, but because his appearance there had been advertised in the newspapers, he decided to go, lest he disappoint those expecting him. The play, *Our American Cousin*, a comedy, began promptly at 8 P.M. despite the fact that the president had not yet arrived. The Lincoln party was late getting started, and it was close to

8:30 before they took their seats in the playhouse, filled with an audience of a thousand people.

They entered through the front door of the theater, led by John Parker, a Washington policeman assigned to guard the president at Ford's, with Lincoln and the others a couple of steps behind. They could be seen walking down the open second level corridor to the right, the so-called dress circle. As theater patrons began to notice the prestigious guests' arrival, they began to stand and applaud. Even the actors stopped, turned toward the presidential box and applauded. The band began playing "Hail to the Chief." After several minutes the president took his seat, the cheering stopped and the play resumed.

Lincoln and the others were seated in a second level box to the right of the audience, directly above the floor of the stage. Actually, it was a combination of two boxes, with a partition removed for the occasion. The two portals of the box looking out were framed with heavy decorative lace and satin drapery. Two American flags stood at the exterior of either end, while two more flags were arranged to hang down from the railings; centered between them was a framed portrait of George Washington. Just below these was a Treasury Guard's flag displaying its eagle.

Inside, as one looked out over the stage, were placed a rocking chair upholstered in dark red satin, with a floral pattern. To its right were two stuffed chairs and a sofa. Behind them were six straight cane chairs for any possible guests who might sit with the president. Lincoln sat in the rocker. Mrs. Lincoln was in a cane chair to the president's right, Miss Harris occupied another chair to her right, and Major Rathbone was on the sofa to the right of her. Presidential valet Charles Forbes was seated on a straight chair to the right of the sofa. Outside the presidential suite, through two unlocked white doors, was a small anteroom, through which anyone wishing to enter the boxes would have to pass. In this anteroom was seated the guard Parker.

The actor John Wilkes Booth was well known at Ford's Theatre, having played there many times. He was free to enter at any time. Consequently, he aroused no suspicion when he came down the slightly sloping dress circle to the right of the stage toward the president's box. Along the way he passed by patrons seated at the railing watching the play.

As he pushed open the door to the anteroom the police guard was not there. Booth would not have to contend with him, for Parker had earlier moved out into the gallery of spectators to watch the play, then around 9 P.M. had left the playhouse. He asked Francis Burns, the president's carriage driver, who was dozing in the carriage in front of the theater, if he would like to go for a beer. Burns said yes just as valet Forbes was also exiting the theater. The three walked together to a nearby tavern for drinks.

Booth jammed shut the door to the anteroom behind him with a piece of wood. To the left were the two doors to the expanded presidential box. The left one was directly behind the Lincolns.

Booth peered through the peephole he had carved into it earlier that day. He could see the back of Lincoln's head just four feet behind the door. Now he waited for a precise moment in the play when he knew only one actor would be on stage. That occurred when actor Harry Hawk recited the lines, "Don't know the manners of good society, eh? Well, I guess I know enough to turn you inside out, you sockdologizing old mantrap."

As Hawk began to speak, Booth pulled a small derringer from his coat pocket and turned the doorknob. It was 10:13 P.M. The door opened inward. He moved forward along the box's wall to the left. The president was leaning forward, looking down at the audience, his head turned slightly to the left. Booth raised the pistol to within four or five inches of the back of Lincoln's head and fired, the bullet striking him behind the left ear. The audience was laughing at the actor's lines. The sound was augmented by the sound of the shot.

A small cloud of gunsmoke rose into the air of the box. The major sprang from his seat and tried to grab Booth, who lost his hat, dropped the pistol and pulled out a dagger, which he plunged into Rathbone's upper left arm. Mrs. Lincoln was shocked and confused. The assailant moved toward the rail as the major came at him again. He pushed Rathbone away and vaulted over the railing, holding on with his arms. He lowered himself, then dropped the twelve feet to the stage. But he jumped slightly off balance, causing the spur of his right boot to catch in the Treasury flag. The banner ripped and fell to the stage.[2] Booth landed rigidly on his left foot, falling forward and catching himself with his arms. The awkward landing caused his tibia (the bone between the knee and the ankle) to fracture just above the ankle.

On stage, Harry Hawk had stopped his soliloquy at the sound of the shot and looked up at the president's box. Booth got up and ran limping past the astonished Hawk, fell, then rose again. At some point on stage, Booth is said to have shouted, "Sic semper tyran-

Assassination of Abraham Lincoln by John Wilkes Booth in the presidential box at Ford's Theatre. Booth fires at the president's head. To Lincoln's right are Mrs. Lincoln, Major Henry Rathbone and his fiancée, Clara Harris. (Library of Congress)

nis," Latin for "Thus always to tyrants," but this is in dispute.[3] Most witnesses heard him shout, "The South is avenged!" The audience was confused. Mrs. Lincoln screamed loudly and shrieked, "Help! Help!" Rathbone shouted, "Stop that man!" as did Miss Harris. Booth exited stage right, brushing past an actress and the orchestra leader, and brandishing a knife as he went by.

Confusion reigned in the theater as the audience slowly began to realize that something terrible had happened in the president's box, that this was not part of the play. A loud hubbub arose in the theater. Miss Harris called out for water. Major Rathbone yelled out, "He has shot the president!" Chaos ensued. People left their seats, shouted, moved about the aisles, and some rushed up to the stage. A group of men ran to the box entrance but could not get in until the major removed the bar Booth had braced against the outside door.

Booth limped through the rear stage door exit and mounted a waiting horse. He escaped southward, crossing the Potomac River into Virginia.

Meanwhile, a man who identified himself as a doctor pressed forward outside the president's box and was pushed into it. Dr. Charles A. Leale, a twenty-three-year-old army surgeon, had been seated on the second level not far away. Major Rathbone pleaded for help for his bleeding arm, but the doctor turned his immediate attention to the president. Mr. Lincoln was slumped in his chair, and Mrs. Lincoln had her head on his chest. "Oh, doctor, can he recover?" she cried. "I will do what I can," he replied. She was removed to the sofa in the back of the box, where she sat with Miss Harris.

President Lincoln appeared lifeless. There was no pulse, and he took only an occasional breath. Men held matches until a better light could be found. Dr. Leale at first suspected a stab wound. He ordered some soldiers in the crowded box to lay the president down on the floor. Using a small knife he cut away Lincoln's collar and coat. He could find no wound until he held the president's head and felt a clot of blood behind one ear. He stuck a finger into the wound, causing blood to flow out and the breathing to improve.

Another doctor in the audience got onto the stage and was lifted into the box by a group of men. This was twenty-three-year-old Charles S. Taft. A bit later he was joined by a Dr. Africanus F. King and Dr. Charles A. Gatch. Leale administered mouth-to-mouth respiration. The breathing became stronger. But, realizing that Lincoln had sustained a serious wound to the brain, he said to the other doctors, "His wound is mortal. It is impossible for him to recover."

Soldiers cleared the box. Among the frenzied audience, word spread that an actor named Booth was the assailant. Some shouted to burn down the theater, sensing a conspiracy by the owner. Outside, people had been roused out of their houses by the noise, as some theater patrons ran shouting from the building. The street outside became a mass of people. As word spread further about the incident, citizens throughout the city became frightened. They did not know exactly what was happening. A rebel attack? Many were terrified and bolted their doors. Scores of rumors spread.[4]

Dr. Leale wanted Lincoln taken to the nearest bed. A spoonful of brandy was given to the dying man. The actress Laura Keene arrived and used a wet cloth to wipe the president's face. Messengers were sent out to nearby hospitals for medical supplies.

Dr. Leale ordered two soldiers to grab Lincoln's legs, while two others formed a sling under his torso. Dr. King grabbed the president's left shoulder,

The presidential box above the stage at Ford's Theatre days after President Lincoln was shot. The chair in which Lincoln was sitting can be seen in the right portal. Farther to the right is the ghostly image of one of the soldiers sent to the theater to guard it. (Library of Congress)

and Leale held his head. They lifted him up as a squad of soldiers cleared the way out of the box, downstairs and out of the theater. It was Leale's intention to carry the patient to a bed in a nearby house — any house. The soldiers cleared a path across the dirt street as the body emerged from Ford's. Lincoln was carried into a house across the street at the summons of a young boarder. "Bring him in here," shouted Henry Safford. The president was carried into the boarding house of William Petersen, a German tailor, and into the first floor bedroom of another boarder, army private William T. Clark. It was 10:30 P.M.

The bed in the little room was small, so Lincoln was laid diagonally across it. Dr. Leale knew that this was a death watch, and that nothing could be done to save the life of his famous patient. The idea was to make the dying president as comfortable as possible.

The shooting of Lincoln was part of a larger conspiracy to murder high government officials. Booth's co-conspirators were Lewis Powell (alias Lewis Paine), George Atzerodt, and David Herold. The same night Booth attacked Lincoln, Powell stabbed Secretary of State William Seward in his Washington home, almost killing him. Herold had waited outside as Powell did his deed, but deserted him. Atzerodt backed out of a plan to kill Vice President Andrew Johnson. Others had been part of a plot to kidnap Lincoln and exchange him for Confederate prisoners of war. But when it became obvious that the South would soon lose the war, Booth changed that plan to one of murder.

Dr. Leale cleared the room of everyone except the three other doctors. He told Safford to fill bottles with hot water. The four physicians discussed a plan of action. Meanwhile, Mrs. Lincoln, Clara Harris and Major Rathbone had made it across the street from the theater. Miss Harris sent for a carriage to take her and Rathbone away. The weeping, distraught First Lady was ushered to a front room where she lay prostrate on a sofa, heavily sobbing and occasionally letting out a loud wail. Outside, a murmuring crowd of thousands packed the street.

The doctors undressed the president, revealing a surprisingly fit physique. He appeared unhurt except for the head wound, from which he continually bled. Bottles of hot water were placed along his legs, as they had grown cold due to lack of circulation. Mustard plasters were applied over almost the entire body, and he was covered with hot woolen army blankets.

Shortly after Lincoln was taken to the Petersen house, various officials and medical men began arriving, alerted by messenger or by the clamor in the streets. In all, more than sixteen doctors were present in the sick room at one time or another. Occasionally, amidst all the confusion, an ordinary citizen made his way into the house from off the street to catch a glimpse of the dying man. More than sixty people came and went from the room during that fateful night.[5]

Secretary of War Stanton had been summoned. When he arrived he took control of the situation in the Petersen house — and in the nation. Though he was third in line to succeed to the presidency, the second, Secretary of State Seward, lay gravely wounded, and the first in line, Vice President Johnson, had no constitutional authority to assume control while Lincoln was alive. Technically, neither did Stanton, but he controlled the armed forces. He gave orders and sent out telegrams. The country had to be informed and the attackers caught. With him was a District of Columbia judge who began interviewing witnesses concerning the crime.[6]

Every available District policeman was put on duty in the streets, as were army cavalrymen. All saloons and theaters were closed by the mayor. Ferries were halted, trains searched, roads around the capital closed, and guards put around the homes of government officials.[7]

Eventually, those present in the Petersen house at any one time included dozens of people. Son Robert Todd Lincoln, summoned to the house, joined his mother. Doctors numbered a dozen, including Surgeon General Joseph K. Barnes, Lincoln family physician Robert K. Stone, and Mary Lincoln's cousin Lyman B. Todd.[8]

Vice President Johnson, when informed of the situation, was persuaded to remain in his apartment at Kirkwood House in the city. But by 2 A.M. he insisted on going to the Petersen house. He walked the few blocks there, escorted unrecognized through streets still filled with people. In the sickroom he stood staring sternly for a few minutes at the unconscious Lincoln upon the bed, gave condolences to son Robert, said a few words to Stanton, held Mrs. Lincoln's hand for a moment and went back home.

During the long night people continually moved in and out of the room. Mrs. Lincoln from time to time asked to be taken to see her husband. She would weep and wail pitifully, at one time asking to be killed, too. During one visit she fainted and fell to the floor, and after that the doctors barred her from the tiny bedroom.

The doctors could do little to save Lincoln's life. They basically tried to keep him comfortable. His right eye turned black. His breathing at times was deep, snoring and rattling, at other times shallow. He had occasional muscle spasms. Still there was a pulse.

As morning light came, a crowd of people still stood outside the house, even though a cold rain had begun to fall. By 7 A.M. Lincoln's breathing had become very sporadic, and the end seemed near. Mrs. Lincoln was led into the room, weak and sobbing, to take a last look, then quickly led away by son Robert.[9]

Lincoln took a deep breath and exhaled. Another did not come. Dr. Barnes lifted an eyelid, then put his ear to the patient's chest but detected no heartbeat. He took Lincoln's hands and placed them across the now lifeless breast. "He is gone. He is dead." It was 7:22 A.M., Saturday, April 15, 1865. The doctor took two coins from his vest and placed them over Lincoln's eyes. After a couple of minutes of utter silence, the Rev. Dr. Phineas T. Gurley, pastor of Lincoln's church in Washington, recited a brief prayer. Secretary Stanton, crying, said either, "He belongs to the angels now," or, "Now he belongs to the ages." Popular history favors the latter. Robert Lincoln left to get his mother and led her into the bedroom. The distraught widow threw herself on her husband and cried out, "Oh, my God! I have given my husband to die!" She was carried out of the room. Though improbable, but about twenty persons are identified as being in the tiny room when Lincoln died. They included four cabinet secretaries, six army officers and three doctors. One of the physicians present, James C. Hall, has a unique place in history, having also been present at or near the deathbeds of William Henry Harrison and Zachary Taylor.[10]

Word of President Lincoln's death spread outside the house to the crowded street outside. Messengers rushed to the newspaper and telegraph offices, and within minutes news of the president's demise was flashed to every corner of the country. Church and city bells began to toll in Washington — and everywhere else. Secretary of War Stanton had notices sent to military commanders and held a cabinet meeting at the Petersen house.[11]

Several sets of orders were sent to the military branches informing them of the commander-in-chief's death and the accession of President Johnson. They also instructed posts to carry out various mourning rituals, including the wearing of mourning badges, the flying of flags at half staff, and the draping of headquarters buildings in mourning for thirty days.

Engraving of the death of Lincoln in Petersen House. It shows 26 men present, but the tiny bedroom was so small that only a fraction of them could have squeezed into it at any one time. (Library of Congress)

In the financial capital of New York, the stock and commodity exchanges and banks did little business and closed by noon. Saturday was a full work day in America in 1865. The exchanges would reopen for Monday and Tuesday, but still there was a paucity of trading. On Wednesday, the national day of mourning, everything remained shut. Yet a collapse of the financial markets did not occur, attesting to the strength of the economy and the confidence of the businessmen that the world would not end.[12]

In short order, an official notice containing the signatures of the cabinet officers, except for the wounded Seward, was personally delivered by Attorney General James Speed to Andrew Johnson at Kirkwood House, formally informing Mr. Johnson of President Lincoln's death. The new president was asked when and where he would prefer to take the oath of office. He requested that the ceremony take place in his apartment at 10 A.M.[13]

Chief Justice Salmon P. Chase was notified and went to Kirkwood House, accompanied by Secretary of the Treasury Hugh McCullough, Attorney General Speed, J.P. and Montgomery Blair, General John Farnsworth, and senators Foot, Hale, Ramsay, Stewart and Yates. At 11 A.M., before these ten men, Chase administered the oath to the new president. President Johnson immediately made some brief remarks in which he expressed confidence that the principles of free government would triumph, and asked for help in seeing "the government through its present perils."[14] Johnson was congratulated by all in the room and engaged in brief conversation.

At noon the president held his first cabinet meeting at the Treasury Building. He said he would retain the current cabinet, and appointed William Seward's son Frederick acting secretary of state. All government business was then suspended for the day.

As news of the shooting, then death, spread throughout Washington, then the rest of the country, sensationalist reporting by the newspapers inflamed the populace. In the ensuing hours, thousands of incidents of attacks against perceived Southern sympathizers, or even anyone who had ever made a critical comment about Mr. Lincoln, occurred. Some killings were reported. Accused assassin John Wilkes Booth's brother Junius fled for his life from a Cincinnati hotel. In New York City, former First Lady Julia Tyler's home was invaded and a Confederate flag taken from her parlor.[15]

In Buffalo, mud was thrown at former president Millard Fillmore's house. It displayed no signs of mourning, and he had a history of opposition to Lincoln's policies. In Concord, New Hampshire, a mob gathered outside the home of former president Franklin Pierce and demanded to know why he did not display a flag in mourning.[16] Pierce had been respectful of the South during his presidency. In the South, reaction for the most part was not one of glee, but of sadness and concern, for the late Lincoln had been expected to treat the defeated states with a degree of compassion.

For his part, Secretary of War Stanton believed the Confederates were behind everything, saying, "It was nothing but a Southern plot, a conspiracy deliberately planned and set afoot by the rebels."[17] A massive manhunt throughout the U.S. for the assassin and any possible co-conspirators involved troops, police and private detectives. A national witch hunt soon developed.

Hundreds of people were arrested — not only those making disparaging remarks about Lincoln, or rebel sympathizers, but also Booth's brother-in-law and two brothers.[18] Most of the actors and employees of Ford's Theatre were arrested.[19]

And at the Petersen house, most of those in attendance had slowly left for their own homes. General Thomas Vincent stayed with the body. He ordered an officer to procure a coffin, hearse and an honor guard to take the body to the White House.

Mary Lincoln was driven back to the Executive Mansion. She would not enter her or her husband's bedrooms, choosing another room and lying on the bed weeping. She was attended by her black maid, a doctor, her sons Robert and Tad, and especially by Dr. Anson G. Henry, an old family friend who stayed with her for the next six weeks.[20]

A few minutes after Mrs. Lincoln left the Petersen house, soldiers placed the dead president's corpse in a pine box and wrapped that in an American flag. At 9:30 A.M. it was carried to the hearse and escorted to the White House by several mounted cavalrymen and a group of officers walking behind in the rain. Despite the downpour, the streets were crowded with people as the contingent moved up Tenth to G Street to the mansion, accompanied by the citywide tolling of bells. On this gloomy day, all businesses were closed, flags flew at half mast and the people were busy draping buildings in mourning.

The coffin was carried up to the guest room in the northwest corner of the second floor of the White House and placed on two boards laid across two wooden horses. During the morning hours several men gathered in the room to perform an autopsy on the body. It was conducted by two pathologists from the Army Medical Museum, Dr. J. Janvier Woodward and Dr. Edward Curtis. Observing the procedure were Surgeon General Barnes, Lincoln's personal physician Dr. Stone, Drs. William Notson, Charles Taft and Charles Crane, General Daniel H. Rucker, and the late president's friend Orville Browning. It began at 11 A.M.

The area around Lincoln's eyes was bruised. The brain was removed and the track of the bullet wound examined. The missile was found just behind the right eye. There was no doubt that the wound had been mortal and the immediate cause of death. A tuft of his hair was cut off at the request of the widow for the family. The doctors present also received a lock.[21]

After the post mortem was completed, Henry P. Cattell of the mortuary firm Brown and Alexander began embalming the body.[22] The doctors remained until the work was done.[23] Entering the room for a few minutes was President Johnson. The body was then covered in a white cloth and a handkerchief placed upon the face. Later, Secretary Stanton came in to supervise the clothing of the body. Lincoln was dressed in the black suit he had worn at his second inauguration just six weeks earlier. White gloves were placed on the hands. Lincoln's cheeks looked bruised, but Stanton decided not to have them cosmetically covered, calling it part of the history of the event.[24] The cost of the embalming and preparation was one hundred dollars.[25]

The body was placed in a fifteen-hundred-dollar walnut coffin lined with lead and covered in black broadcloth. It was six feet six inches long, with a white satin quilted lining, and the late president's head rested on a white silk pillow. It was ornamented with four silver handles, four silver shamrocks and a silver star at each end. A silver plate on the coffin was inscribed:

ABRAHAM LINCOLN
SIXTEENTH PRESIDENT OF THE UNITED STATES
BORN FEBRUARY 12, 1809
DIED APRIL 15, 1865

When all was done, white flowers were placed upon the pillow and over the breast.

The coffin had been specially built, and was ordered by the family and Benjamin B. French, the federal commissioner of public buildings.[26] Assistant Treasury Secretary Emerson C. Harrington was appointed by the new president to take charge of the general arrangements for the funeral. Mr. French was given charge of affairs pertaining to the body, and General Christopher C. Augur was ordered to carry out military arrangements.[27]

Plans had been made to take the coffin downstairs to the East Room on Monday, allow public viewing on Tuesday, conduct a funeral ceremony the next day, then present a lying in state at the Capitol until Friday. Burial would be in Lincoln's home town of Springfield, Illinois. The State Department issued a public statement announcing the Wednesday White House funeral and urging all citizens to assemble at their places of worship on that day. Americans would also gather to worship on Sunday, which was Easter Day and came to be called Black Easter.

Over the next several days, telegrams and letters of condolence came in to the White House from around the country and from many nations abroad, expressing grief and sympathy.

As prostrate with grief as Mary Lincoln was, she had to make the final decision as to the disposition of her husband's remains. A cousin and Secretary Stanton met with her to ascertain her wishes.[28] Some wanted Lincoln to be buried in Springfield, others in Washington, either at the Congressional Cemetery or in the Capitol's basement vault originally intended for George Washington. Yet another suggestion favored New York City.[29]

From the start, the widow wanted her husband to lie in a peaceful spot, since he had told her of his desire to rest in a quiet, rural place. A bucolic cemetery in Springfield was her choice.[30] At first she was not sure about

Springfield, since she had quarreled with friends and family back home and vowed never to return there. She considered a quiet cemetery in Chicago on the shore of Lake Michigan. But in the end she chose Springfield's Oak Ridge Cemetery, where her husband's body was to be placed in the public receiving vault, then later moved to a permanent spot of her choice. However, city authorities decided that Lincoln should be buried in the center of town. They bought a lot and quickly began erecting a burial vault on it. Mrs. Lincoln learned of it six days before the scheduled burial and insisted that her husband would be buried in Oak Ridge; if not, she would have the body transferred to Chicago. This made enemies for her in Springfield, a city that apparently thought Abraham Lincoln was its property.[31]

Mrs. Lincoln reluctantly agreed to processions in Washington and the lying-in-state at the Rotunda. The route of the rail journey to Illinois would follow that of Lincoln's inaugural trip to Washington, but in reverse. The federal government was flooded with requests from the cities that had hosted Lincoln on his 1861 trip to have the body removed from the train and lie in state in those communities. Though Mrs. Lincoln was against this, friends and relatives convinced her that it was in the national interest, and she acquiesced. Secretary Stanton appointed two railway officials to work out an itinerary. Scheduling would not be a problem because the federal government, in one of many actions contrary to the Constitution, had seized control of rail operations during the war.[32]

An elaborate catafalque was built in the East Room under the direction of Mr. French. When completed it stood eleven feet high and measured ten by sixteen feet. A raised dais on which the coffin would rest in the center was six by eleven feet and two feet high, about three feet off the floor. This was covered in black broadcloth. Seven-foot-high posts at each corner of the dais supported an arched canopy of black alpaca lined with white satin. Black crepe curtains swept down at each corner and were tied to the bottom of each post. Sixteen rosettes, connected with black ribbons, adorned the sides of the canopy.

The East Room itself, measuring an enormous forty by eighty feet and twenty-two feet high, was darkly decorated. The deep red window curtains were drawn. The chandeliers, mirrors and mantels were heavily hung in black, with white cloth covering the glass of the mirrors. The exterior of the White House was also draped in black.

Lincoln's coffin was carried down to the East Room by eight soldiers. Very early on Tuesday, April 17, people began forming a line at the south entrance of the Executive Mansion, for it had been announced that the public would be allowed to view the body beginning at 9:30 A.M. By that time the line had grown a mile long, with several abreast. The crowd was guided into the East Room where it was separated into two lines, one to pass on each side of the catafalque, with the mourners stepping up onto a platform and walking alongside the coffin to view Lincoln's features. The top third of the body was exposed, with the coffin lid removed. A great deal of sobbing could be heard among the men, women and children.

At 5:30 P.M. the doors were shut, and for the next two hours only special groups were allowed in. Afterward, a team of carpenters came into the East Room and began constructing a series of stairs all around the room, roughly in the form of an amphitheater, so that guests could clearly view the ceremonies the next day. Each section was reserved for a particular group.

During Monday and Tuesday the rail companies added special trains to Washington, and they were full to bursting with people interested in viewing Lincoln's body and attending the funeral ceremonies. Spectators also drove into the city in carriages and wagons. Among them were farmers and small towners from rural America, city dwellers and the well-to-do, and the African Americans. Rooms were scarce. Many thousands slept on hotel floors, in public buildings, on lawns or in their carriages. Officially invited VIPs and delegations reported to Washington City Hall.[33] The streets were busy day and night. A hundred thousand people poured into the city.

Almost all the stores, businesses and government offices in the nation's capital were closed from Saturday through Wednesday. Only a few places opened for a short time for essential reasons, but none on Wednesday, the day of the official White House funeral.

Wednesday was a warm, bright, sunny day. Almost every building in Washington, from the most opulent to the roughest shack, was decorated in dark mourning. Throngs of people began gathering outside the president's house at daybreak. Windows of nearby buildings were filled with spectators. Cannons began booming at forts surrounding D.C. and church bells tolled.

Thousands of soldiers formed into marching units on streets nearby. Their flags were draped in mourning, as were their swords and instruments. Carriages for use in the procession were lined up, as was an impressive hearse. Lincoln's old friend Ward H. Lamon had planned this part of the ceremonies.

At around 11 o'clock invited guests began arriving in the East Room, beginning with a contingent of sixty clergymen of all denominations. Eventually, all manner of high-ranking government officials had gathered within: members of the Supreme Court, foreign diplomats, governors, military officers (including General Grant and Admiral Farragut), House and Senate members, department heads and assistants, and state delegations. Fifteen newspaper reporters were there. Also present were a few members of civic organizations, and Lincoln family and friends. Of the hundreds of people there, only seven were women. It was a decidedly male group, in keeping with the custom of the time. Mrs. Lincoln and her young son Tad stayed upstairs.

Son Robert Lincoln, in his military uniform and terribly distraught, was at the foot of the catafalque. Present also were two cousins of Mrs. Lincoln and two of her brothers-in-law. Near them were the late president's two personal secretaries, John Nicolay and John Hay. General Grant stood at the head of the coffin.

At two minutes to noon President Johnson and his close friend, former New York senator Preston King, entered, followed by former vice president Hannibal Hamlin and the cabinet. They took places to one side of the catafalque near the Supreme Court justices. About six hundred people in all were gathered in the room.

Leaning against the head of the coffin was a cross of lilies, at the foot a wilting arrangement of white roses and lily of the valley. A wealth of evergreens, orange blossoms and camellias looped around the casket, and sprigs of green and flower blossoms were spread over the closed part. Five army officers stood near the catafalque as an honor guard. Lincoln's face was described as being in a peaceful sleep.

A few minutes after noon, President Johnson and Mr. King stepped up to the coffin, looked upon Mr. Lincoln's face for a moment, then stepped back down to their places. At ten minutes past, the Rev. Charles H. Hall of the Episcopal Church began the obsequies with an opening prayer: "I am the Resurrection and the Life..." Bishop Matthew Simpson of the Methodist Episcopal Church followed with a prayer, comparing Lincoln to Moses.

The family pastor, the Rev. Phineas T. Gurley of the Presbyterian Church, then delivered a lengthy oration that consumed more than an hour. Many in the audience had to sit on the steps upon which they stood, for relief.[34] Finally, the Rev. Dr. Edwin H. Gray, Baptist chaplain, gave a short closing prayer, asking God's blessing on the family and government in that trying time.

When the government had announced plans for the Washington noontime ceremony, it had requested the people "meet at their respective houses of worship at that hour." And this they did. All across the nation people crowded into churches to hear memorial services.

With the White House solemnities concluded, the assembled guests left the dim gloom of the East Room and went outside into the bright daylight. Undertaker Frank T. Sands closed the coffin, and a team of army sergeants carried it out of the north entrance and into the waiting hearse. This group of twelve sergeants would be the only ones to lift the casket, all the way to the burial vault in Springfield.

The funeral car was grand, canopied as it was with black cloth surmounted by a gold eagle. The coffin rested atop an eleven foot high platform covered in black cloth down to the ground. Six gray-white horses attended by grooms were harnessed to it, and two drivers sat in the front seat.

The procession moved out as minute guns began thundering and church

4. Abraham Lincoln

bells commenced ringing. First came a detachment of black infantry soldiers that, upon arriving late, quite accidentally took the lead spot in the already moving march. Thousands of other military men, both mounted and on foot, followed. Then came Ward Lamon, acting as marshal, clergymen, doctors who had attended the dying president, and the twenty-two honorary pallbearers that included General Grant and Admiral Farragut, several other military officers, and various congressmen.

The hearse followed, surrounded by a contingent of the military in charge of escorting the body. Next came a riderless gray steed led by a groom, boots reversed in the stirrups. Then came covered carriages carrying Robert and Tad Lincoln and the family, but not Mary Lincoln. After that was President Johnson's carriage and those of the cabinet members, diplomats and the Supreme Court justices. Congressmen and numerous other delegations, representing both government and civilian entities, followed, most on foot. About 30,000 to 40,000 marchers participated in a procession so long that it stretched for more than the one-and-a-half-mile distance down Pennsylvania Avenue from the White House to the Capitol.

The sights and sounds were magnificent. There were the muffled drums and dirges played by thirty different bands, the clattering horse hooves and wheels over the cobblestones, the booming of artillery, and the ringing of all manner of bells throughout the city. Thousands of citizens were lined along the streets, five and ten deep. Many had tears in their eyes. Others watched from windows and porches of buildings decked out in patriotic mourning. The wounded secretary of war, William Seward, was one of them, looking out from the window of his house. Some people climbed into trees for a better view. This was probably the largest public demonstration held in Washington up to that time.

It was 3:30 before the funeral car reached the east front of the Capitol, just as the tail end of the procession was leaving the vicinity of the White House. The beautiful Capitol, whose dome had recently been completed, was also decked in mourning. The pillars and windows were draped in black, and the statue Liberty atop the dome was encircled in black.

All the military units formed into ranks in the plaza in front of the building. The honorary pallbearers and a guard of honor formed a double line up the stairs to the Rotunda. Eight of the sergeants who had walked alongside the hearse carried the coffin on their shoulders up the steps between the line of guards. It was from this very spot just a few weeks earlier that Lincoln had been sworn in as president for a second term.

Only a few men followed the coffin into the Rotunda, where it was set on a specially built catafalque. These included Building Commissioner French, President Johnson, family members, the doctors, secretaries Nicolay and Hay, three army officers and a contingent from the Kentucky and Illinois delegations. Soldiers encircled the coffin and mourners. The Reverend Gurley was there, and he read a short passage. After a few minutes, those present departed, except for an honor guard. Eventually, all marchers and spectators dispersed from the Capitol area.

The Rotunda was dark, with black cloth covering the statues and the eight large paintings depicting scenes from American history. From the tops of the columns to the top of the interior of the dome, black streamers were connected, making the large space seem funereal.

The catafalque was covered in black cloth fringed in silver and decorated with silver stars. Rifles, pistols and swords lay alongside the bier, and bundled rods tied with silver bands stood at each corner.

At 8 A.M. on a rainy Thursday the doors were opened and the public was allowed to enter the Rotunda in two columns through the west entrance, passing by on either side of the coffin, guarded by the military, and exiting through the east entrance. People spoke in hushed tones as they shuffled by, three thousand per hour, for a total of 40,000 before the building was closed at 9:00 P.M.

At about 6 o'clock the next morning, those designated to escort the coffin to the Baltimore and Ohio railway station three blocks away began to assemble in the Rotunda. Most were military officers, and the escort party included General Grant. The Reverend Gurley recited a short prayer, then the military body bearers carried the casket down the Capitol steps into a drizzling rain and placed it in the hearse.

The contingent that escorted the remains was much smaller than the one from two days prior. It consisted of several hundred military men, the pallbearers, and government officials, including the carriage of President Johnson. It was a silent cortege, with no music and no muffled drums, accompanied only by the clatter it made as it moved along the streets.

The station was heavily guarded by federal troops. The coffin was carried between ranks of soldiers through the depot to the waiting train. A brand new engine, all decorated in black, and with a portrait of the late president above the cowcatcher, headed nine cars. Six were new passenger cars, while one was a baggage car. The last car was for the guard of honor and the family. Mr. Lincoln had ridden in it on occasion. The second to last one was the funeral car, newly built months before as the presidential car, richly and plushly furnished. That day its handsome exterior was draped in black mourning with silver fringe. The interior furnishings were covered in black. It was in the front section of this car on a raised dais that the coffin was placed, covered with an American flag and banked with flower arrangements.

At the rear of the car rested the casket of Willie Lincoln, the president's son who had died in 1863 at age twelve. His body had been removed from Oak Hill Cemetery in Washington to be reinterred in Springfield with his father.

At 8 A.M. the Reverend Gurley said a prayer, then bells tolled and the engine slowly huffed out of the station. The cars carried about three hundred passengers. They included the two brothers-in-law and two cousins of Mrs. Lincoln and Robert Lincoln, the only family members to make the trip. Also onboard were the Reverend Gurley, the embalmer Brown and the undertaker Sands, various government officials (including several congressmen), Ward Lamon, Associate Justice David Davis, a few reporters and scores of military men.

The train chugged toward Baltimore at twenty miles per hour. A pilot engine ran some distance ahead. This was the speed set for the entire journey. It would allow spectators to properly view the train as it passed along the tracks. And there were many spectators along the way. Farmers and woodsmen stood at the tracks in the less populated areas, and crowds massed in stations and along the rails at every small town and large city.

This somber funeral train would stop at every city that Lincoln had visited during his inaugural trip except Cincinnati and Pittsburgh. At each stop the coffin would be removed and opened to lay in state in a public hall so that the populace could come and pay its respects.

The first stop was Baltimore, reached in about two hours, close to 10 A.M. According to the schedule, Baltimore had only four hours to venerate the dead president. The Camden Street station and surrounding area was a mass of uniformed soldiers and civilian mourners. Tens of thousands lined the route of the procession to the Merchants' Exchange where the body was placed for viewing. The station, exchange and every building in the area was draped in mourning. All business was suspended in the city.

A hard rain fell as bells tolled and cannons boomed. The sergeants carried the coffin off the train and into an elaborate hearse with plate glass sides. A cast of thousands took part in the procession. It took three hours for the coffin to reach the exchange. The cover was removed and the doors of the building were open for only an hour and a half. Only ten thousand were able to view the remains, disappointing tens of thousands more. The coffin was ceremoniously taken to the President Street station where it was placed back in the funeral car and left for its next stop, Harrisburg. Actually, the train would make other occasional stops to take on water or allow different dignitaries to board. At each state, the governor of that particular state came aboard.[35]

The train was slightly reconfigured as other distinguished men boarded to ride at least to the next stop, and others left to return to Washington. All along the tracks the crowds continued to solemnly greet the train as it passed by their towns, villages and farms. At a short stop in York, Pennsylvania, as at many other stops, a group was allowed to carry a floral arrangement onto the funeral car.

Ninety miles to the north of Baltimore the Pennsylvania capital city of Harrisburg was reached just past 8 P.M. amidst a driving rainstorm, accompanied by thunder and lightning. So bad was the weather that the large procession planned through city streets was scaled back. Yet a huge mass of humanity packed the railroad station and the route to the state Capitol.

The coffin was removed to the waiting ornate hearse, specially built for this occasion (as was the case in each city where Lincoln would lay). Artillery roared and bells tolled as the soaked procession moved out, the route lit by specially installed chemical lights that gave out a yellow glow.[36]

Once the casket was deposited in the bedecked hall of the state House of Representatives, the public was immediately allowed inside to view the body, beginning at 9:30 P.M. and lasting until midnight. At seven the next morning the doors were reopened for three hours, then the coffin was closed and escorted back to the rail station, once again in the rain. At 11:15 the train headed east for Philadelphia. As it passed slowly through Lancaster, the station was packed with mourners. Among them was the city's most distinguished citizen, former president James Buchanan, who sat in his buggy at the depot.[37]

The engine pulled into Philadelphia at around 4:30 P.M. on Saturday. Here, in the nation's second largest city, a huge throng of half a million people crowded around the station in the downtown streets. As in Baltimore and Harrisburg, military formations were arranged at and near the station. Also gathered were the civic organizations and VIPs who would march with the casket, this time to Independence Hall. The usual booming cannons, bells and dirges were heard. And, as at the other places, a specially built hearse awaited, and all buildings sported black decorations. Such sights and sounds were to be repeated at each city each time the body was removed from the train.

It was 6:30 by the time the procession got underway, and past eight before the black-canopied hearse pulled into Independence Square. Sixty calcium lights provided illumination in red, white and blue.[38] The coffin was carried inside Independence Hall through ranks of the Union League civic group. It was placed inside, where the Declaration of Independence was introduced and where the Constitution was written. Lincoln lay on a dais not far from the Liberty Bell, which was shrouded in black, and against which a large flower arrangement had been propped.

At 10 P.M. the hall was opened to holders of special passes, remaining open until about 1 A.M. During the whole time a choir sang hymns out front. At 5 A.M. the general public, some of whom had waited in the streets all night, was allowed in to view the remains. On this Sunday morning the crush of people was overwhelming and got out of hand. Some attempted to cut into the three mile long line, pickpockets operated, there was pushing and shoving, clothes were torn, and fights erupted. Eventually, the police and troops restored order. It was just after 1 A.M. on Monday that the doors were closed, and city officials claimed 300,000 had passed through the hall.

The undertakers dusted off the coffin and the corpse, and applied a bit of cosmetics to the face.[39] At 2:30 the coffin was placed back in the hearse and conveyed to another rail station and loaded back onto the train. An hour and a half later it chugged out for its next destination, New York.

After a brief breakfast stop at the station in Trenton, New Jersey, the train arrived at Jersey City at 10 A.M. There the coffin was transported in a small hearse to a ferry. As at other stops, ceremonies were held. Choirs sang, bands played, guns were fired and everything in the area was bedecked in mourning as thousands looked on. The ferry crossed the Hudson River, and two other large ferries carried the dark brown funeral rail car and crimson officials' car.

The ferries docked in Manhattan around eleven, and the coffin was carried to a hearse. The people were everywhere, not only on the streets but on rooftops, in windows, in trees, on lamp posts, and on carriages. Every building in sight was suitably decorated. The procession moved up Broadway and eventually reached city hall, decked in mourning streamers and sporting the words "The Nation Mourns" in large white letters on black over the entrance. When the hearse arrived the coffin was carried into the city hall rotunda, up a flight of stairs and placed on a dais on a landing just outside the entrance to the Governor's Room.

The coffin had been rattled about during the trip, so the undertakers took half an hour to put things in order, including redressing the body in a clean shirt and collar.[40] Then a photographer, Jeremiah Gurney, was allowed to come in to take pictures of the open casket. Later, Secretary of War Stanton learned of the photographs and ordered them destroyed. Mrs. Lincoln had been adamant in her prohibition of photographs of the body.[41] One survived and was found among Stanton's papers in 1887 after his death. It was then forgotten until being rediscovered in 1952, the only known photograph of Abraham Lincoln in death.[42]

At 1 P.M. the doors opened to the public. The line snaked maddeningly through a basement entrance and dark hallways, up narrow staircases, into the rotunda and up twenty-two stairs to pass by the bier. The area was dimly lit, with four gaslight chandeliers putting out some illumination. Viewers were kept moving without stopping, and occasionally someone would sneak a touch of the body.

Some newspapers reported that Lincoln's face looked gaunt, shrunken and discolored. Others said the countenance was quite well preserved. Yet others called it dry, leathery and coarse. Accounts that the coffin would not be reopened after New York because of deterioration of the body were false.[43]

Hour after hour the line crept by, all through the night. Finally, just before noon on Tuesday, April 25, the building was closed. A few diplomats and prominent citizens were then allowed a viewing. At one o'clock the coffin was closed, then the sergeants carried it down the stairs and placed it in a new hearse. This was a huge fourteen-by-seven-foot, indescribably elaborate canopied vehicle drawn by sixteen gray horses caparisoned in black.

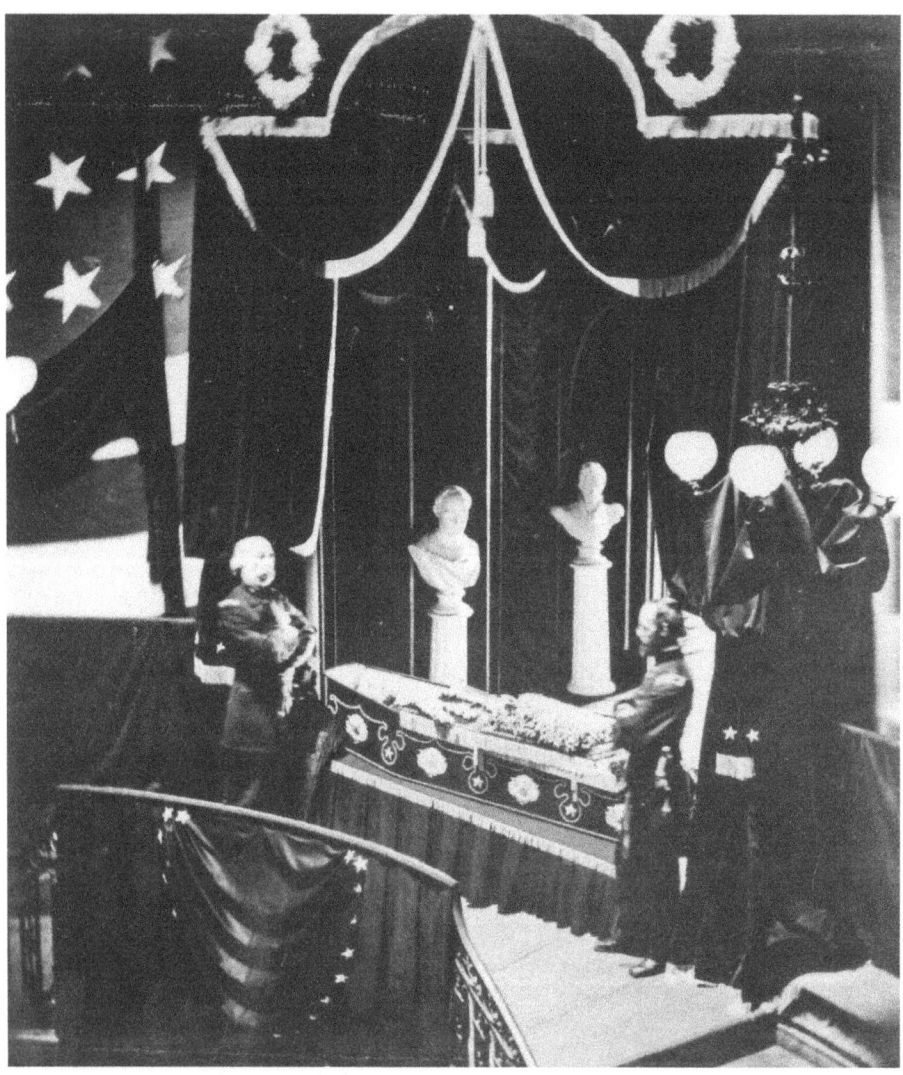

The only surviving photograph of Abraham Lincoln in death, lying in state in New York's city hall on April 24, 1865. It was one of several taken by photographer Jeremiah Gurney, but the negatives were seized by Secretary of War Edwin Stanton, and only one survived. (Abraham Lincoln Presidential Library & Museum [ALPLM])

An hour later, one hour behind schedule, it headed up Broadway as part of the by-now-customary funeral procession with all its participants, onlookers, pomp and ceremony. Near Union Square, the young boy Theodore Roosevelt observed the parade below from his grandfather's second story window. Eventually the front end reached the Hudson River railroad depot. The body was put back in the funeral car, and just past 4 P.M. the train moved out. It took a few hours for the cortege to end, long after the train had left for its next destination.

The engine steamed up the bucolic Hudson River valley to Albany, capital of the Empire State. All along the way the tracks were lined with onlookers, and mourners formed at each station through which it passed. During the night, torches lit the scenes.

During a brief stop at Garrison, across from West Point, young cadets were allowed to walk through the funeral car past the coffin. At East Albany, reached at 11 P.M., the coffin was put in a glass sarcophagus and ferried across the river to Albany proper. It was carried into the Assembly Chamber of the State House and placed in front of the speaker's stand. At 1:15 the room was opened to the public. All through the darkness and into the morning light the mourners filed through, and by the time the doors closed at 1:30 in the afternoon, it was estimated that 50,000 had visited. It was on this day that Abraham Lincoln's murderer was finally surrounded and killed. The next day's papers carried the news.

At 2:00 P.M. a grand foot procession escorted a hearse to the Albany railway station, which was reached almost two hours later. Once again the coffin

Stereoscopic view of the hearse carrying Lincoln's body down Broadway in New York City, April 25, 1865. (Library of Congress)

was lifted into the funeral car, and the train headed west for Buffalo, clear across the state. Through rural farmland, small towns and bustling cities like Utica, Syracuse and Rochester, the train was met by the now-common sight of mourners paying their respects.

When the train stopped at 5 A.M. in Batavia, former president Millard Fillmore and other prominent Buffalonians came aboard.[44] Near seven, the engine pulled into Buffalo's Exchange Street station downtown. Compared to other cities, Buffalo's procession was not lengthy. Lincoln's body was transported on an impressive hearse a short distance to St. James Hall.

The reason for the lesser pomp and circumstance in Buffalo was twofold. On the day of the Washington funeral the city had held an emotional grand funeral, minus the body of Mr. Lincoln, complete with canopied funeral car and every manner of VIP and military display. The city decided not to repeat the scene. Also, they correctly surmised that shortened ceremonies would enable more people to visit the bier of the deceased.[45]

And for eleven hours the citizens came — a hundred thousand strong. It was noted that the Buffalo crowds were the most courteous, and the arrangements more superior, than at any previous stop. Among the mourners paying their respects at the hall were former president Fillmore, who had campaigned against Lincoln in 1864, and twenty-eight-year-old Grover Cleveland, a less than enthusiastic supporter of the martyred president, who would, twenty years hence, rival Honest Abe's reputation for morality in the White House.[46] It was also while the venerated dead was in Buffalo that the nation received word of John Wilkes Booth's capture.

The coffin was taken back to the station, and the train pulled out of Buffalo shortly after 10 P.M. At seven the next morning, Friday, April 28, a full week since the body had left Washington, it pulled into Cleveland's Euclid Street depot. Once more the coffin was borne to a waiting ornate hearse. This time it was taken to a specially built, covered, open air pavilion in Monument Square. The coffin was laid on a dais banked with flowers.

From 9 A.M. until 11 P.M. two double lines passed by to view the body. Though rain began in the morning and grew heavier during the day, all under the canopied structure remained dry. Though the umbrellaed crowds waiting in line got wet, 150,000 came through, accompanied by the sounds of cannons and funeral dirges played by bands on hotel balconies surrounding the square. Before midnight the coffin was conveyed back to the train, which promptly left the station for its next destination, Ohio's capital city of Columbus.

Heavy rain fell throughout the night, but the people would not be deterred from standing trackside to watch the train pass. It rolled into Columbus' station around 7:30 in the morning of April 29. The funeral car was halted across High Street so that the coffin could be carried to the hearse without passing through the depot. The special horse-drawn vehicle carried the casket through the streets, and people packed in everywhere. Flowers were the order of the day. Lilacs were strewn on the road near the Soldier's Home, and people threw roses before the approaching hearse.

When it reached the Capitol building, the coffin was taken inside and placed on a flower-bedecked open catafalque, which displayed at the head and foot the name "Lincoln." Around the rotunda were arranged more flowers. From 8:30 A.M. until 6 P.M. the public was allowed to pass the bier. The coffin was taken back to the station, and the train pulled out at 8 P.M.

The next stop would be Indianapolis, bypassing Cincinnati — to the sad disappointment of that city, which had, after all, hosted Lincoln as president-elect during his trip to Washington in 1861. Pittsburgh, likewise, had been denied a visit by the funeral train. These were the only two cities on the inaugural run four years prior that were excluded.

The train arrived at 7 A.M. Sunday in Indianapolis in a driving rain. Because of this, the greater portion of the planned procession was abbreviated. Nevertheless, many thousands packed the streets and buildings along the route to the state Capitol, where the coffin was deposited. It was carried from the elegantly simple canopied hearse through a specially constructed, gaudily covered walkway and into the great hall. Until ten at night, 100,000 citizens walked past the coffin to gaze upon Lincoln's features. Again the coffin was re-closed and taken back to the train in a huge procession. It left the station at midnight.

Instead of heading directly west to Lincoln's hometown of Springfield, Illinois, in reverse order of the inaugural route, the train was scheduled to stop in Chicago first. This was the most important commercial metropolis in the midwest and the largest city in Illinois, so the planners had added Chicago to the list of places to host the body.

On Monday morning, May 1, before it reached the Windy City, the train paused in Michigan City, Indiana, for one of its normal stops to allow passengers to have breakfast at the station, take on and discharge dignitaries, and take on water and food. At many of these intermediate stops small groups were allowed to enter the funeral car to lay flowers at the coffin. But the coffin remained closed. But at Michigan City the rule was broken and the cover opened. A limited amount of citizens were allowed in to view the body during the thirty minutes the train was stopped, while a short but impressive funeral service was held right there at the lavishly bedecked station. Among the mourners was future vice president Schuyler Colfax.[47]

At 8:30 A.M. the train resumed its journey to Chicago, arriving at eleven o'clock and stopping a mile south of downtown Union Station. The coffin was carried off the train and placed on a dais under a huge triple mourning arch built over Park Place. No prayers or eulogies were read. Thirty-six young ladies placed one flower each on the casket as requiems were played, then it was lifted onto a grand hearse. A huge procession escorted the body to the court house.

Chicago's tribute was equal to that of New York's in size and grandeur.[48] All streets, rooves, porches, windows, and trees on the route were packed with people. All buildings in the city were decorated in black mourning, the court house simply and tastefully so. It was late afternoon before the public was admitted. Seven thousand per hour filed by the raised, canopied catafalque in the dim hall.

Here it was clear that a black discoloration around Lincoln's eyes had spread over much of the face, and the body appeared to be shrunken and shriveled.[49]

All through the night and into Tuesday the steady stream continued through the court house, even after rain began falling. Viewing was stopped at eight in the evening, and a procession re-formed to escort the remains back to the train station, lit by a thousand torches. At 9:30 the train left for its final destination.

This last portion of the long journey was the most touching, for Abraham Lincoln was now coming home. And that is a word that, along the tracks and at the stations, one began to see displayed more and more — "home." The train rolled into the Springfield station on Wednesday, May 3, at 8:40 A.M., just forty minutes behind the schedule that had been set more than two weeks earlier, after a trek of almost 1700 miles.[50]

Knowing that their city would be the focal point of the entire extended national funeral, officials urged all residents to decorate the city's buildings in proper decor. The two points of interest for everyone were the Lincoln home and the state Capitol building. Care was especially taken to make sure the edifices of these were tastefully and appropriately decorated in mourning.

A grand procession escorted the coffin to the State House, and it was placed upstairs in the Hall of Representatives. It was laid upon a tilted black velvet dais under a black canopy at the top of four stair steps. The gas-lit hall itself was also draped in mourning emblems, and was heavy with evergreens that imparted their distinctive scent.

Tens of thousands of people had gathered in the city for the viewing and ceremonies. Every hotel room and every private room available was occupied. Halls were open to serve meals. At 10 A.M. the crowds were admitted to see the body — in one entrance and out another and back onto the streets. Many commuted by train from nearby communities, viewed the body and immediately returned home. Others wandered the streets awaiting the next day's burial ceremony. Of course, all businesses save the hotels were closed until after the funeral.

Though it was reported that Lincoln's corpse appeared as natural and lifelike as could be expected, many described it as ghastly, shriveled and decaying. The undertakers were very concerned about the blackened face, and a local mortician, Thomas Lynch, applied a thick coat of rouge and amber to hide the discoloration.[51]

Embalming of the dead before the Civil War was a rarity. It was not seen as necessary, nor was it affordable for most Americans. In order to preserve a body for later viewing, if desired, it was packed in ice, somewhat of a problem in warm weather. But during the war, embalming was promoted in the North as a way to preserve the bodies of dead soldiers for transport home from Southern battlefields. That is, if the family could afford it and the process on the corpse could be started in time.

The Lincoln family agreed to have his remains transported and displayed in the extended funeral journey across the country, which necessitated the embalming of his body. The chemicals injected into the corpse made it rock hard and statuesque. Details of the process were reported in newspapers.[52] The embalming did the trick of preserving the remains, but in 1865 this could only go so far. By the time of the Springfield funeral, reports of deterioration of the body became more numerous, yet polite observers still called the countenance peaceful and pleasant with a slight smile.

Lincoln was the first president, whether he died in office or not, whose body was embalmed. The publicity surrounding the preservation of his remains made embalming a common and accepted funeral practice right through to the present day.

Thursday, May 4, 1865, dawned hot and sunny. Twenty days after the assassination, on this day all that was mortal of Abraham Lincoln was to be committed to the grave. Around 10 A.M. the line of mourners to view the body was halted and the State House doors closed. Guns had begun firing at dawn at ten minute intervals, and participants in the funeral procession

The hearse, on loan from St. Louis, that was used to carry Abraham Lincoln's body to its grave in Springfield, Illinois. (Library of Congress)

began to gather near the Capitol during the morning hours and form into their assigned groups. The streets and every vantage point on the route to the cemetery were clogged with onlookers. Around noon the coffin was removed to an ornate funeral hearse by the army sergeants, to the accompaniment of a choir and band playing a hymn.

The hearse used in Springfield was not a specially built one for the occasion, as had been the case in all the other cities. This one was an elegant carriage sent by the city of St. Louis. It was ornamented in silver and gold trim, topped by flowered plumes and enclosed in glass panels, through which the flag-draped coffin could be seen. It was pulled by six black horses with black plumes attached to their heads.

General Joseph Hooker led the march to the burial ground. A formation of more than a thousand soldiers marched behind, with drummers pounding out the mournful, muffled beat. Following them came Lincoln's horse, Old Bob, covered in a black shroud and led by a groom, then an honor guard and carriages carrying family and friends, including Robert Lincoln and cousin John Hanks, and several relations from the widow's side. Hanks represented Sarah Lincoln, the late president's stepmother, who was too infirm to come to Springfield.[53] Missing too were Mary Lincoln and son Tad, who remained in Washington.

Following the family came government officials, including congressmen, governors of several states, and city authorities. The officiating clergymen were there also, the Reverend Gurley and Bishop Matthew Simpson. Then came various civic groups and ordinary citizens, with the "colored persons" bringing up the rear.

The route took the procession past Lincoln's house and wound its way down the country road to the cemetery two miles distant. The military band played hymns and dirges, some of them specially composed for this day. The head of the column finally reached Oak Ridge Cemetery at 1 P.M.—before the last marchers had even left the Capitol.

The procession passed under an evergreen arch at the cemetery's entrance. This was the quiet, rural place that the widow had chosen for her husband's final resting place. But today it was anything *but* quiet. Spectators occupied every inch of the hillsides and rises near the receiving vault that would take the late president's remains, including the knoll immediately behind the vault.

This burial vault was built into a hillside. The exterior was about fifteen feet by fifteen feet, of limestone, with two columns supporting a Doric gable. Its interior wall, ceiling and floor were of brick. Leaks in the ceiling had to be patched, and a new sturdy set of doors had been installed.[54] For this ceremony, the interior ceiling and walls were covered in black velvet, and it was decorated with evergreen sprigs and floral pieces.

Abraham Lincoln's original tomb in Oak Ridge Cemetery in Springfield, Illinois, on the day of the burial, May 4, 1865. Spectators have taken positions around it for the later ceremony. (Library of Congress)

Already placed on a small marble slab on a brick foundation in the tomb was the coffin of Lincoln's son Willie. A larger one next to it awaited the president's. Outside, to the front left of the vault, was constructed a platform for a choir and band. To the right was a small speaker's stand.

As soon as the hearse stopped in front of the tomb, Lincoln's coffin was carried inside and placed on the marble slab. Family and friends stood and sat in front of the tomb, Robert Lincoln front and center, as a hymn was sung. Many of the mourners gathered in the cemetery held umbrellas against the hot sun on a beautiful spring afternoon, with bushes and trees just beginning to bud. The religious obsequies started, with the Rev. Albert Hale of the Presbyterian Church reading a prayer, followed by a hymn. Then came a reading of the Scriptures by the Rev. N.W. Miner of the Baptist Church. After another hymn, the Rev. A.C. Hubbard recited Lincoln's entire second inaugural address. At the conclusion, another hymn was sung, which was followed by a eulogy by Bishop Simpson, which at times drew applause and lasted more than an hour. After another hymn, the Reverend Gurley then pronounced the benediction, which was followed by a hymn (with lyrics composed by the clergyman), followed by yet one more.[55]

The iron gates and heavy doors of the burial vault were closed and locked. The key was given to Robert Lincoln. The marchers re-formed their procession and returned to the city as the people covering the hillsides of the cemetery began to disperse. Soldiers were left to guard the tomb.

The Union's long orgy of grief came to an end. An estimated one million persons had seen Lincoln's body, and millions more had watched the train pass by their communities or taken part in various funeral pageants.

The cost of the entire extravaganza to the federal government was only $30,000. States and local municipalities had to pay the expenses for the ceremonies held in their jurisdictions.[56]

The consequences of the assassination of Abraham Lincoln were just as great as the consequences of his decision to wage a civil war against the Southern states. President Lincoln intended to welcome the rebellious states and their citizens back into the Union "with malice toward none, with charity for all," as he put it in his second inaugural address.

But Congress was controlled by a faction called the radical Republicans, who favored harsher treatment and punishment for the South. Lincoln, with his great popularity in the North, his powers of persuasion, and the bully pulpit of the presidency, probably could have succeeded in implementing his benevolent plans for reconstruction and reunion of America.

But his successor was Andrew Johnson, who was hated by the radical Republicans for two reasons: He was a Democrat and he was a Southerner. In 1864 the Republicans, in order to attract votes, rechristened their party the National Union Party and chose Johnson for vice president. He had remained loyal to the Union after his native Tennessee had seceded.

Johnson's attempts to follow Lincoln's plans in reconstructing the South were rebuffed by the radicals, who sought to punish the former Confederacy. And they had an ally in the administration in Secretary of War Stanton, who undermined Johnson at every opportunity.

President Johnson was in an impossible situation, for he could never measure up to the sainted Lincoln, even if he were not a Southern Democrat. For a hundred years the harsh Reconstruction policies implemented kept a wedge between North and South, and even today their consequences are felt.

The man recognized as the assassin of Abraham Lincoln, John Wilkes Booth, was never brought to trial, for he was surrounded and fatally shot by an army sergeant before he could be captured. Booth, a rebel sympathizer from Maryland, had conceived a plot to kidnap Lincoln and exchange him for Confederate prisoners. He attracted a group of shady characters and conspired with them to carry it out, but after Lee surrendered to Grant, he realized that his plans were futile. He instead came up with the idea to kill the president in the hope that the South would be inspired to continue to fight.

From the moment of the assassination it was thought that it was part of a plot by the Confederate government to kill the president and high-ranking government officials. Indeed, Booth's accomplices were assigned to kill Vice President Johnson and the third in line to the presidency, Secretary of State William Seward, but those plans failed. But Confederate involvement was never substantiated, though from circumstantial evidence it seemed plausible. Other conspiracy theories arose, from a Roman Catholic plot to the involvement of Andrew Johnson, and most significantly the implication that Secretary of War Stanton had blood on his hands. Circumstances point to the possibility that Stanton was behind the assassination, not the least of which was the fact that the top three officials of the government, President Lincoln, Vice President Johnson, and Secretary of State Seward, if killed, would have made Stanton president of the United States. And he would have loved the job. He was vain, dictatorial and power hungry. He opposed Lincoln's proposed leniency toward the South, favoring vengeance and the accompanying opportunity to enrich both the Northern business interests and himself. But like theories about Confederate involvement, Stanton's role cannot be proved.

From the start, Secretary Stanton began handling the assassination as a military matter. The new president, Andrew Johnson, was in no position to oppose this, given the tenor of the times and his relative impotence due to the swift march of events. Thus, the civilian government of the District of Columbia would have no jurisdiction in the matter. In the muddled legal atmosphere of the Civil War, things like following the law and the Constitution took a back seat to the suppression of the Southern insurrection. The United States would see the shameful scene of civilian American citizens tried in a military court for crimes committed against civilians.

The assassin himself was killed and could not be brought before any court, but eight of his alleged co-conspirators were captured. In July 1865 they were tried before a military tribunal on charges of treason and conspiracy to commit the murder of the president of the United States and other government officials. These seven men and one woman were treated harshly in prison, kept shackled and hooded most of the time. They were denied access to counsel, and were confronted by witnesses who were coerced or simply liars. There was never any doubt that they would be found guilty. The only question was whether any would be spared the death penalty. In the end, four were condemned to hang: Lewis Powell (alias Paine), David E. Herold, George Atzerodt and Mary Surratt. Four others received prison sentences: Michael O'Laughlin, Edman Spangler, Samuel Arnold and Dr. Samuel Mudd. One who escaped, John Surratt, was tried by a civilian court in 1867, but no verdict could be reached.

Many artifacts connected with the Lincoln assassination exist today. Among them is Ford's Theatre. After the assassination, it ceased to be a playhouse, was bought by the War Department and converted to a three-story office building. The entire interior was gutted and the contents destroyed, including the box where Lincoln was shot. In 1893 the floors collapsed, killing twenty-two people. For thirty-five years it remained a shell, then was used for storage by the precursor of the National Park Service. In 1932 a Lincoln museum opened in it. Finally, in 1964 work on restoring it to its 1865 appearance began, including rebuilding the presidential box. Today it is again a theater, combined with a museum.

The Petersen House where Lincoln died was rented out as a Lincoln Museum, and in 1896 the federal government purchased it. Renovations began in 1932 to restore it to its authentic 1865 appearance, and is today open to visitors.[57]

Articles associated with the events include the catafalque upon which Lincoln's coffin rested in the Capitol Rotunda. It is still used today for lying in state ceremonies there. The Chicago History Museum has the bed and mattress upon which Lincoln died, Mrs. Lincoln's blood-stained cloak, the silver dollars laid upon Lincoln's eyes after he died, locks of his hair, a fragment of Petersen House floor board, and molding from Ford's Theatre. The Henry Ford Museum in Dearborn, Michigan, has the blood-stained rocking chair in which the president was sitting when he was shot. The contents of Lincoln's pockets the night he was shot are at the Library of Congress, and his top hat resides at the Smithsonian. The National Museum of Health and Medicine has fragments of his skull removed at autopsy. Ford's theater has Booth's pistol, knife and diary, and the original door to the presidential theater box. Petersen House displays the bloody pillow upon which Lincoln's head lay when he died.

Abraham Lincoln died without a will. His friend, Supreme Court Justice David Davis, was appointed administrator of the late president's estate. At the time of Lincoln's death, it was worth $83,000, a substantial sum in 1865. Through shrewd investments, Davis increased its value to almost $111,000 upon its distribution in 1867.[58] This was divided equally among the widow Mary Lincoln and the Lincolns' two surviving sons, Tad and Robert.[59] Mrs. Lincoln also received a $25,000 lump sum from the federal government and a pension of three thousand dollars per year, later increased to five thousand dollars.

The body of Abraham Lincoln was not to rest in peace for another thirty-six years after it was first placed in the Springfield burial vault. It is estimated that his body was moved seventeen times during that time span.[60]

On December 21, 1865, Lincoln's body was moved to a new vault nearby, in the presence of his widow and son Robert.[61] The coffin was opened by plumber Leon P. Hopkins, and six men looked in to identify the body. They were members of the national Lincoln Monument Association, a group of friends formed to construct and maintain a fitting burial place for the late president within the cemetery. The coffin was enclosed in an iron outer casket.

The memorial was begun in 1869, and ten years later the new tomb had progressed far enough to house the body of Lincoln. Again Hopkins opened the casket, and six men looked in before it was put in a sarcophagus.

In 1874 a new marble sarcophagus was finished, but the iron casket was too long for it. So Lincoln's remains in the old coffin were then placed in a lead coffin, which was put into a cedar coffin. But before this was done, the old coffin was again opened, and an undertaker identified the body as that of Abraham Lincoln. It was placed in the sarcophagus.

On November 7, 1876, two men, accompanied by a third who was a police informant, broke into the tomb in an attempt to steal the body. They had removed the cover, sawed through the end of the sarcophagus and partially pulled out the casket when they were surprised by police officers and eventually captured. They were counterfeiters who planned to hold Lincoln's body for a $200,000 ransom and release of one of their friends from prison.[62]

Two days after the break-in, the coffin was shoved back into the sarcophagus and repairs were made. Members of the Monument Association, which eventually morphed into the Lincoln Guard of Honor, were so alarmed by the attempted theft that on November 15 they had the coffin removed from the sarcophagus and carried down to the basement of the tomb. A wooden box was constructed around the outer cedar box. The plan was to bury all this in a grave dug into the basement floor. But water was struck, so the box was simply covered with a pile of old scrap lumber.

More than a year later, on November 18, 1878, another, shallower grave was dug in the basement and the body placed in it. Four days later the box was covered with dirt.

On July 16, 1882, Mary Lincoln died, probably from a stroke due to diabetes, and her body was deposited in a crypt in the wall of the interior of the monument, near her sons Eddie, Willie and Tad. Still in the center of the room was Abraham Lincoln's marble sarcophagus, empty. For years visitors passed by the tomb, thinking that it contained Lincoln's body, though rumors had circulated that the body had been removed. The night of her funeral, Mary's body was carried down to the basement and placed in a shallow grave next to that of her husband.

In 1884 a portion of the ceiling of the monument collapsed, and repair work had to be undertaken, including installation of a ventilation shaft in the basement, during which workmen trampled over the unmarked, secret graves of the Lincolns.

On April 14, 1887, their coffins were removed from the basement and transferred to a new brick-lined grave cut into the floor of the monument interior. Once again plumber Hopkins opened Mr. Lincoln's coffin, peeling back the lead inner coffin to reveal Lincoln's well-preserved face, described as dark bronze in color. It was resealed, then cement was poured into the new grave, completely encasing the two coffins.

By 1900 the Lincoln Monument was in very bad shape and had to be rebuilt. On March 10, after a week's work, the Lincolns' bodies were again removed, put in new wooden crates and lifted by crane to a nearby twelve-foot-square cement-lined grave outdoors. Also placed in the grave were the bodies of the three Lincoln sons and a grandson who had also rested in a crypt in the tomb. Stone slabs were placed over the coffins, then a thirty foot high pile of earth, stone and brick was placed over that. The monument was completely rebuilt over a period of eighteen months.[63]

In April 1901, President Lincoln's remains were unearthed and placed in the marble sarcophagus in the memorial room of the monument, the same sarcophagus that had been vandalized twenty-five years earlier.[64] The other family members were placed in crypts in the wall. Robert Lincoln objected. He wanted something more secure for his father.

A crane lifts the box containing the coffin of Abraham Lincoln from its tomb within the Lincoln Memorial in Oak Ridge Cemetery in Springfield, Illinois, on April 30, 1901. The body was removed so that the memorial could be reconstructed. (Library of Congress)

His wishes were as follows. His father's coffin, encased in the one of red cedar, was to be enclosed in another wooden box, then encased in a steel cage of flat steel bars. A ten-foot-deep hole was to be dug in the floor of the catacomb and a twenty-inch concrete slab placed in it. The caged coffin would then be lowered into the hole and covered with wet cement.

On September 26, 1901, exactly one week after the burial of the assassinated President William McKinley, twenty-three individuals gathered in the monument room before a wooden crate containing Lincoln's body, with the newly dug hole near it. Despite Robert Lincoln's request that the coffin remain closed, those present decided to have it opened. Once again the plumber Hopkins opened the boxes and cut through the lead lining. A pungent odor escaped. The people gazed in and saw the remarkably well preserved, bronze colored face of the sixteenth president. The lead was soldered and the boxes reclosed. After the witnesses left the chamber, workmen immediately lowered the coffin into the grave and covered it with cement. There it has lain since, undisturbed, behind and below a huge polished red marble marker.[65]

Robert Todd Lincoln

The president's son, Robert Todd Lincoln, did not simply fade away. Rather, he had quite a distinguished career. The only one of Abraham Lincoln's four children to survive to adulthood, Robert became a Harvard-educated lawyer who served as secretary of war in the Garfield and Arthur administrations, and was appointed ambassador to England by President Benjamin Harrison. Lincoln was often mentioned as a presidential candidate but never sought the office. His real success came in the business world, primarily as chief attorney, president and chief executive of the Pullman Rail Car Company, a maker of railway cars. He became a rich man.

A few coincidences connecting Robert T. Lincoln to presidential deaths and assassinations are quite remarkable, even eerie. Around 1864 young Lincoln was at the railway station in Jersey City, New Jersey. He was standing in line next to a railroad car to purchase a ticket from the conductor. He was accidentally pushed against the rail car, which began to move, causing him to twist and drop into the space between the car and platform. He was quickly pulled up by his coat collar, which probably saved his life. Turning to thank his rescuer, he saw that it was the famous actor Edwin Booth. It was said that this deed gave Edwin comfort after his younger brother John Wilkes murdered Robert's father.[66]

Robert Lincoln was probably invited to accompany his parents to Ford's Theatre on that fateful night in 1865, but he did not attend. When word reached him of the shooting, he was at the White House a few blocks away and rushed to the boarding house where his father lay insensible. He was present there when President Lincoln died the following morning. Robert purportedly regretted not having gone to the theater, thinking that he may have been able to save his father's life.[67]

Robert Lincoln was appointed secretary of war in 1881 by new president James A. Garfield. On July 2 the president was walking through the Baltimore and Potomac railroad station in Washington on his way to board a train. Secretary Lincoln was on the platform waiting to see off Garfield when someone shouted, "The president is shot." Lincoln rushed to the scene in the station's waiting room and took Garfield's hand for a moment. For the next three days Lincoln spent long hours at the White House where the wounded president lay. When Garfield died two months later, it was Secretary of War Lincoln who had to officially notify the army of his demise, and he took part in plans for the state funeral.[68]

President William McKinley invited Robert Lincoln to join him at the Pan American Exposition in Buffalo on September 6, 1901. Lincoln and his

Standing left to right at the dedication of the Lincoln Memorial on May 30, 1922, are Chief Justice William Howard Taft, President Warren G. Harding, and Robert Todd Lincoln, son of the late president. (Library of Congress)

wife were still onboard their train, arriving at the exposition station, when word came to them that McKinley had just been shot.[69] Lincoln later visited the wounded president's bedside, and also talked to Vice President Theodore Roosevelt, who had rushed to Buffalo.[70]

After this, Robert Lincoln supposedly refused invitations by other presidents to visit them, so as not to put them in danger. How serious he was about himself being a jinx is not known. It may have been a convenient reason for him to avoid such visits, for he was a man who did not seek the limelight. In any event, he broke his self-imposed moratorium and was in the presence of President Warren G. Harding at the dedication of the Lincoln Memorial in Washington in 1922.[71] Harding, of course, would die in office the following year.

In 1926, Robert Todd Lincoln died. He had once written that he expected to be interred in the Lincoln Tomb in Springfield, Illinois, but apparently his wife favored Arlington National Cemetery, and he was buried there.[72] Four decades later the remains of the fourth assassinated U.S. president, John F. Kennedy, would be buried nearby.

John Wilkes Booth

John Wilkes Booth was born in Maryland in 1838. His father and two brothers were accomplished actors, and so was John Wilkes, known for his dashing good looks. He lived in Maryland during the Civil War, a slave state that had remained in the Union, but Booth was a supporter of the Confederacy. He visited Canada where he supposedly met with Confederate spies, and purportedly was involved in smuggling medical supplies to the South.

In 1864 he came up with his plan to kidnap President Lincoln. He recruited accomplices, and an attempt in March 1865 failed. When he changed the plan to one of murder, most of those who had conspired with him disapproved of this change. Nevertheless, Booth, Lewis Powell, David Herold and George Atzerodt, on the night of April 14, 1865, put plans in motion to kill Secretary of State William Seward, Vice President Andrew Johnson and President Lincoln.

After shooting Lincoln at Ford's Theatre,

John Wilkes Booth, noted actor and assassin of President Abraham Lincoln. (Library of Congress)

Booth jumped to the stage and broke his ankle. He limped out the back stage door and escaped on horseback, eventually meeting fellow conspirator Herold and escaping together into Virginia.

Union soldiers were in hot pursuit of the two men, who had been staying in safe houses owned by people that Booth knew. On April 26, 1865, the two were sleeping in a barn on the property of Richard Garrett near Port Royal, Virginia. At 2 A.M. the federal troops surrounded the barn. Herold surrendered. Booth refused, so the soldiers set fire to the barn to flush him out. A shot rang out, Booth fell, and was dragged out and onto the porch of the nearby farmhouse. Sergeant Boston Corbett took credit for shooting the fugitive, against orders, though there is a probability that Booth committed suicide.[73] He died at 7:15 A.M. on the porch, moaning, "Tell Mother I died for my country. My hands..." Someone held up one of his hands. "Useless, useless," he murmured.

Booth's body was transported to Washington. Aboard a navy vessel on the Potomac River it was positively identified, and an autopsy was performed. The body was removed to the federal arsenal in D.C. and buried under the floor of a prison cell in the penitentiary. When the prison was torn down in 1867, the body was removed to a pine box and buried in a locked storage room in another building on the grounds, along with the bodies of the four co-conspirators who had been hanged.[74]

In 1869 the Booth family petitioned President Johnson to have Booth's body removed for a decent burial, and the request was granted. He was reburied in the family plot in Greenmount Cemetery in Baltimore, Maryland. His grave is unmarked but is located behind the Booth obelisk.

In the years since Booth's death, stories have circulated that he escaped and the body in Greenmount Cemetery is not his. He was reported to have escaped to England, India, China or Mexico. A man living in Granbury, Texas, was believed to be Booth. A mummy once displayed at carnivals in the early twentieth century was purportedly that of the assassin and is now believed to be in the possession of a private collector. Legal attempts to exhume the body from Greenmount Cemetery for positive identification have been unsuccessful.[75]

Chapter 5

James Abram Garfield

20TH PRESIDENT OF THE UNITED STATES
TERM OF OFFICE: MARCH 4, 1881, TO SEPTEMBER 19, 1881
BORN: NOVEMBER 19, 1831; DIED: SEPTEMBER 19, 1881
AGE AT DEATH: 49 YEARS, 304 DAYS
PLACE OF DEATH: ELBERON, NEW JERSEY
CAUSE OF DEATH: BLOOD POISONING DUE TO GUNSHOT WOUND
BURIAL PLACE: CLEVELAND, OHIO

James A. Garfield was the surprise Republican nominee for president in 1880 when the convention deadlocked over the leading candidates. He went on to win the general election and became our twentieth chief executive.

Garfield was born in a log cabin near Cleveland, Ohio. He went to seminary, but ultimately became a lawyer and involved himself in politics. He was a general in the Civil War and was a hero of the Battle of Chickamauga.

Garfield was a robust, fit man who stood six feet tall, growing up fatherless on the Ohio frontier and becoming physically tough. He was bothered by severe headaches as a child, and boils, rheumatism and a delicate digestive system plagued him throughout his life.[1] As a teen, young Garfield was a canal worker, which he gave up after a few near-drownings and a severe attack of fever and possible malaria.[2] During his war service, in addition to the hardships of battle, he suffered from camp fever, colds, dysentery, and hemorrhoids, for which he needed surgery in 1875.[3]

Elected to the House of Representatives, he served there for seventeen years before becoming president. As had been the practice since the spoils system was introduced by Andrew Jackson in the 1820s, in the early months of 1881 the new president was besieged by men seeking appointments to federal jobs. Every position, down to the lowest clerk, was subject to be filled by the president, regardless of skill or merit. Virtually anyone could visit the White House and request a meeting with the president.

One such office seeker was Charles J. Guiteau, a mentally unbalanced drifter of some disrepute. He was not a big Garfield supporter, but he had printed up a speech during the election of 1880 which he believed was responsible for the president's election. This, he thought, should be rewarded by an appointment to an important position in the government. He preferred Minister to Austria or Consul General in Paris. He actually succeeded in having a short meeting with the president to press his case in person, but his obviously strange behavior left Garfield perplexed. Further attempts to see Garfield were rebuffed. Guiteau also managed to buttonhole Vice President-Elect Chester A. Arthur, Secretary of State James G. Blaine and a couple of senators, but they were equally put off by this strange man who was an obvious crank and not worthy of any further attention. Guiteau grew discouraged over these rejections, and also over the ongoing feud within the Republican Party between the Stalwarts, whom he favored, and the president and his supporters. In late May the idea that he should kill Garfield, thereby thrusting the Stalwart Vice President Arthur into the presidency, entered his mind.

For weeks Guiteau, armed with a .44 caliber pistol, stalked the president, waiting for the right time and place to strike, and trying to summon his courage. It would not be that difficult a task to carry out. Sixteen years after the assassination of Abraham Lincoln, the president went about unprotected. That killing was thought to be an anomaly due to the passions of the Civil War. It was felt that the leader of a democracy should be free to come in direct contact with the citizenry. There was no Secret Service, military bodyguard, or police protection outside of the White House. Garfield sometimes walked down the street completely alone, and he himself believed that he should be unguarded.

On the morning of Saturday, July 2, the president and his teenage sons Harry and James prepared to leave Washington by special train for New York where they would meet Mrs. Garfield and daughter Mollie, who were resting at Long Branch, New Jersey. The five of them were to go to Williams College in Massachusetts where the president was to deliver the commencement address and the boys were to attend classes.

Garfield invited Secretary of State Blaine to ride with him to the railroad station and see him off. Harry and James had gone ahead in another carriage. The coachman pulled up in front of the Baltimore and Potomac station, located a few blocks from the White House at B Street (now Constitution Avenue) and Sixth Street on the mall, at 9:20 A.M. The two men were greeted by police officer Patrick Kearney, who was on duty outside the depot. They alighted from their carriage and walked arm in arm, as was the custom of the time, into the building through the waiting room entrance.

Deep in conversation, they did not notice the bearded, neatly dressed Guiteau, broad-brimmed black hat pulled down low, who was standing just inside the doorway. Upon entering the station, Blaine and Garfield dropped

Probably the most accurate depiction of the shooting of President Garfield in the ladies' waiting room of the Baltimore and Potomac Railroad Station on July 2, 1881. The assassin Guiteau shoots the president in the back as Secretary of State James G. Blaine and other startled onlookers witness the crime. (Library of Congress)

their arms as they turned slightly to the right, then left through a row of seats on their way to the main concourse toward the train platform. Blaine was on the president's right and Guiteau to their rear.

Guiteau pulled his gun from his pocket and fired at the president from a distance of six or seven feet. This shot passed through Garfield's right overcoat sleeve and lodged in a workman's tool box. Guiteau quickly stepped two paces forward and fired another shot into the president's back. Garfield's hands flew into the air and his hat fell off as he exclaimed, "My God! What is this?" He twisted to the right and collapsed to the floor, unconscious and vomiting.[4]

Blaine and the dozen or so other people in the room, including the Venezuelan minister to the United States,[5] were startled and shocked. Guiteau put the pistol back in his pocket and attempted to leave the station, but the secretary called out for someone to stop him. Another man ran out to the concourse and shouted, "Murder! Murder!" Officer Kearney, who was entering the station in response to the gunshots, grabbed Guiteau and was met by another officer. They escorted him out of the building to the nearby police station.

The president was tended by the waiting room attendant, who lifted his head upon her lap. Others ran calling for a doctor and police. A physician who was in the station gave the wounded man some brandy and spirits of ammonia, which revived him. A crowd had pushed into the room. Among the throng were the president's sons, the postmaster general and secretaries of the treasury, navy and war, who had been scheduled to travel with Garfield and were waiting near the train. The secretary of war was Robert Lincoln, the late president's son, who had been present at the deathbed of his father sixteen years earlier.[6]

Garfield was in obvious shock. The physician told him he did not think it was serious. Garfield replied, "I thank you doctor, but I am a dead man." More doctors arrived, and the president was placed on a mattress and moved upstairs to the station superintendent's office. The hallway outside became clogged with people. The cabinet members and about twenty doctors were present in the room. Dr. D.W. Bliss, a prominent Washington surgeon, was chosen by Secretary Lincoln to take charge of the patient, and introduced a probe and his finger in an attempt to locate the bullet. He mistakenly thought he found the bullet's path and probed this channel repeatedly, but could not find the projectile. All this was done without sterilization or anesthesia. He decided to dress the wound and have Garfield moved to the White House. Mattresses were placed in the back of a delivery wagon, and the president was carried to it and driven to the Executive Mansion.

Twenty-five to thirty physicians were present in the White House. The president was in a second floor bedroom in such poor condition that he was not expected to live out the day. The doctors could not agree on what to do, and may have been reluctant to suggest any unusual course of action, afraid to further injure such an esteemed patient. Signs of internal hemorrhage were present, and they thought the liver had been damaged. His vital signs were weak, but he was lucid, and from time to time he was given stimulants. Friends and colleagues came in to visit, most believing it to be their final farewell. That night Mrs. Garfield arrived by special train from New Jersey and comforted her husband, joined by daughter Mollie and sons Harry and James.

The assassin Guiteau had been escorted by the police on foot to the police station near the railroad depot and jailed. Upon being apprehended, he said, "Arthur is president of the United States now. I am a Stalwart. I have a letter that will tell you about it."

He gave the letter to one of the police officers, and in it Guiteau explained his actions. He did not struggle or attempt to escape. His demeanor in his cell was one of complete calm.

As word spread after the shooting, thousands of people converged on the White House, anxious for news. They also crowded around newspaper bulletin boards in hotel windows for the latest dispatches. Elsewhere, people gathered at newspaper and telegraph offices in cities throughout the nation, and at railway stations in small towns, waiting for the latest information to be posted. Evening newspapers of July 2 carried news of the incident. From time to time that first day the doctors issued bulletins regarding the president's condition. The cabinet members had promptly notified Vice President Arthur of the situation, and he arrived in Washington from his home in New York City the next day. During the coming days, expressions of sympathy poured in from governments around the world.

Surprisingly, the patient survived the night. The next morning his vital signs were improved, and he felt rested and cheerful. Garfield chose Dr. Bliss, an old boyhood friend, to remain in charge. Bliss, in turn, selected five other prominent physicians to assist him, including army surgeon J.J. Woodward and Surgeon General J.K. Barnes, who, along with Bliss, had attended to the dying President Lincoln in 1865. Among the doctors dismissed by Dr. Bliss was Garfield's White House physician, Jedediah H. Baxter, who was quite miffed at the decision.[7]

Since there appeared to be no injury to the internal organs, and the patient had stabilized, the doctors hoped for a slow, steady recovery. During the next few days the president was moved to another room, and an innovative air conditioning system was devised to keep the room cool in the stifling summer heat. He had trouble keeping down solid food, so he was put on a liquid diet with oatmeal and an occasional piece of meat. The doctors, a female nurse and male attendants kept an around-the-clock vigil. Other than they and the family, Garfield was denied most visitors, and this made him lonely. He was allowed to hold one cabinet meeting during the course of his illness, in the sick room, and signed only one document.

A routine of issuing two daily bulletins was established. The doctors daily dressed, drained and probed the wound. Occasionally the patient could sit up. Attendants had to shift his position several times a day to prevent bedsores, to feed him, clean him, and change him like a baby. Painkillers were often injected to ease the pain. The doctors remained obsessed with finding the bullet. An early metal detector, devised and operated by Alexander Graham Bell, failed to conclusively locate it.

On July 23 the president suffered a setback. He was stricken with chills and fever, indicative of serious infection. A pus sac in the wound was discovered and an incision made to drain it. He improved for a few days, but on August 8 another attack necessitated more surgery, the doctors making the wound much larger. But Garfield became weaker, at times delirious, and could not keep down any food. Pus sacs appeared in his ear canal and other areas, signs of a general blood poisoning. Nutrient enemas were given. His death appeared imminent by late August, by which time government business was at a near standstill; but he rallied again. Racked by pain, fever, vomiting, and wasting away, the sick man begged the doctors for a change of scene. They ultimately allowed him to be taken to his favorite seaside resort, Elberon, an enclave near Long Branch, New Jersey.[8]

On September 6, by special carriage and rail car, the president was carefully transported 230 miles in seven hours to Francklyn Cottage at Elberon, a 23-room house a hundred yards from the sea. A three-thousand-foot rail spur had been built to the door of the cottage the night before by two thousand workmen, and the car was pulled along this.[9] The home had been put at Garfield's disposal by its wealthy English owner. His bed was situated in a second floor room where he had a clear view of the ocean. He was content and seemed to improve. "Thank God. It is good to be here," he said. Doctors, family and aides also stayed there. A horde of reporters took up residence at the Elberon Hotel next door, and army sentinels were posted around the house. Four cabinet members stayed at another hotel in Long Branch.

The president's relief was only temporary. On the sixteenth he weakened. The next day he began suffering from chills, fever, a racing pulse, coughing, and chest pains. The doctors knew the end was near.

On Monday, September 19, he slept most of the day, though the symptoms remained the same. A few minutes after 10 P.M. Garfield awoke and complained of a pain in the chest. "Oh, Swaim, this terrible pain!" he moaned to his aide David Swaim, who, along with the president's body servant Daniel Spriggs, was present in the candlelit room. Garfield asked for some water, then complained again of the pain, "Oh, Swaim, can't you stop this? Oh, Swaim!" The president slipped into unconsciousness, his breathing loud and labored. Swaim sent Spriggs to rouse the household. Dr. Bliss came in, then Mrs. Garfield and Mollie, aide Colonel J.M. Rockwell and his wife and daughter, Dr. Hayes Agnew, the president's private secretary, J. Stanley Brown, Executive Secretary to the President Warren Young, and Spriggs.

"He is dying," Bliss declared. He injected brandy into the region of the heart. Mrs. Garfield cried, "Oh, why am I made to suffer this cruel wrong?" She took hold of her husband's hand. Mollie put a hand on his shoulder. Bliss could feel no pulse, but by putting his ear on Garfield's chest he could detect a slight fluttering of the heart. This soon stopped. At 10:35 P.M. the doctor raised his head and said, "It is over," turning away from the bed.[10] One by one the people left the room, leaving Mrs. Garfield and Mollie alone with the body. The new widow stayed in the room for three hours before someone came to get her.[11]

President Garfield had survived for eighty days following the shooting. His administration lasted for 200 days. He bore his fight for life with stoicism and courage, through excruciating pain, illness and discomfort. In the end, this healthy 210-pound man had wasted away to 130 pounds. He died on the nineteenth anniversary of his heroism at the Battle of Chickamauga.

After 10 P.M. one of the cottage's doorkeepers had been sent to get Dr. Silas Boynton from the Elberon Hotel. There had already been a warning of some crisis when various lights at the house were turned on. The two men and a reporter hurried to the cottage and were met near the front door by

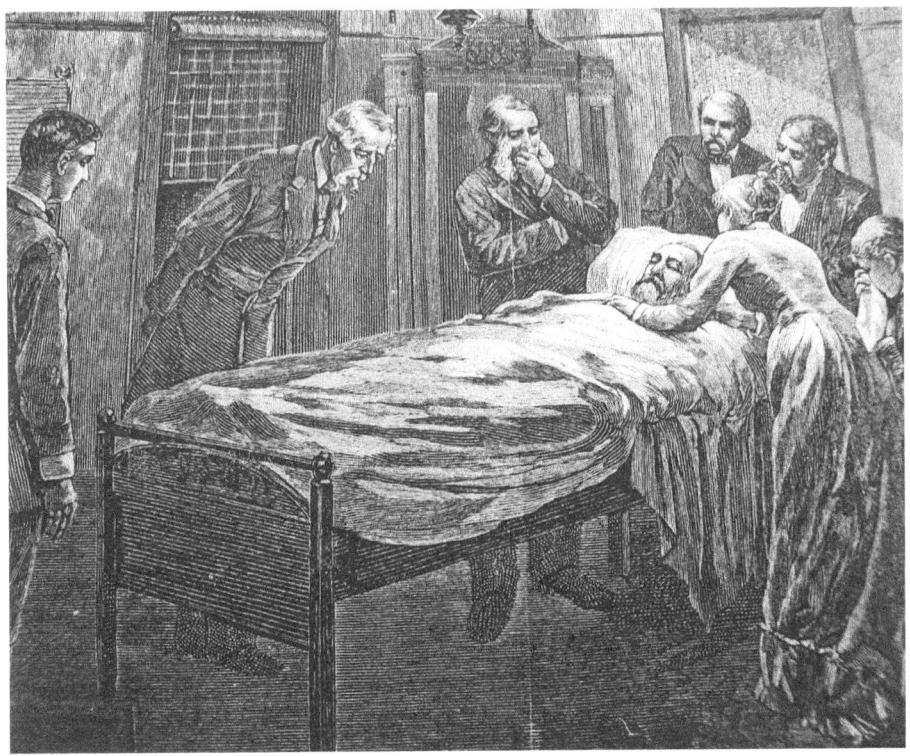

Death of President Garfield. Doctors observe the dying president as Mrs. Garfield comforts him and daughter Mollie cries. (author's collection)

Warren Young, who was asked, "Is it worse?" "Yes, worse. It is all over. He is dead," came the reply.[12]

Young went to the hotel and repeated the news to the other reporters, who made a mad dash in carriages to the West End Hotel where they sent telegrams to all parts of the country and the world. Young was carrying a warrant allowing him to take possession of the telegraph at the Elberon Hotel for the government. One telegram was sent to Garfield's sons at Williams College, and another to his mother in Ohio. Attorney General Wayne McVeagh, who was staying at the Elberon, and the four other cabinet members who were at the West End, were summoned to the cottage.[13]

Within an hour of the president's death the news had been received and posted on newspaper and telegraph office bulletin boards in every city in the country. Some newspapers had special editions on the streets within a few minutes of receiving the communication. Church and fire bells began ringing. Those awakened by the sound instinctively knew what it must mean. Many people left their houses for the newspaper offices.

At 11 P.M. in Elberon the attorney general appeared at the hotel and sent the official news of the death to President Arthur in New York. Secretary of State Blaine and Secretary of War Lincoln, who were in New England, were also notified. The attorney general also read a lengthy statement to reporters with details of the last moments. At 11:30 the last official bulletin on the president's condition was released. It simply stated the circumstances of his death, and read in part: "The President died at 10:35 P.M. At 10 o'clock he awoke complaining of a severe pain above the region of his heart. He almost immediately became unconscious, and ceased to breathe at 10:35." It was signed by Drs. Bliss and Agnew, and Frank Hamilton.

Chester A. Arthur was at his townhouse in Manhattan, and was receiving regular messages and bulletins concerning President Garfield's condition. At 11:30 on the night of September 19 a newspaper reporter appeared at the house and told Arthur the president was dead. Though not unexpected, considering the information coming out of Elberon, Arthur replied, "Oh. It cannot be true. It cannot be. I have heard nothing."

The reporter explained that his paper had received a dispatch. "I hope, my God, I do hope it is a mistake." He went back into the house to tell friend Elihu Root and District Attorney Daniel G. Rollins, Police Commissioner Stephen French and his secretary John Reed, who were with him.[14]

At 12:25 A.M. the official notice of Garfield's death was received by the new president. It was signed by the five cabinet secretaries then in Elberon, and read as follows:

> It becomes our painful duty to inform you of the death of President Garfield and to advise you to take the oath of office as President of the United States without delay. If it concurs with your judgment we will be very glad if you come down on the earliest train tomorrow morning.

President Arthur sat with his head buried in his hands for several minutes. He then sent a reply indicating he had received the message and extending his sympathies to the widow. Two policemen took up positions outside the house. Arthur's companions left to find a judge to administer the oath of office. Shortly before 2 A.M. they returned, first with New York State Supreme Court Justice John F. Brady, then Justice Donohue of the same court. Justice Brady, arriving first, was asked to perform the swearing-in. This he did at 2:15 A.M. in the first floor front parlor. The ceremony was witnessed by the aforementioned men, plus Arthur's friend Dr. Pierce Van Wyck, the new president's son Chester, and a valet. It was dawn by the time Arthur got any sleep.[15]

The accession of Chester A. Arthur to the presidency was met with some concern. He was chosen for the vice presidency by the Republicans because he was from the Stalwart faction, the more conservative wing of the party, in

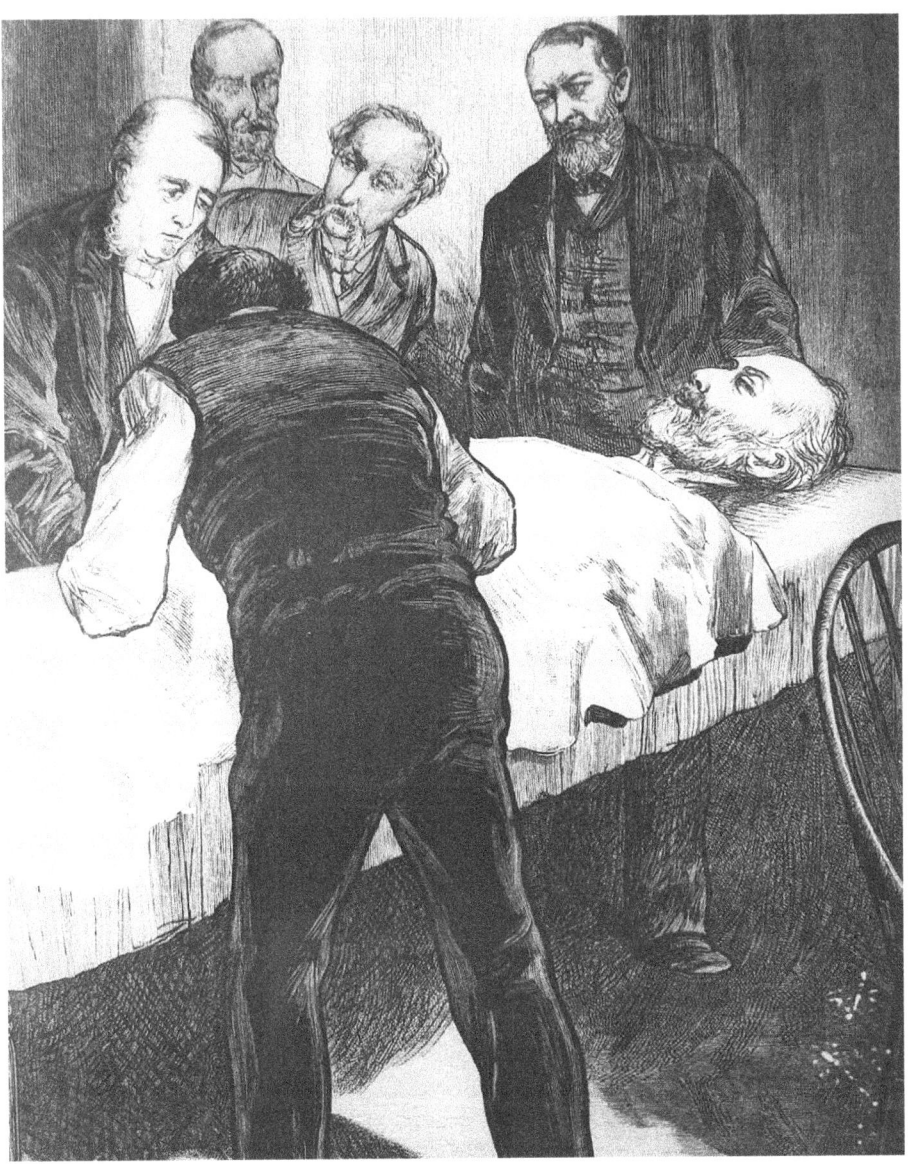

Doctors perform an autopsy on the remains of President Garfield. (author's collection)

order to balance the ticket and unify support against the Democrats. Arthur had a reputation as a political hack and tool of the party bosses, and charges of corruption had been leveled against him The fact that the assassin Guiteau had claimed that he was a Stalwart added to the concerns. To some, it almost seemed like a coup d'etat had taken place. President Arthur, however, would alleviate those concerns by his demeanor and actions in office.

At noon on September 20, President Arthur made the short train trip to Long Branch and met with all seven members of the cabinet. He also visited Francklyn Cottage where he expressed his sympathies to the family, along with former president Ulysses S. Grant, who had also arrived in town. Arthur left to return to New York at 4 P.M. with Grant.

Meanwhile, thousands of messages of condolence were pouring in to the widow and to the White House from governments all over the world, and from political, civic and governmental bodies throughout the United States.

In Elberon, a local undertaker had been put in charge of the body, pending arrival from New York City of another undertaker and an embalmer. The embalming took place on a table at the cottage, beginning at noon.

At 4 P.M. an autopsy on the body was begun. Mrs. Garfield had been much opposed to it, but when told that it was required by New Jersey law, she, of course, relented. Eight doctors, including those present at the death, were present for the procedure, which was primarily performed by army surgeon Dr. D.S. Lamb. It lasted close to four hours. At 11:30 P.M. the results were released and read aloud in the lobby of the Elberon Hotel. The examination revealed that the bullet was not located to the lower right of the spine, where it had been repeatedly probed for, but to the left and higher, ten inches away. It had shattered a rib, passed through part of a vertebra, supposedly tore the splenic artery and lodged behind the pancreas. The repeated probings of the long, false channel by the doctors had caused infection, leading to blood poisoning and pneumonia. The immediate cause of death was aneurysm of a pus sac formed by blood from the splenic artery. The bullet lodged in fatty tissue and was harmlessly encapsulated. The report was signed by the eight physicians.[16]

During the day orders had been given to the armed forces, and the next day the official announcement of the death of the commander in chief and the assumption of his duties by President Arthur was read to the troops. Flags were ordered to half staff until after the funeral, officers to wear a mourning badge on the left arm, colors to be draped in mourning for six months, and guns to be fired at dawn and dusk, and at thirty minute intervals during the day, for thirty days.

In cities and towns throughout the land, buildings were draped in black mourning cloth. Many entertainments and amusements were cancelled on the day of the death. New York City theaters were closed. The stock exchanges opened briefly but shut down at noon.

Instances of threats and the forming of vigilante groups against the assassin Guiteau were reported in many places. The few people who dared speak out against the late President Garfield were sometimes met with violence, but those reports were very few in number. One Democratic-leaning newspaper in New Jersey was marched on by indignant citizens after printing comments critical of the late president.

Plans for the funeral were put into place on Tuesday the twentieth and followed the wishes of Mrs. Garfield: A special train would take the body to Washington to lie in state in the Capitol, then on to Cleveland to lie in state in the public square, followed by interment in Lake View Cemetery in that city, where the late president had expressed a wish to be buried and where relatives already lay. Viewing of the body would be permitted, including the next morning at Elberon.

Early Wednesday, a crowd gathered near the heavily guarded cottage, and at 8:30 they were formed into a line of three thousand and admitted inside. A couple of hours earlier, Garfield's body had been placed in a chestnut coffin secured from New York. It was inlaid with black cloth, and ornamented with silver handles and a plate on top that read:

> JAMES ABRAM GARFIELD
> Born November 19th, 1831,
> Died President of the United States,
> September 19th, 1881.

The president was dressed in the same outfit that he had worn at his inauguration just a few months earlier: a long, black, double-breasted frock coat, dark vest and trousers, and black necktie. His left hand was laid across his breast, tucked into his coat, the right arm at his side. The casket had been carried downstairs and placed on two stools draped in black in a hallway near one of the cottage entrances. The upper lid was removed, but a glass plate was in place over the upper body. Two palm fronds lay across the lower portion. The room was plain save for one hanging fern and one flower arrangement. It was dimly lit, and a soldier stood guard in each corner.

As the public entered they were hurried through at a quick pace. They were shocked by the appearance of the body. It was much changed from before, due to the effects of the illness and the autopsy. The undertakers did the best they could, but the face appeared haggard and emaciated. A *New York Times* reporter described the remains:

> The President's face was shockingly ghastly. The skin was drawn tightly over the projecting bones, except on the forehead, where it was deeply corrugated. The lips were apart, disclosing the set teeth. The hair and whiskers had whitened perceptibly ... the face was blotched with black specks, the result, it is said, partly, of the taking of a plaster cast of the face.[17]

At 9:30 the line was stopped and the doors shut. Family, friends and colleagues took a last look, then the lid was closed. The Rev. Charles J. Young of Long Branch read a prayer while the funeral train backed up to the front of the cottage. Then the heavily-veiled Mrs. Garfield, the family, friends and dignitaries walked out the front door and boarded the train. A minute later six undertaker's assistants carried the coffin into a specially arranged funeral car. It was placed on a center dais between two flower arrangements in the black-draped car. Twelve soldiers took places around the casket. The passengers, including the cabinet and chief justice of the United States, Morrison K. Waite, entered another car. The train proceeded up the track a few hundred yards, then stopped alongside another train from New York, whose occupants, including presidents Arthur and Grant, transferred to the funeral train. A little after 10 A.M. it departed for Washington as Long Branch bells tolled.

The train passed through Princeton, where students laid flowers along a hundred yards of track, then through Philadelphia, Wilmington and Baltimore. Huge crowds of mourners stood along the tracks in and near every city and town. The men removed their hats as the train passed by, the coffin clearly visible, but the shades of the passenger cars were pulled down. Even in rural areas farmers stood along the tracks to bid goodbye to the late president.

At 4:30 P.M. the engine pulled into the Baltimore and Potomac depot in the nation's capital. Upon the platform were arranged rows of army and navy men, led by General William Tecumseh Sherman. In the nearby streets were thousands of members of military and civic groups that would join in the escort to the Capitol building. The windows of houses and hotels with a view of the tracks were filled with spectators, and thousands stood along the route from the station to the Capitol, and in windows and on rooftops.

The widow descended from her car, accompanied by her son Harry and Secretary Blaine, followed by the other passengers, including Arthur and Grant. The coffin was carried off the train on the shoulders of eight soldiers, passing through the main hall of the terminal—within several feet of the spot where Garfield had been gunned down. Once outside the building, the Marine Band, led by John Phillip Sousa, played "Nearer, My God, to Thee" as the coffin was placed in a hearse.

The impressively decorated canopied funeral car was drawn by six gray horses wearing customary mourning trappings, each led by a uniformed colored groom. The mourners from the train got into carriages. One of them, bearing Mrs. Garfield and two of her children, went directly to the house of Attorney General MacVeagh, whose guests they remained until they left Washington. Preceding the hearse were carriages containing President Arthur, the cabinet, and others. Columns of army and navy officers marched alongside the hearse, and several military companies came after it, followed by other groups. When the order was given to move out, a band commenced playing a dirge, and the carriages were on their way down 6th Street to Pennsylvania Avenue.

The thousands of spectators were kept to the sides of the streets by police officers along the ¾ mile route. The procession pulled up to the east portico of the Capitol a little after 5 P.M. The grounds around the building were a

From left to right, Secretary of State James G. Blaine, President Chester A. Arthur, and former presidents Rutherford B. Hayes and Ulysses S. Grant pay their respects at the coffin of the late President Garfield in the Capitol Rotunda. (author's collection)

mass of people. "Nearer, My God, to Thee" was played as the coffin was borne up the steps into the Rotunda and placed on a catafalque, the same one that had been used for President Lincoln sixteen years earlier. Behind the casket walked a contingent of congressmen that had greeted the procession upon arrival, followed by President Arthur and the others.

When everyone was inside, the lid of the coffin was opened. President Arthur, Secretary Blaine and General Grant approached and looked upon the face of the late president, then passed out of the hall, again through the east entrance, and into their carriages. They were followed by other guests in the funeral party. Once the carriages had driven away, the assembled troops dispersed to their respective headquarters.

The public was then admitted into the Rotunda. The exterior of the Capitol had been draped in black cloth, and likewise the interior. A few floral arrangements were in place around the catafalque. A massive wreath sent by Queen Victoria of England especially stood out. A detail of D.C. police and a contingent of army veterans stood guard. Rich and poor, black and white, young and old, the people reverently passed the bier in two single lines, in through the east door and out the west. The line snaked for a long distance outside the entrance. Vendors hawked photographs, snacks and lemonade. All through the night and into Thursday the mourners shuffled by.

At noon on Thursday several carriages pulled up to the Senate wing of the capitol, and the occupants alighted and entered the building through a basement entrance. The group included President Arthur, Chief Justice Waite, former president Grant and former president Rutherford B. Hayes, who had arrived from his Ohio home, and several other government officials. They gathered in the Vice President's Room at the rear of the Senate chamber, where Arthur took the presidential oath of office from Chief Justice Waite. There was no legal necessity to do so, since the Constitution does not designate an official to swear in a president. Any person authorized to administer oaths may do it, and that is what happened two days earlier in the president's New York apartment when Judge Brady swore him in. However, to be absolutely certain that all requirements had been met, Arthur was advised to take the oath again, administered by the Chief Justice.

All the cabinet members tendered their resignations, but the president asked them to remain at their posts, at least for the time being. He also issued a proclamation that designated Monday, September 26, 1881, the day of the burial, as a "day of humiliation and mourning."

Congress was not in session, but a group of representatives issued a eulogy and letter of condolence. A group of senators decided not to adopt any similar resolution until the Senate met in regular session. Both houses agreed to send eight members each to the funeral ceremonies at Cleveland.

Because the new Congress was not yet in session, succession to the presidency in case of the death of President Arthur was problematic. The Constitution and the law provided only that the vice president succeed the president, followed by the president pro tempore of the Senate, then the Speaker of the House of Representatives. If no new president pro tem or speaker had yet been chosen, who was next in line? The last president pro tem? The last speaker?[18] President Arthur foresaw the problem, for right after being sworn in in New York, he mailed a letter calling for a special session of the Senate, which could then pick a new president pro tem.[19] In response to this potential crisis, the Presidential Succession Act of 1886 was passed, which put the cabinet officers next in line after the vice president. Today, the offices of president pro tem and Speaker of the House are always filled, in session or not, thus eliminating such a potential problem.

On Thursday, Mrs. Garfield, Mollie and Harry visited the White House to arrange for the removal of the family's personal property to the Garfield home in Mentor, Ohio, near Cleveland. She had no intention of remaining in the mansion, though President Arthur was temporarily staying in a senator's apartment in the city and allowed her to take all the time she needed. The widow appeared deeply emotional and wept when she bade farewell to the staff. The building was draped in deep mourning, inside and out. Police were stationed everywhere outside, and inside the staff tried to conduct business as best they could.

During the afternoon Presidents Grant and Hayes made a brief visit to the Rotunda to view the body. In the early evening the wives of two of the cabinet members visited, and they were shocked at the condition of the body. The face had further deteriorated in appearance, and an unpleasant odor was noticed. Upon their complaint, the lid was placed on the coffin, concealing the body from view.

The lines for the viewing dwindled considerably during the night. The next day the Rotunda was closed to the public at 11 A.M. after an estimated 100,000 people had passed through. A few minutes later everyone, including the honor guard, left the Rotunda. An undertaker opened the coffin, powdered the face, and rearranged the hair and beard. Then Mrs. Garfield entered and was left alone under the vast dome for twenty minutes. She was then escorted out through the Senate wing and did not return for the later funeral service. The lid was put back in place on the coffin, and on request of the widow it was never to be opened again.

Around two in the afternoon 1500 invited guests began arriving in the Rotunda for a memorial service. The gathering included the president and former presidents, the cabinet, former vice presidents Hannibal Hamlin and William P. Wheeler, foreign emissaries, congressmen, military officers, Supreme Court justices and veterans groups. President Arthur was seated facing the head of the coffin, and near it stood a choral group and four clergymen.

At 3 o'clock a hymn opened the ceremony, followed by a reading by the Reverend Rankin of the Congregational Church. This was followed by a prayer read by the Rev. Isaac Errett, a leading Disciples of Christ preacher from Cincinnati, then a eulogy by the Rev. F.D. Power of the Vermont Avenue

Christian Church, which the late president attended. The services closed with a prayer by the Rev. J.G. Butler, Lutheran pastor and chaplain of the House of Representatives. The floral arrangements were removed, save for the wreath and palm leaves that rested upon the coffin. Then six bearers from the Vermont Avenue church carried the coffin out the east door, preceded by a military contingent and followed by all the other mourners. The casket was handed off to military bearers and placed in the waiting hearse as the Marine Band played "Sweet By and By." The principal mourners entered the several carriages parked nearby. Every spot imaginable was packed with humanity, from the Capitol grounds, down Pennsylvania Avenue, to the Baltimore and Potomac station.

The cortege moved off to somber music and muffled drums led by several companies of military, veterans and civic groups in full uniform. Then came the hearse and dozens of carriages. Minute guns were fired. The procession reached the depot around 5 P.M. where the body was once more carried from the hearse, through the station to the awaiting train, and placed in the funeral car, bound for Cleveland. It was difficult to keep the way open against the press of people straining for a glimpse. Members of the funeral party entered the rail cars. President Arthur did not board the train, but stayed in Washington. Mrs. Garfield and her children had earlier arrived and been seated. The congressmen and reporters occupied a second train. In short order the trains left the depot as a fine rain began to fall and a rainbow appeared in the sky.

The engine and all of the nine cars of the funeral train were heavily decorated in mourning. In the funeral car only the wreath and palm branches lay on the coffin. Twelve soldiers were assigned to stand as honor guards.

The tracks along the route were lined with people out to pay their respects. At the stations of every little town or city immense crowds were gathered. Nearly everywhere bells tolled as the train passed.

Seabrook, Bowie, Odenton. The towns flew by. After an hour and a half, Baltimore was reached, where a stop of ten minutes was made to change engines. Among the throng of mourners were the mayor, council, veterans groups and businessmen. Indeed, at each place passed, the prominent citizens were present to pay their respects. All buildings were draped in black.

Coming out of Baltimore and all the way to Pittsburgh, every switch was manned, and a worker was placed every half mile to make sure the tracks were clear. In addition, a pilot engine preceded the funeral train by several miles to insure clear passage.

The train passed into Pennsylvania. York, Goldsboro, Harrisburg. In the country, groups of people gathered at road crossings, despite nightfall. Marysville, Mifflin, Anderson. Bonfires were lit at some points along the route. The train reached Pittsburgh near 6 A.M. on Saturday, where it stopped to switch tracks. As at all the other stations, a mass of people was gathered. Minute guns fired and church bells rang.

Soon the train reached Ohio. Some funeral decorations on one of the cars caught fire, but it was quickly extinguished. In Wellesville, where the train stopped for water, some people were able to shake hands with President Hayes and cabinet secretaries through the windows of their car. Near Salineville the train got stuck going up a steep grade, and another engine had to be called to push it along. Finally, at half past one in the afternoon, the train pulled into Cleveland.

The train stopped at the Euclid Avenue station — not the main station downtown, three miles away — because it was deemed more suitable for the occasion. In the packed depot the passengers began to disembark. Several military officers formed a double line through which passed the officials, friends and relatives of the late president. The widow was immediately taken away to the home of a friend. Then the coffin was passed through the door of the funeral car and placed upon the shoulders of eight artillerymen in white helmets and blue and red uniforms. They carried it out to the waiting hearse, which was a plain but costly vehicle provided by local undertakers. It was led by four black horses caparisoned in black with silver trim, each led by a Negro groom, each of whom had performed this duty at the obsequies of Abraham Lincoln.

When the congressional train arrived minutes later, its occupants joined the other mourners. The scene around the station was impressive. Every building in sight was draped, and a mass of spectators occupied every spot available — on rooftops, in every window, atop coaches and rail cars. Along Euclid Avenue the mansions were covered in folds of black and white material, and large portraits of the late president were frequently displayed. Flags were flown at half staff. This display extended to every part of the city of Cleveland.

In short order the procession to downtown, where the body would lay in state, began. First came three platoons of policemen, a military band with muffled drums, a body of mounted men, the Knights Templar, and then the hearse, alongside of which marched the military pallbearers. Next came more military companies, veterans of Mr. Garfield's old Civil War unit, and a long line of carriages carrying the cabinet, governors, congressmen and others, including friends of the family.

At three o'clock the lead part of the procession reached the black arch that spanned the entry into the downtown square, where the body of Lincoln had rested years earlier. Though the streets leading to the square were blocked with people, no one was allowed into it. Near the center of the square stood the specially built pavilion that would receive the body. It was open-air, 45 feet square, and 30 feet tall. From two sides ramps led up to the viewing area five feet above the ground. Each side of the structure had arched openings 24 feet wide. The facades were ornamented with flowers. Gilded columns at the four corners were graced by minarets topped by flags and banners. At the center of the rooftop was a large gold globe, on which stood a 24-foot-high angel. Several elaborate floral pieces were arranged within the pavilion.

When the procession reached the square the hearse stopped at the pavilion, the carriages were emptied, and the soldiers carried the coffin onto the catafalque at the center of the structure to the sounds of a hymn. Twelve soldiers were placed around the casket, four of whom stood at each corner. They wore tall bearskin hats, and their coats sported fringed epaulets, à la the Buckingham Palace guards in England. At the head of the coffin was a scroll with the words:

> Life's race well run,
> Life's work well done,
> Life's crown well won,
> Now comes rest.

Above that was a portrait of the late president. At the foot, "GARFIELD" was spelled out. Four tall columns stood at each corner of the coffin, topped by huge urn-like decorations. That night, in an early display of electricity, the pavilion and the whole square were illuminated by electric lights.

The late president's mother, 80-year-old Eliza Garfield, had arrived in Cleveland, as had the Garfields' two younger sons, the widow's father, and two sisters. Son James R. Garfield had just recovered from an illness and had arrived from college in Massachusetts.

Early Sunday morning, citizens began to converge on the square and at one end formed a line for access to the pavilion. Soldiers were stationed around the perimeter of the square to prevent entry except by the queue, which, beginning at 9 A.M., was allowed to move forward. The people walked through a large triple arch, appropriately decked in mourning emblems and flowers, up the ramp of the pavilion and past the closed coffin. These were people from the country where Garfield was known best, where he was born and grew into manhood. These were his people.

Early in the day the widow, accompanied by a few others, made the carriage ride to Lake View Cemetery to personally view and approve the site for her husband's final resting place and memorial. Workmen were constructing a canopy near the cemetery association vault, where Garfield's remains would be placed pending removal to the completed memorial.

Late in the afternoon the Marine Band entered the square and played a few selections. Various organizations were allowed into the pavilion as a body to view the coffin. At one point it rained for several minutes and a rainbow formed. At nightfall the lights were turned on. All through the night the people kept coming, until the square closed at 9:10 A.M. the next morning — after an estimated 200,000 had visited the bier.

During the preceding days, people from all parts of the country, especially within easy reach of Cleveland, had been arriving in the city, occupying every hotel room and staying at private houses. These included not only officials and VIPs, but common citizens of enough means to be able to attend.

This being the day of mourning declared by President Arthur, memorial services were held in churches throughout America and in many cities worldwide. Games and amusements were cancelled in many places. The New York Stock Exchange closed. In Cleveland all business was suspended for the day. In Washington all business was halted after 2 P.M., and President Arthur attended a church service.

Years later an undertaker revealed that at some point after arriving in Cleveland, Garfield's body was secretly removed from its coffin and taken to a funeral establishment in an attempt to make the face more presentable. It was desired that the people of Cleveland be allowed to view it. Despite morticians working throughout the night, the discoloration of the face, caused by an embalming fluid used to preserve bodies for post-mortem examination — but not for viewing, was unable to be sufficiently corrected. It was too late to return the body to the casket because the crowd had already begun to pass by the bier. It was late Sunday night before the remains were surreptitiously returned. Many thousands of people had unknowingly paid their respects to an empty coffin.[20]

During the 9 A.M. hour on Monday the distinguished guests arrived to take their places in the Cleveland square. About one thousand seats had been placed near the pavilion for them, and they were led by Chief Justice Waite, former president Hayes, generals Sherman and Philip Sheridan, and the congressmen. An impressive hearse was drawn into the square by twelve black horses, harnesses four abreast and led by six grooms. It was twenty feet long, with a twenty-foot-high canopy supported by six columns festooned with black and white flowers, flags draped in crape and a raised dais for the coffin.

All around the square were arranged the thousands of participants for the march to the cemetery. The Marine Band, singers and the Knights Templar had places near the pavilion. In the streets nearby were columns of military and civic groups. Several carriages came into the square, and from them exited the widow and her two eldest sons, the president's mother, other family members, the cabinet, and five clergymen. They all took seats in the pavilion. Mother Garfield lay her head upon the coffin and cried.

Close to 11 o'clock the services began with a hymn, followed by a Bible reading and a prayer, during which a fire alarm was sounded as a signal for minute guns to begin firing from a nearby park. A clergyman gave a lengthy reading, followed by a hymn. At this point the Rev. Charles Pomeroy, scheduled to recite the last prayer, was asked to keep it short, since some ladies were fainting. It was a hot, sunny day, and the people were dressed in the heavy, covered style of the late nineteenth century. After little more than an hour the service ended.

As the Marine Band played "Nearer, My God, to Thee," the coffin was carried from the pavilion by the soldiers and placed in the hearse. Then the principal mourners, many of them weeping, came down and entered their carriages. The grand procession formed and passed out down Euclid Avenue toward the cemetery, five miles to the east. A special committee had made provisions to supply the marchers with 20,000 sandwiches and ice water. Barrels of water were placed at intervals for the use of all. The crowd along the street was immense, once again occupying every possible spot.

The order of the procession was essentially the same as two days earlier, except the family was present in the line of carriages, and it consisted of a larger numbers of troops. The marching bands played hymns and dirges, accompanied by muffled drums, and the sound of carriage wheels and horse hooves were punctuated by the sound of the minute guns. Soldiers kept the spectators back from the center of the avenue. Men doffed their hats as the hearse passed by.

The head of the procession reached Lake View Cemetery at 2 P.M., but it was 3:30 before the hearse arrived, so lengthy was the line of march. Rain had been falling for nearly an hour, and the marchers and spectators became soaked. The archway set up at the cemetery entrance, as well as other decorations, and the black canopy erected in front of the burial vault became drenched. The marchers took places in the cemetery, and the hearse pulled up to the vault entrance, where flower-bedecked gates stood open. In front of it, under the canopy, was laid a carpet of evergreen branches, with flowers strewn among them. A large tarpaulin was laid upon the wet evergreens, and an inclined plane was placed at the rear of the hearse.

The carriage containing President Garfield's widow, mother and sons Harry and James pulled up near the vault. Harry and James got out, but the two women remained seated inside. The eight artillerymen removed the coffin, marching down the plane and over the evergreen carpet and into the vault where the casket was placed on supports. They remained in place beside it. The widow covered her face and wept. The Marine Band once more played "Nearer, My God, to Thee," and her face turned bright. The Rev. J.H. Jones spoke, a choir sang, and a representative of the relatives thanked everyone for their support. After a short prayer the long journey of James A. Garfield was over. People picked up flowers or pieces of branches as souvenirs as they left. Some approached the carriage and briefly spoke to the family. All the carriages and troops returned to downtown Cleveland. A round-the-clock

Funeral scene at Lake View Cemetery in Cleveland. In front of the receiving vault, a minister with upraised hand blesses the coffin of James A. Garfield, still on the hearse to the far left. In the background is the carriage containing the widow, with Garfield sons Harry and James standing beside it. (author's collection)

guard of Cleveland police was assigned to watch over the vault. They were replaced by federal troops three days later.

In the following days many visitors stopped at the cemetery to look at the coffin through the vault's gates. Rumors of a plot to steal the body proved unfounded, apparently the result of a visit to the cemetery by four drunken men the night of the funeral.[21] Hundreds also visited the downtown pavilion and the funeral car parked near it, which remained in place for thirty days.

For months after the funeral, memorial addresses were given by distinguished persons around the country. None was more moving than that delivered by Garfield's friend and secretary of state, James G. Blaine, before a joint session of Congress and President Arthur on February 27, 1882.

The doctors' treatment of the president was second-guessed, questioned and criticized from within days of the shooting until long after his death — in newspapers, magazines, medical publications and by the public at large. The physicians were accused of withholding information from the public, and this was true. In many cases the bulletins they issued were more optimistic than warranted because they did not want to dishearten their patient with unfavorable reports, about which he was sure to find out. The doctors who treated Garfield defended themselves, as did other physicians, but many were very critical.

It should be remembered that in 1881, medical science was only nearing the dawn of what could be called "modern" medicine. Doctors relied much more on their experience, suppositions, and best calculations, which, of course, led to more diverse opinions as to the course of treatment than would exist today. Surgical gloves were not used; instruments and hands were not sterilized. Antiseptics were only starting to be used. There were no antibiotics, intravenous treatments, or x-rays. Ether to ease the pain during procedures was only infrequently employed. In Garfield's case only a weak topical antiseptic was administered. His wound was probed dozens of times by unsterile fingers and instruments in an unsuccessful attempt to locate the bullet. This was undoubtedly the cause of the infection and fatal blood poisoning.

The doctors were obsessed with finding the bullet, probably believing that its removal would help heal the patient, and that the missile itself would cause infection. However, it had often been the practice for years to leave a deeply buried bullet in the body, where it would become harmlessly encapsulated, and hope that no vital organs had been damaged. This was not done in Garfield's case. The autopsy reported that the bullet tore the splenic artery, which healed itself and caused a pus sac to be formed around the coagulated blood, then later burst and killed the president. But others argued that the pus sac was formed as a result of the blood poisoning spreading throughout the body, for if the artery had been pierced by the bullet, the victim would surely have died in a short time.

The doctors and other caregivers sent their bills for services rendered to the United States government. Congress was outraged that the government and not the Garfield estate should be billed. Never before had it paid the medical bills of a civilian federal employee, other than routine care provided the president by the White House physician. The care given to Abraham Lincoln during his last hours was covered by the War Department, but that was because the nation was considered to be at war and Lincoln was the com-

Opposite: Montage of scenes from the assassination of President Garfield. In the center is the Baltimore and Potomac Railroad Station where the crime took place. Clockwise from center top: President Garfield; the waiting room where the assassin stood; Dr. Townshend, one of the attending physicians; the assassin's weapon; the assassin Guiteau; the president's coffin in the Capitol Rotunda; Dr. D.W. Bliss, lead physician in the treatment of the president; the waiting room showing the spot where the president fell after being shot. (Library of Congress)

mander-in-chief. That the patient, James A. Garfield, had been the president of the United States did not matter. The government did not pay the bills of private citizens. After much debate and denunciation of the doctors as "quacks," about $35,000 was paid out, roughly a third of what had been asked.[22] This set the precedent of government financial obligation for the medical care of the president in such cases.[23]

Protection of the president was not enhanced following the assassination of President Garfield. Three policemen continued to be assigned to the White House staff, as they had been for years. The feeling that the president should be free to mingle with the citizenry, and not be isolated from them by a palace guard, prevailed.

Garfield's assassination by the "disappointed office seeker" Guiteau led to the signing of the Pendleton Civil Service Reform Act by President Arthur in 1883. This was the first meaningful law to control the corrupt spoils system, though even today the positions the assassin sought are not covered by civil service law, but are presidential appointments. It is also ironic that Arthur, who was part of the party machine and benefitted greatly from the old system, became a reformer and signed the bill into law.

At the Baltimore and Potomac railway station a commemorative plaque was affixed to the wall near the spot where Garfield was shot. The building was torn down in 1908 after a new Union Station opened in the nation's capital. The National Gallery of Art now occupies the spot.[24] A section of the floor where the president fell is preserved at the Smithsonian Institution.[25] Francklyn Cottage in Elberon was razed around 1900. A statue of Garfield stood for many years near its former location, but was moved inland to stand with statues of other presidents who vacationed in Long Branch–Elberon. The railroad ties used on the rail spur to the cottage were made into a cabin that still stands today as a privately owned tool shed. The section of Garfield's vertebra that the bullet penetrated, as well as some of his internal organs, were sent to the Army Medical Museum, now the National Museum of Health and Medicine in Washington.[26]

Late in the evening of October 5, 1881, within the vault, Garfield's body was transferred from its original coffin to one of elegant bronze.[27] On October 22 the casket was transferred to the Scofield private vault at the cemetery.[28] In 1882 complaints surfaced that the officer in charge of the detail guarding the vault was opening the coffin for certain visitors and allowing them to view the remains.[29] On February 6, 1886, in the presence of the late president's son James, the coffin was placed in an expensive outer bronze sarcophagus, but kept in the vault.[30] In June 1887 the military guard was discontinued.

By the spring of 1890 the Garfield Monument in the cemetery was completed. It is an impressive light brown circular stone structure rising 180 feet.

Upon ascending the stairs and entering, one encounters a beautiful life-size marble statue of the late President. Around the exterior runs a frieze depicting various phases of his life. One floor below, in the crypt, behind iron gates, lies the flag-draped coffin of President Garfield, and next to it that of his wife.

On the rainy morning of May 20, several carriages and a hearse arrived

The Garfield Memorial in Lake View Cemetery in Cleveland. (M. Nowak)

at the Scofield vault. An undertaker and cemetery official entered and opened the outer sarcophagus and the inside coffin, revealing the face of the deceased. It looked little changed in nine years. The covers were refastened, then the casket was carried out and transported to the new monument. Witnessed by sons James and Harry Garfield, their father's remains were carried into the building and lowered into the crypt by means of ropes and derrick.[31]

Ten days later, on Memorial Day, the dedication of the Garfield Memorial was held. The cemetery was filled with thousands of people who heard speeches by President Benjamin Harrison, Vice President Levi P. Morton, former president Hayes, and then-representative and future president William McKinley.[32]

President Garfield's widow, Lucretia Rudolph Garfield, survived twenty-six years after her husband's death. She continued to live at the homestead in Mentor, but spent winters at a second home in Pasadena, California. She died there of pneumonia on March 14, 1918, at age 85. Several days later her body was placed in the crypt at the Garfield Memorial beside the president.

James A. Garfield had died without a will. His assets of $61,000, including the farm at Mentor, near Cleveland, "Lawnfield," were divided among his heirs according to Ohio law. The widow was the beneficiary of life insurance policies worth thousands of dollars, and a public subscription raised over $350,000 for her and her children.[33]

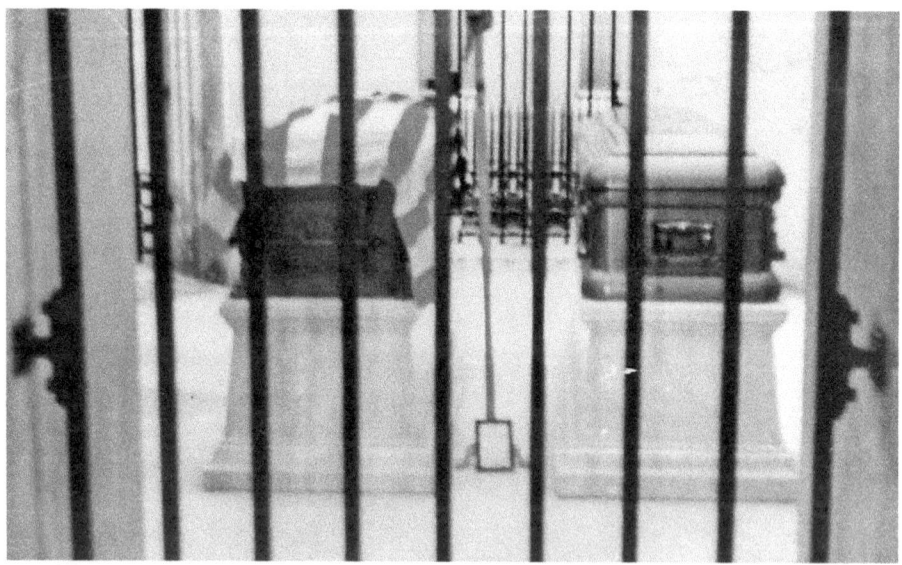

The flag-draped casket of James A. Garfield lies next to that of his wife in the basement crypt of the Garfield Memorial in Lake View Cemetery, Cleveland. (M. Nowak)

Charles Julius Guiteau

"He must have been crazy. None but an insane person could have done such a thing. What could he have wanted to shoot me for?" said James Garfield, after asking who shot him. He apparently did not remember the persistent job applicant. But Secretary of State Blaine did. Chester A. Arthur remembered seeing him several times.

Charles J. Guiteau was born in Illinois in 1841. He was a mentally unbalanced shyster who managed to pass a bar examination, was an itinerant preacher and imagined himself an important politician. Believing that God commanded him to kill the president, he claimed he did it to save the Republican Party and America.

Two attempts were made on the assassin's life while in custody for the shooting. He went on trial for Garfield's murder on November 14, 1881, in District of Columbia Supreme Court. His brother-in-law was one of the attorneys defending him. Another was Charles H. Reed, who was co-prosecutor in the case of the men who attempted to steal Abraham Lincoln's body in 1876. The judge was Walter S. Cox, who had been legal counsel to two of Booth's confederates in the Lincoln murder trial. Guiteau's ten-week trial was a sensation, with the defendant often leaping to his feet and making impromptu, sometimes senseless comments. At one point the section of Garfield's backbone hit by the bullet was introduced as evidence, and was reportedly handled by Guiteau. Spectators were noisy and unruly. It was a circus.

Though probably insane, as testified to by such an eminent psychiatrist as Edward C. Spitzka, Guiteau was found to be sane; and when the arguments ended, he was quickly found guilty. He was sentenced to hang, and appeals, including one to President Arthur, were denied. The sentence was carried out on June 30, 1882, at the D.C. jail. He went to his death reciting a poem he had written.

Afterward, the body was autopsied. The government refused to release the body to the family. Technically, Guiteau had willed it to a friend, who relinquished possession to the federal government. It reportedly was buried under the jail at 19th Street and Independence Avenue SE, but there are also stories that it was stripped to the bones for eventual public display. The skeleton, spleen and brain are now stored at the National Museum of Health and Medicine in Washington.[34] The public bought souvenirs: pictures of the hanging, pieces of the hanging rope, and replicas of the bullet that struck Garfield.

Chapter 6

William McKinley

25TH PRESIDENT OF THE UNITED STATES
TERM OF OFFICE: MARCH 4, 1897, TO SEPTEMBER 14, 1901
BORN: JANUARY 29, 1843; DIED: SEPTEMBER 14, 1901
AGE AT DEATH: 58 YEARS, 228 DAYS
PLACE OF DEATH: BUFFALO, NEW YORK
CAUSE OF DEATH: GANGRENE DUE TO GUNSHOT WOUND
BURIAL PLACE: CANTON, OHIO

By the end of the nineteenth century America was known throughout the world for its Wild West culture. Western cowboys, ranchers, outlaws, lawmen, soldiers and American Indians were cultural icons famous for their gun battles, both real and fictitious. The United States had even changed presidents twice with the bullet. Any hopes that the dawn of the twentieth century would change this "tradition" were dashed when another president fell victim to an assassin's gun in 1901.

William McKinley had been a healthy child who enjoyed outdoor activities with enthusiasm. When he was a small boy he nearly drowned. At age seventeen he suffered an attack of physical exhaustion while attending college.

He served in the army during the Civil War, and his commander was Rutherford B. Hayes, the future president. After the war, McKinley became a lawyer and entered politics. In 1876 he was elected to the U.S. House of Representatives. After losing that seat in 1891, he was elected governor of his native Ohio. Having established a prominent national reputation, and being well liked, he was nominated by the Republicans for president in 1896 and won the election.

The most significant event that occurred during the McKinley administration was the Spanish-American War, which resulted in the United States acquiring the Philippines, Guam and Puerto Rico. America truly became a player on the world stage.

President McKinley was admired by the American people because of his courteous, friendly and thoughtful manner. They were especially touched by his devotion to his wife Ida, who suffered from fits of epilepsy.

Early in the evening of September 4, 1901, the president arrived in Buffalo, New York, to attend the Pan-American Exposition, which was the world's fair of its time. His train was welcomed by an overenthusiastic cannon shot that blew out some of the windows of the presidential car and completely unnerved Mrs. McKinley. He gave a speech on international relations on the grounds the following day, and on Friday morning he visited Niagara Falls. He returned to the Buffalo Exposition that afternoon, where he was scheduled to greet the public in the Temple of Music building.

The ornate Temple of Music was one of dozens of structures built for the exposition in a theme of varied colors. The Temple's exterior was of a salmon hue, with red trim and touches of aqua, which contrasted with the blues, greens, yellows and other colors of the different buildings on the beautiful 350-acre grounds. Gaudy yet opulent, the grounds were studded with gardens, fountains and canals, and featured a brilliant, massive display of the new electric lighting each night. Topped by a gilded dome, and built in the Spanish Renaissance style, the 180-foot-high rotund Temple of Music seated 2,200 and featured concert performances and speeches. On the afternoon of September 6 it was to host a receiving line for the public, who could enter the building, greet the president and shake his hand. The reception was scheduled to start at 4 P.M.

George B. Cortelyou, the president's personal secretary, decided that the reception would last only ten minutes. He had some concern for his boss' safety, and advised McKinley to cancel the event; but not wanting to disappoint the people, the president thrice refused, answering, "Why should I? No one would wish to hurt me."[1]

In 1901 no elaborate Secret Service detail existed to protect the president, although they did accompany him on all trips outside of Washington. On this trip to Buffalo, three men were assigned to McKinley. But the safety of the president was mostly in the hands of local police, both in the nation's capital and on his travels.

Impeccably dressed in a black frock coat, with trademark red carnation in the lapel, and sporting a black tie, white vest and top hat, McKinley arrived in an open carriage at the Temple of Music at 4 P.M., accompanied by Cortelyou and John G. Milburn, president of the Exposition. As he alighted from the vehicle, President McKinley bowed and smiled to the cheering crowd of 20,000 that had gathered round the building. Only a couple of hundred of them who had waited all day in the sunny, unseasonable, eighty-degree heat would actually get to shake the president's hand. Meanwhile, 3,000 people had been admitted to observe the reception, and they filled the galleries and many of the seats on the main floor.

This is said to be the last photograph ever taken of President William McKinley, as he arrives at the Temple of Music at the Pan-American Exposition in Buffalo a few minutes before being shot. He is seated in the carriage to the left. Next to him is John Milburn, president of the Exposition. (Collection of Buffalo and Erie County Historical Society; used by permission)

From inside the Temple came the strains of the "Star Spangled Banner," and the people made way for the president to enter the south entrance of the building. McKinley took his place in the ornate interior. He was positioned at the bend of a curving aisle that was formed by chair backs hung with light blue cloth. This aisle ran from the east entrance, where the public would enter, toward the center of the building, where the president stood, turned and continued out to the south entrance where the people were to exit. Directly behind McKinley and his party were several potted palms and two bay trees. In back of this was a huge wooden frame over which a large American flag was decoratively hung as a backdrop. Farther away, past rows of wooden chairs, was the Temple's stage, and a large flag was hung from its ceiling, as well as from the balconies at its sides. Mr. Milburn was directly to his left and Cortelyou to his right. Four Buffalo plainclothes detectives stood near the president, one immediately behind him. Two Secret Service agents were positioned directly across the aisle from McKinley, facing him, and another was ten feet down the aisle to his right. Two unarmed army soldiers stood to Milburn's left and two to Cortelyou's right. Another seven unarmed soldiers and eighteen uniformed Exposition guards formed a double line from the east entrance up to the presidential party, through which the public passed. In addition, a dozen guards were on duty outside the building.

As a Bach sonata played softly on the house organ, the doors were opened and the public was admitted. As they made their way down the aisle through the phalanx of guards, the people formed into a single file. Famous for his fifty-a-minute handshake, McKinley found the greeters advancing too slowly, and word was sent to hurry them along. With the line moving along so quickly, it was hard for the guards to carefully observe each person.

One of the people in line approaching the president was Leon F. Czolgosz, a former wire mill worker from Ohio. Czolgosz, who was probably mentally disturbed, had become a drifter and professed to be an anarchist. He had attended anarchist meetings and read their literature, but was not accepted by them — they considered him to be a government spy. At the turn of the century, anarchism was considered to be a great evil movement, comparable to communism. European anarchists had in recent years killed the president of France and the king of Italy, but there was no proof that the American anarchists sanctioned violence.

Czolgosz had arrived in Buffalo on August 31 and taken a room. He purchased a .32 caliber Iver-Johnson revolver and made his plans to meet the president. On September 5 he attended the Exposition and was present near the front of the crowd when McKinley gave his President's Day speech, but was prevented from taking action by the crush of the crowd and security guards. He also claimed to have followed the president to Niagara Falls the next morning, but made no attempt to approach him.

So it was that Czolgosz took his place among the well-wishers at the Temple of Music on Friday, September 6. A little girl passed the president, to whom he gave his lapel carnation. Then came a man who seemed to linger after shaking hands and was hurried along by the guards, drawing their attention for a second or two. Immediately on his heels was Czolgosz, who had put his revolver in his right hand, then wrapped a handkerchief around the hand, making it appear to be bandaged. This apparently aroused no suspicion, because many people had handkerchiefs out on that warm afternoon, mopping their brows. Also, a man who had passed in line earlier had a bandaged right hand.

It was 4:07 P.M. One of the Secret Service agents who stood just three feet in front of McKinley put his hand on Czolgosz's shoulder as if to move him along. The president's right hand reached for Czolgosz's left hand, but Czolgosz struck it aside and rapidly fired two shots through the handkerchief

With a revolver concealed in a handkerchief, Leon Czolgosz shoots President McKinley at the Temple of Music at the Pan-American Exposition in Buffalo. Startled guards and spectators look on in disbelief. (Library of Congress)

at McKinley's midsection. The first was deflected by a button on the president's vest and did no real damage, but McKinley straightened up to his full height as a look of astonishment came over his face. The second shot tore through his body, and he staggered backward, clutching his stomach. He was caught by Detective John J. Geary of the Buffalo police.

Utter chaos erupted in the Temple of Music. Cortelyou helped the president to a nearby chair. The assailant was instantly disarmed, knocked to the floor and beaten by guards and a tall African American who had followed him in line. Panic gripped the crowd as screams and shouts pierced the air. There was a rush for the exits as others from outside tried to get in to see what the commotion was all about.[2]

Czolgosz was dragged to the center of the building as McKinley pleaded, "Let no one hurt him." The president was seated in a chair, and the men about him were fanning him with their hats and trying to comfort him. They removed his collar and unbuttoned his shirt. Guards were clearing the public from the Temple as an ambulance was summoned. McKinley thought of his wife Ida as he whispered to his secretary, "My wife. Be careful, Cortelyou, how you tell her. Oh, be careful."[3]

Czolgosz was taken to a small room to the left of the stage. Meanwhile, Exposition doctor George M. Hall and two interns arrived at the scene aboard an electric ambulance from the Exposition field hospital. With bell clanging, it pulled up at 4:18. The wounded president, still conscious and not bleeding very much, was placed on a stretcher and carried out to the ambulance as onlookers moaned. The vehicle sped away to the hospital and arrived there in a few minutes.

The small Exposition hospital was staffed mostly by interns, nurses and medical students. It was intended to handle emergencies, but not major surgery, though it did have an operating room. As the president was laid on an operating table and undressed, a bullet fell from his clothes. This was from the first, non-lethal shot. A senior medical student ordered a nurse to administer painkillers, and an antiseptic was swabbed on the wound.

The first surgeon arrived at the hospital at 4:45, Dr. Herman Mynter, accompanied by Dr. Eugene Wasdin. After examining the patient and talking to others doctors who had come in, Mynter agreed that immediate surgery was necessary. McKinley, still conscious, was so informed and gave his consent. A few minutes later Dr. Matthew Mann, a noted gynecologist, arrived. Dr. Roswell Park, one of the country's leading surgeons, and medical director of the Exposition, was summoned, but he was eighteen miles away performing an operation in Niagara Falls. He started for Buffalo as soon as he could. It was deemed inadvisable to wait for Dr. Park, or to move the patient to a better equipped hospital, so Dr. Mann was chosen to perform the surgery there at the Exposition hospital.

At 5:20 ether anesthetic was administered with a gauze mask. Dr. Mann, four other physicians, one medical student and seven nurses who would assist in the operation scrubbed their hands and arms and put on sterile gowns. They did not wear caps or surgical masks or surgical gloves, as these were not yet generally used during surgeries. Five other doctors observed the procedure.

It was noted that there was an abrasion near the sternum, obviously caused by the deflected bullet that had fallen from McKinley's clothing. The other wound was half-way on a line between the left nipple and navel, and was very deep. An incision was made to open the abdomen.

It was discovered that the bullet had passed through both the front and rear walls of the stomach. Dr. Mann sutured these wounds. He then introduced his hand behind the stomach in a futile attempt to locate the bullet and its path, but stopped when it seemed to have a bad reaction on the patient. The doctors declined to use one of the new x-ray machines to find the bullet. They believed it was not necessary to find and remove it. The area of the stomach was cleansed with a saline solution, then the abdominal wall was sewn closed and bandaged. Dr. Mann decided not to allow the wound to drain.

The operation was conducted in poor conditions. Inadequate instruments were available, and the lighting was bad. Despite the fact that the Pan-American Exposition was a glittering display of electric lighting, only a few dim bulbs were in use in the hospital. Gaslights were not turned on because of the highly flammable ether anesthetic. Dr. Presley Rixey, the president's personal physician who had been traveling with him, arrived during the operation and made himself useful by using a mirror to deflect the rays of the fading sunlight onto the incision, thereby aiding visibility. Dr. Park arrived as the operation was coming to an end at 6:50 P.M. McKinley was taken by ambulance to Mr. Milburn's house, not far from the Exposition grounds, where he had been staying.[4]

Back at the Temple of Music the assailant Czolgosz had been handcuffed, taken from the building and placed in a carriage. Police and soldiers had to fight to keep back the angry crowd, which shouted cries of "Lynch him!" He was driven to Buffalo police headquarters.

The news of the shooting was quickly disseminated throughout the country by the press. About three minutes after the shots were fired, Associated Press wires had already picked up the story, though it was a bare statement with no details. It made the late editions of many city newspapers. Mrs. McKinley was gently told that her husband had had an accident, then shortly afterward she was given the full story. She took it quite well.

With some difficulty, Vice President Theodore Roosevelt was located in a remote part of northern New York State's Adirondack Mountains, and he started for Buffalo on a special train. Officials in Washington, of course, had been immediately informed of the events.

In the evening, the doctors released two bulletins indicating that the president was rallying and resting comfortably. People throughout the nation gathered outside newspaper offices to read the latest releases concerning the events in Buffalo.

By Saturday morning, authorities had cordoned off the area around the Milburn residence. An army regiment was camped across the street in a vacant lot, guarding the house, along with local police. Tents and a large election booth were set up nearby for the press. The house next door took in clerks and stenographers to handle mail. Vice President Roosevelt, cabinet members and other high government officials arrived throughout the day. They made their headquarters at the exclusive Buffalo Club down the street. A special wire connected them to the Milburn house, which in turn was connected to the White House.

Inside, the Milburn residence became a private hospital. McKinley rested on a hospital bed in a second floor bedroom and was attended by nurses and doctors. The first floor was a reception area for government officials, relatives and friends, including the president's two sisters and brother.

Messages were received from governments around the world expressing their revulsion at the attack on McKinley and their hopes for a speedy recovery. On Sunday, America's churches offered prayers for the stricken president.

Newspapers denounced the anarchist movement, and many of them called for the wholesale arrest and prosecution of anarchists, as well as the denial of freedom of speech and assembly to them. Around the country many of these completely innocent people were hunted down and jailed without charges. Many citizens who spoke ill of the president or expressed glee at his shooting were beaten by their fellows or the police, arrested and jailed. Temperance crusader Carry Nation was booed when she said during a speech that she was not sorry for McKinley because he was in favor of the alcohol trade.[5] Two men with Polish surnames who had registered at Czolgosz's hotel in Buffalo on the same day as he were taken in for questioning, but later released.

Bulletins were released by the doctors every few hours, usually three times a day, briefly describing the president's condition, a summary of the treatment being given, and the patient's pulse, temperature and respiration. They were signed by the physicians and Cortelyou, then carried out to the newspaper tents. The reporters telegraphed or telephoned the information to their newspapers' offices where notices were posted in the windows for the public and printed in their next editions.

By Tuesday, these bulletins became quite reassuring regarding the president's condition. Based on them, and especially on statements by a New York City attending physician, the well known Dr. Charles McBurney, the newspapers had begun to paint a rosy picture of McKinley's recovery.[6] On Tuesday and Wednesday, many of the government officials, including the vice president, left Buffalo, convinced that the worst was over and the president was no longer in danger.

The patient became alert and wanted to talk. However, visits were restricted to brief forays by Mrs. McKinley and Cortelyou. McKinley was denied newspapers and the cigar he asked for. The doctors and nurses continued to administer drugs and nutritive enemas, and to cleanse the wound. But drugs to control infection did not yet exist.

On Thursday morning the president was given solid food for the first time. He seemed to tolerate it well, but around 3 P.M. he complained of nausea, fatigue and headache. He had a racing pulse. The doctors ascribed the discomfort to indigestion, but it soon became obvious that it was much more serious. The doctors administered cathartics and enemas in the belief that it was an attack of intestinal toxemia, but the heart began to weaken and failed to respond to digitalis and strychnine.

By Friday morning the condition of the president was extremely serious. Saline solutions, whiskey adrenalin and camphorated oil were administered, all to no avail. The pulse grew steadily weaker. Heart specialists were summoned. Telegrams went out to call back the family and friends, government officials and the vice president, who had left Buffalo in high hopes just a couple of days before. The mood of the nation grew gloomier as the papers relayed the alarming news.

By Friday afternoon the president began to slip into unconsciousness, but he came out of it every once in a while. Oxygen was administered. It was all to no avail. About 6 o'clock a rumor circulated that McKinley was dead, but it was not yet true. A 6:30 P.M. bulletin issued by the doctors said that "the end is only a question of time."

At one point the dying man said to the doctors, "It is useless gentlemen. We ought to have prayer." At about 7 o'clock he asked to see his wife. For several minutes she was left alone with him and a nurse. She leaned over the bed and held his hands, and kissed and caressed him. He put an arm around her and smiled. In a feeble voice McKinley said, "Good-bye. Goodbye all. It is God's way. His will be done, not ours."

Then he faintly began to whisper the words of the hymn "Nearer, My God, to Thee." Mrs. McKinley began sobbing and was led away. Dr. Rixey came in, and McKinley soon fell back into a coma. Family, friends and cabinet members were led in to say good-bye, each one kissing the president or clasping his hand. Particularly moving was Senator Marcus Hanna's good-bye. Tearfully at the bedside he called out to his old friend, "Mr. President! Mr. President! Can't you hear me? Don't you know me?" Receiving no response, he cried out, "William! William!"[7]

President McKinley never regained consciousness, though his head would at times move from side to side and his hand reach out as if to grasp something. At that point Dr. Rixey would take his hand. At 8 P.M. the pulse was gone, and by nine the heart was barely audible. The extremities became cold and his breathing became a death rattle. The respiration ceased at 2:15 A.M. Saturday, September 14, 1901. Dr. Rixey put his stethoscope on the president's chest. He raised his head and said, "The president is dead."

Those present in the room beside the attending physicians were the president's two sisters; his brother Abner; several nieces and nephews; Webb Hayes, who was the son of former President Hayes and a McKinley confidant; W.C. Brown, who was the law partner of Abner McKinley; Charles G. Dawes, who was comptroller of the currency and a future vice president; and Cortelyou — twenty people in all.[8]

Cortelyou went downstairs and sadly announced to those gathered in the parlor, "Gentlemen, the president has passed away." He then signed the final bulletin, which simply read, "The president is dead."

Vice President Roosevelt had not yet reached Buffalo. Late Friday he had finally been reached at the remote mountain retreat in northern New York State to which he had returned. Upon receiving the news of the president's relapse, he immediately raced for the nearest railroad station by horse and buggy. When he reached the station at dawn he learned that he had succeeded to the presidency. He refused to make any comment, and rode on a speeding train to Buffalo, secluded in a compartment.[9]

As word of McKinley's death spread by telegram, telephone, and finally the morning newspapers, the nation entered into mourning. Various shows, festivals and sporting events were cancelled or postponed. Thousands of messages of condolence began flowing in from all corners of the country and the world.

In the days that followed, isolated instances of beatings and arrests of persons uttering critical remarks about the late president continued. Men in the street, as well as some in posts of authority, including the pulpit, ranted against freedom of speech and assembly for anarchists.[10] Some newspapers advocated wholly irresponsible measures, such as the *National Tribune* of Washington, D.C., which said, "This is one of the occasions when the aroused public vengeance should have full sway, unfettered by legal impediments, and any proclaimed anarchist have no further grace than the time to take him to the nearest tree."[11] A New York City pastor advocated the lynching of Czolgosz. The pastor of McKinley's church in Washington said, "I would have blown the scoundrel to atoms."[12] Many persons even accused newspapers that in the past had been critical of McKinley as being guilty of aiding the crime. The Buffalo police headquarters where the assassin Czolgosz was being held became the target of mobs of vigilantes, but police successfully countered attempts to rush the jail.

The Pan-American Exposition closed early on Friday night, and all electric illumination was shut off. It remained closed through Sunday.

Theodore Roosevelt arrived in Buffalo just before 2 P.M. Saturday. After lunch at the mansion of his friend Ansley Wilcox, he was driven to the Milburn house, where he expressed his sympathies to the family. Roosevelt did not see Mrs. McKinley, however, who was in seclusion.

Roosevelt then was driven the few blocks down the street back to the Wilcox mansion. Secretary of War Elihu Root had made arrangements for a swearing in ceremony. He had also been present at the swearing in of Chester A. Arthur in New York twenty years before when the latter succeeded to the presidency upon the death of James A. Garfield. U.S. District Judge John R. Hazel had been called to administer the oath of office to the new president. Gathered in the small library of the Wilcox home, amid furniture in dust covers and walls lined with bookcases, were five cabinet members, all except Secretary of State John Hay and Secretary of the Treasury Lyman Gage, who remained in Washington. A few other government officials and invited guests were also present. At Roosevelt's request, about twenty members of the press were allowed to observe. Forty-three persons bore witness to the event. Mr.

Root paid an emotional tribute to the late president, then asked Roosevelt to take the oath. Roosevelt, standing in a bay window alcove, quite seriously and sternly, but with his voice breaking at first, said, "I am ready to take the oath. I wish to state that it shall be my aim to continue absolutely unbroken the policy of President McKinley for the peace, prosperity and honor of our beloved country."[13]

Judge Hazel then commanded, "Theodore Roosevelt, hold up your right hand." Roosevelt then repeated the Constitutional oath of office. He had become the twenty-sixth president of the United States, and, at 42, the youngest ever to hold the office.

A cabinet meeting was held, and it was agreed that all officers would retain their positions for the time being. Roosevelt's first official act was to declare Thursday, the planned day of McKinley's funeral, a national day of mourning in an official proclamation that also eulogized the fallen leader.

On Saturday evening the funeral arrangements were announced. A prayer service was to be held in the Milburn house on Sunday, after which the body would be conveyed to Buffalo's City Hall, where it would lie in state. On Monday it was to be transported to Washington, where it would repose in the White House, then be taken to the Capitol for a public ceremony. Burial would be in Canton, Ohio, on Thursday.

The secretary of state sent a notice to foreign diplomats informing them of the succession of Theodore Roosevelt to the presidency upon the death of William McKinley. The secretaries of war and navy officially informed the military and ordered the armed services to render appropriate honors. These included, for the army, a formal reading of the news to the troops, the firing of guns at thirty minute intervals on that day, and placing the flag at half staff until after the funeral. All activity was to cease at noon on the day of the burial. Badges of mourning would be displayed for thirty days. Similar orders were given to all ships and naval stations.

President McKinley's body remained in the bedroom where death had occurred. Military hospital corpsmen had been detailed to guard the remains since shortly after his passing. Senator Hanna went to undertakers Drullard and Koch in downtown Buffalo to order a casket.

At the Milburn house, beginning at 11:45 A.M. on Saturday, an autopsy was conducted by Dr. Harvey Gaylord and Dr. Herman Metzinger, two pathologists who had not taken part in the treatment of the patient. Also present during the procedure were other doctors, including two U.S. Army surgeons and most of those physicians who had tended to the dying man, the district attorney, and his stenographer, who took minutes. Two orderlies lifted the body from the bed onto an operating table that had been brought into the room, and the operation began. The procedure lasted more than three hours and was halted at the request of Mrs. McKinley, who did not want the corpse injured any further.[14] The pathologists stopped before they found the bullet, and the family would not permit any tissue to be removed from the body for further examination and testing. The doctors and coroner, James T. Wilson, signed the autopsy report, which stated that there was a fatty degeneration of the heart muscle, that the tissue around each bullet hole in the stomach had become gangrenous, and that the bullet had passed through the back walls of the abdomen and hit the upper end of the right kidney. Part of the bullet track was also gangrenous, as was the pancreas, located directly behind the stomach. A major finding was that the pancreas had also been hit by the bullet. The report concluded, "There was no evidence of any attempt at repair on the part of nature and death resulted from the gangrene, which affected the stomach around the bullet wounds, as well as the tissues around the further course of the bullet. Death was unavoidable by any surgical or medical treatment and was the direct result of the bullet wound."

Though it sounded conclusive, the post-mortem report raised more questions than it answered. Coroner Wilson issued the certificate of death of the late president, stating the cause of death as "gangrene of both walls of stomach and pancreas following gunshot wound."

Undertakers from Drullard and Koch in Buffalo were called in to prepare the remains for the funeral.[15] Young mortician Arthur Legg was given the job of embalming President McKinley's body.[16] A death mask of his face was made.[17] Friends and relatives were asked not to view the body until Sunday morning, after it was placed in the casket and taken downstairs.

At nine in the morning on Sunday, September 15, a large group of Buffalo police officers arrived at the Milburn house and were stationed around the outside of it. A military detachment was quietly marched to the house, and took positions both inside and outside. The troops came from Fort Porter in Buffalo, the Exposition, the New York National Guard, and the gunboat *Michigan*. Guests began arriving for a scheduled 11 A.M. service. They included intimate friends and associates of the late president, as well as local and national government figures—about one hundred persons in all. All the cabinet members save Secretary Hay were there.

The president's body had been laid in a casket of hand carved black mahogany, with his name and dates of birth and death carved on top. The interior was lined with cream-colored silk. It was carried downstairs and placed in the drawing room between two windows. The upper lid was opened. Red roses, white chrysanthemums and wreathes of purple violets rested atop an American flag, which was draped in folds over the foot of the coffin. The late president had been dressed in a black frock coat, his usual suit in life, and his left hand rested on his breast. His face purportedly showed the suffering he had recently endured in his struggle for life. A soldier and a sailor were stationed behind the coffin.

Prior to the arrival of guests, Mrs. McKinley was led into the library by Dr. Rixey. The first lady, in a black gown, was composed as she gazed upon her husband's face and touched it. She then retreated to the head of the stairs on the second floor, where she joined other family members.

President Roosevelt was the last mourner to arrive at the house. With solemn demeanor he took his place near the head of the coffin as everyone rose. After a moment, Methodist minister the Rev. Dr. Charles E. Locke, who had been pastor to the McKinley family back in Canton, began the service. It started with a quartet from the First Presbyterian Church in Buffalo singing "Lead, Kindly Light."

The singers were stationed in the hall outside the library, and the Reverend Locke was positioned in the doorway between the hall and library so that the family at the head of the stairs could hear his words. When the quartet finished, the minister read a chapter from the Bible, and after that they sang the hymn that had been upon the president's lips as he lay near death, "Nearer, My God, to Thee." The Reverend Locke then raised his hands and offered a brief closing prayer. The simple ceremony lasted about twenty-five minutes.

Senator Hanna moved forward to the bier to look upon his friend's face for a moment, then the casket was closed. Colonel Theodore A. Bingham, an aide to President Roosevelt, motioned, whereupon four soldiers and four sailors who had been stationed near the library stepped in and lifted the coffin upon their shoulders, carrying it out of the house. It was followed closely by President Roosevelt, the cabinet, then the others, except for the family, which remained behind.

It had been very cloudy all morning, but when the soldiers emerged from the house, a ray of sunshine broke through to illuminate the scene. The 65th Regiment band across the street played "Nearer, My God, to Thee" as the flag- and flower-bedecked coffin was carried down the walkway and placed in a windowed black hearse drawn by four black horses draped in white netting.

The strains of Chopin's "Funeral March" filled the air as a platoon of mounted policemen took its place at the head of the procession to Buffalo's city hall. The distinguished mourners entered waiting carriages.

The procession moved out in the following order: the police, an army band playing dirges, army infantry and Marines, the hearse, about a hundred Grand Army of the Republic veterans, more soldiers and sailors, and several carriages (the first being that of President Roosevelt). The funeral cortege moved out slowly, in time to the solemn music, straight down Delaware Avenue, the grandest street in the city, lined with stately homes and mansions. All along the two-and-a-half-mile route, about fifty thousand people stood to watch the last journey of Mr. McKinley begin. Many looked from

A hearse carrying the body of the late President McKinley leaves the Milburn House in Buffalo. The president died in a second floor bedroom eight days after being wounded by the assassin Czolgosz. (Collection of Buffalo and Erie County Historical Society; used by permission)

windows or were grouped on front porches or even on rooftops. The buildings were draped with flags and mourning cloth.

Upon reaching the downtown area, the procession turned toward city hall, where, after a two-hour drive, the hearse came to a stop in the front driveway of the east entrance of the gray stone building. Here, where favorite son Grover Cleveland had occupied the mayor's office two decades earlier, the pallbearers lifted the coffin onto their shoulders and carried it up the stone stairway into the building. A plain black catafalque was set in the main corridor, and upon this the coffin was placed. The hall was draped with black bunting and American flags, four of which hung straight down above the coffin and formed a cross.

President Roosevelt, the cabinet and other mourners stood near the coffin as its upper lid was removed. The lower part of the casket was covered by an American flag, on which were laid arrangements of white and red roses. Only a few other floral pieces were placed nearby. After paying their respects, the principal mourners left, and a military honor guard took positions around the coffin. Then the public was admitted. A huge crowd had massed near the building, standing for hours in sometimes heavy rain that began about the time the cortege reached city hall.

The people passed by the coffin in two columns, one on either side. They came in through the east and left by the west entrance, shuffling down the corridor. At times the lines extended back for half a mile. Many mourners left a flower at the catafalque as they passed. Among those in line were 125 American Indians who had been part of the Indian Congress at the Pan-American Exposition. In native dress, with painted faces, they too paid tribute to "the Great Chief of the Nation." The hall was open for ten hours, during which an estimated 80,000 to 100,000 persons paid their respects.

The bier was guarded through the night. Just past 7 A.M. on Monday morning the front door of the building reopened. Companies of sailors and Marines arrived, as well as the hearse. Five cabinet officers drew up in two carriages. At precisely 7:45 the call "Present arms!" was shouted by the commander. The coffin, borne by the four soldiers and four sailors, emerged from the doorway. On their shoulders was the flag-draped coffin of their chief, which they placed in the hearse to the strains of mournful music.

The area around city hall and along the short route to the railroad station was crowded with thousands of citizens. The procession moved out. First came the military, then the cabinet's carriages, followed by the Grand Army veterans and a local militia marching to the sad pace of the music and tolling church bells. Turning down Main Street, the line moved past the black-draped buildings and finally arrived at the station after thirty minutes. There the cortege met the carriage of President Roosevelt.

The invited guests of the funeral had arrived at the train station before President McKinley's body. They came from their various guest houses, with the heavily-veiled widow leaving the Milburn house early, and were already aboard the train, save President Roosevelt and a few others who escorted the casket to the train. The coffin was placed in the observation car. A sheaf of wheat rested on the coffin's flag, and several floral displays were arranged inside the car. The train consisted of a locomotive and seven cars; only the locomotive and observation car were draped in mourning, but not profusely.

The train rolled out for the nation's capital at 8:30 A.M., preceded ten minutes earlier by a pilot engine to clear the tracks. The funeral train's route took it through Harrisburg and Baltimore. At every city, town and settlement along the way, the local citizens lined the tracks as it passed, the coffin, guarded by a soldier and a sailor, visible to all. Men and women, young and old, some in their work clothes, took time to meet the train. Many knelt in prayer. Some sang hymns. Civil War veterans stood in their old uniforms. Almost every railway station along the 450-mile route was decorated in mourning.

During one long stretch between stations the bereaved widow entered the funeral car with her sister and Dr. Rixey. The lid of the coffin was turned back, and Mrs. McKinley knelt at the bier. Calm and composed, she remained there for one hour before returning to her own car.

The train finally arrived in Washington at 8:30 P.M. Military companies and policemen occupied the area around the station, as well as inside. A cannon boomed at five-minute intervals. Greeting the train were secretaries Hay and Gage and a few White House staffers.

When the family disembarked, they were driven to the White House. President Roosevelt and the other dignitaries lined themselves in two rows facing each other just outside the station entrance, where a hearse stood ready. The coffin was removed through the window of the railway car and carried to the hearse by eight military pallbearers.

In the darkness, the full procession stepped out from Sixth Street onto Pennsylvania Avenue, which was packed with mourners. The hearse was drawn by six black horses, each led by a Negro groom. At 9:30 the line reached the Executive Mansion. A woman across the street began singing "Nearer, My God, to Thee," and soon the whole crowd joined in. The body was carried into the East Room where President Roosevelt and the cabinet stood for a moment with bowed heads, then left. Two Marines, a soldier and a sailor stood guard throughout the night while four veterans were seated nearby. Mrs. McKinley occupied her old room, and President Roosevelt spent the night at his sister's house in the city.

Just after 9 o'clock the next morning the body of the late president was borne to the Capitol from the White House. The coffin had been placed in the hearse, led by the same six black horses with attendant grooms as on the previous night. As the procession moved out, a band played "Nearer, My God, to Thee." At almost the same time the gray skies began to rain. This did not deter the throngs of citizens gathered along the route to the Capitol. All along Pennsylvania Avenue stood thousands of men and women. Balconies and upper floors of structures, which were draped in black, were filled with onlookers, some of whom sang the hymn. It was only private buildings that were adorned, however. A federal law in effect at the time prohibited U.S. government buildings from being decorated.

The line proceeded in the following order: companies of foot and horse soldiers (including military bands), clergymen, physicians, veterans, and the hearse, alongside of which marched the military guard of honor and pallbearers, followed by carriages containing the family (but not the widow, who remained in the White House). Next came the carriages of former president Cleveland, President and Mrs. Roosevelt, the cabinet, diplomats, the Supreme Court justices, congressmen, governors and various other government officials.

The procession passed around the north side of the Capitol, and the hearse halted in front of the steps of the east entrance. Again from the bands were heard the strains of "Nearer, My God, to Thee," and then once more the eight men lifted the casket from the hearse and carried it upon their shoulders, up the steps and into the Rotunda through a military cordon. The rest of the funeral party followed.

At this time the large crowd that had been watching the events surged forward toward the Capitol steps, apparently to secure a place in line for admittance to view McKinley's body. Some people fell to the ground. Police and soldiers drew clubs and carbines and shouted for the people to get back. This caused more confusion and panic, and many were pushed down and trampled. Those who were injured were helped to their feet, and order was restored in five minutes.[18]

Inside, a catafalque, the same one on which had rested the coffins of Lincoln and Garfield, had been set up in the center of the Rotunda and 800 wooden chairs arranged about it. Most of the seats were already occupied by guests who had arrived earlier. They were now joined by those coming in from the procession. President and Mrs. Roosevelt, President Cleveland, and the cabinet occupied the row in front of the catafalque. The diplomatic corps and military officers were seated behind them. The Supreme Court and congressional leaders also occupied prominent places.

Everyone was on his feet as the coffin was carried in and lowered onto the catafalque. What followed was a Methodist funeral mass conducted by two clergymen, accompanied by a small organ and a choir. The eulogy praised Mr. McKinley as a man of "incorruptible personal and political integrity."

At the conclusion of the services the guests left the Rotunda through the Senate door. The chairs were moved out of the way, and the undertaker removed the upper lid of the coffin in preparation for the admittance of the public.

President McKinley's body lies in state in the Capitol Rotunda. (Library of Congress)

Once again, outside the east entrance the public surged forward toward the steps, and the trampling and crushing injuries were repeated. Doctors and ambulances were called for, and a couple of dozen of the injured were treated in a room below the Rotunda. Another twenty-two were conveyed to area hospitals.[19]

When the crowd was finally allowed to enter, it passed by the coffin in two streams, one on each side, entering from the east door and exiting through the west. From the crush outside, scores of men and women were shoved into the Rotunda in a bewildered or fainting state, clothing lost or torn. It was reported that one woman reached the catafalque with her dress completely gone.

From noon onwards, thousands of citizens passed through after waiting in long lines and enduring intermittent rain. Then abruptly, at 6:25 P.M., the doors were shut, and the police shouted that it was all over. Those thousands denied entry were outraged after hours of waiting, and an effort was made to charge toward the Capitol, but this was stopped by the police, who pushed back and threatened to use force.[20]

Just a few minutes later, in the early darkness of a stormy night, the sounds of marching troops and horses were heard. The escort for the late president's journey from the Capitol to the Pennsylvania railroad station was forming. At 7 o'clock the boom of cannons and the sound of drums were heard, and the casket was carried down the Capitol steps under electric lights placed there. This was the only lighted area, and it looked quite impressive to the throng of onlookers gathered beyond the plaza.

Once the body was placed in the hearse, the procession moved down Pennsylvania Avenue to the station. Once again, the dark, rainy streets were filled with mourners. At the station the crowd was immense, both outside and inside. The soldiers and sailors carried the casket through the station and into the funeral car. President Roosevelt and the cabinet, most of the guests who came down from Buffalo, additional mourners, and a large body of the military were already aboard three trains. The first was made up of eight cars, the second of seven (which was the funeral train), and the third of five cars, which was occupied by the military. Mrs. McKinley arrived a few minutes late, owing to the fact that her driver had trouble finding the right gate. At 8 P.M. the trains departed.

The interior of the funeral car was flooded with light, allowing onlookers to see the flag-draped coffin, with floral arrangements, and the soldier and sailor who guarded it. The trains headed through the rain and the darkness to Baltimore, York, and Harrisburg. Despite the late hour, enormous crowds waited at each station and at various crossings along the way to pay their respects. At some stations the trains stopped to change crews or engines.

In Pittsburgh the next morning it was estimated that 250,000 jammed the stations and lined the tracks, and crowded onto vessels in the Allegheny River, as the trains crossed. They finally reached Canton, Ohio, around noon on Wednesday the 18th. The tracks leading to the station and the nearby streets were packed with people. Out of towners co-mingled with what must have been the entire population of President McKinley's home town, a mass of humanity estimated at 100,000.

For days, thousands of Canton citizens had labored to make arrangements for this day. Nearly every business and home was draped in black mourning of some type, the notable exception being the late president's home, the only one not so decorated. On the wall of a factory overlooking the railroad station was painted a thirty-foot-high black-bordered shield with a portrait of President McKinley in the center.[21]

The interior of the station had been kept clear of the public. Outside, the area immediately near the station was kept clear by soldiers at ten foot intervals. Nearby stood ranks of cavalrymen mounted on black chargers.

Once the trains stopped, a local committee approached the funeral car. The late president's brother Abner and Dr. Rixey appeared, half carrying the sobbing, convulsing figure of Mrs. McKinley from the train to a nearby carriage. She was immediately driven to her home. The sight had men and women in the crowd weeping.

The funeral car's window was removed and the floral pieces taken out. In the meantime, President Roosevelt and his entourage emerged from the car ahead and took their places nearby. The eight body bearers took their places, and the flag-draped coffin was lifted out of the car and onto their shoulders. An army colonel, followed by the local committee, led the casket past the president and to a waiting hearse as a requiem sounded on a bugle. Once the coffin was placed in the hearse in front of the station, trumpeters signaled the procession to move forward.

Led by a Grand Army of the Republic band playing "Nearer, My God, to Thee," the line started for the courthouse. Following the band were mounted troops in brilliant uniforms, with tall bearskin hats topped with white pompoms. Then came the hearse, drawn by four black horses; the carriages of President Roosevelt, the cabinet and other guests; and broad ranks of Ohio National Guardsmen bringing up the rear.

The end of the mile-long march was the courthouse in the central city square. The coffin was carried up the wide steps, followed by the president and other officials, including the uniformed military officers, who stood out in contrast to the somberly-dressed spectators gathered in the square.

Once again the strains of "Nearer, My God, to Thee" rang out, and the coffin was placed on a catafalque in the building's rotunda, under a cluster of electric lights (including a single chandelier). The hall was neatly decorated in black crepe. The casket was opened, and Roosevelt, the cabinet and

6. William McKinley

Stereoscopic view of the arrival of President McKinley's remains at the courthouse in his hometown of Canton, Ohio, where it would lie in state. (Library of Congress)

other guests passed by the deceased and back out the building to their carriages. An honor guard consisting of a Knight Templar, national guardsman, a soldier and a sailor was posted at the coffin. Lines of militia formed from the entrance to side exits inside the building, then the public was allowed to enter in two lines. The doors were closed at 6 P.M., and in about five hours, 30,000 people had gone through.

Many mourners commented on the gaunt, pinched appearance of the late president's features. The brow and cheeks and lips had become darkly discolored. The Buffalo undertakers, in town to transfer their duties to a Canton undertaker, felt compelled to explain that the condition of the body after autopsy had made it difficult to properly embalm it.[22]

In the early evening the body was taken by hearse to the McKinley home on Market Street, where the widow waited. The only escorts on this trip had been the uniformed members of the Canton Grand Army of the Republic commandery. The coffin was taken in through the front parlor, and a number of sentries were posted around the house for the night. Mrs. McKinley was allowed to enter the small library where the coffin rested, and for one half-hour she sat beside the flower-draped bier. Though she wanted to look upon her husband's face, her family convinced her that it was not possible. Considering the deteriorating condition of the body, it was best that she did not.

Canton, a small city of 30,000, was inundated with visitors. About 100,000 were expected in town for the funeral. Thousands had to search for a place to spend the night, since Canton's hotel facilities were much too inadequate to handle such a huge influx. Government officials slept in their railroad cars. President Roosevelt stayed at a private residence.

One o'clock in the afternoon of Thursday, September 19, was the time set for the start of the funeral ceremonies. Throughout the morning the dignitaries, the citizen mourners, and the military and civic units had converged on the McKinley residence. Soldiers stood in triple ranks along the curbs of the street, and behind them was a great crush of spectators. In front of the house, along the walkway, stood ranking military officers, a civilian honor escort and many close associates of the late president. Thousands of other procession participants waited in the streets.

Inside, the Rev. C.E. Manchester said brief prayers over the coffin in the presence of the family, while Mrs. McKinley, too stricken to participate in any of the day's events, listened from the half-opened door of her adjoining room.

A troop of mounted cavalry on black chargers came down the street. President Roosevelt and the cabinet arrived, and they took places near the entrance of the house. At 1:15 all the church bells of Canton began ringing. A body-bearing team of eight soldiers and sailors entered the house, raised the casket onto their shoulders, and carried it outside. Decorated with enfolded flags, white roses and lavender orchids, the coffin was placed in the hearse. Marching orders were given, and the procession began.

Led by a squad of mounted police, rank upon rank of Grand Army of the Republic veterans advanced. They were followed by military units and then carriages carrying President Roosevelt and the cabinet. Then came the hearse, which was drawn by black horses with tall black plumes adorning their heads and covered with long black palls. Each horse was led by a soldier. On one side of the hearse marched a line of generals, and on the other a line of admirals. They were followed by a long line of carriages containing the family, congressmen, state governors and officials, and federal civil servants. Also marching were thousands of members of various civic organizations and local officials. The procession stretched for about two miles.

As the bells tolled and funeral dirges played, a vast silent throng of mourners covered every inch of the lawns and curbsides along the way, occupying porches and housetops and every window. They were held back by an unbroken line of soldiers along each side of the street.

It was about 2 P.M. when the hearse drew up in front of the First Methodist Episcopal Church, where President and Mrs. McKinley had been married thirty years earlier. Files of soldiers kept clear a pathway to the entrance as the body was borne inside, followed by the president and other dignitaries, as still others entered through side doors. The organ played Beethoven's "Funeral March" as the coffin was set down upon its bier at the front of the church.

The interior of this house of worship was magnificently decorated. A twenty-foot-high black border with white trim swept completely around the interior. The stained glass windows were framed in black cloth, and black and white streamers formed a canopy above the bier. At the front of the church was a breathtaking floral display at whose center was a black flower–bordered portrait of Mr. McKinley.

A quartet sang a selection, then the Rev. O.B. Milligan began the service with a prayer. The Reverend Manchester delivered an impressive eulogy. A brief prayer was followed by the singing of "Nearer, My God, to Thee." An army chaplain gave the benediction, then the body was borne from the church back to the hearse. The mourners reentered their carriages, and the march to the West Lawn Cemetery about a mile and a half distant, began. Still, the streets and buildings were filled with crowds of people. Homemade funeral arches spanned the street in some areas.

The head of the procession reached the cemetery at 3:30 — before much of it had even begun to move from the church; the hearse arrived about thirty minutes later. Sweet pea blossoms were strewn along the road in the cemetery, and they were collected as souvenirs by marchers and spectators who came later.

The beautiful burial ground was located on a knoll overlooking the city. On this late summer day the trees were beginning to show the first signs of autumn colors. The carriages stopped near the large receiving vault, just inside the cemetery entrance, and the guests alighted and walked up the path to it. Climbing ivory covered most of the gray stone structure, which was banked high with expensive floral pieces spreading a hundred feet on either side of it. The interior was covered with roses and orchids. Three huge wreaths hung near the front entrance, and the late president's baby cradle was placed nearby, covered with asters.

President Roosevelt and other officials formed two columns on each side of the walkway from the vault to the cemetery roadway. The hearse pulled up, and the body bearers, led by three military officers, carried the coffin up the walkway and placed it on a catafalque inside the vault. Mr. McKinley's brother and sisters stood at the front of the casket as Bishop I.W. Joyce of Minneapolis intoned the Methodist burial rites. When he finished his brief pronouncement, a signal went out to eight buglers stationed on a nearby mound, and they played "Taps" in unison. This even had many of the men weeping, for it was the end of the funeral, the final salute to the late commander in chief.

President Roosevelt, the cabinet, army and navy officers, and family members reentered their carriages and left the cemetery. The procession resumed. When the Knights Templar reached the vault, their choir took a place near it and sang a selection of beautiful hymns. The last of the procession passed by the vault near 6 P.M. as darkness approached, and an army guard took up places around it. They were to guard the body until it was moved to a permanent burial place, which was expected to be the family plot in the cemetery.

Memorial services were held all over the United States that day. Citizens gathered in churches and civic halls to hear prayers and eulogies. Also, in foreign capitals, from Havana to Manila, from London to St. Petersburg, the late president was memorialized. Former president Cleveland spoke at two gatherings in Princeton, New Jersey — one at the university, where he was a faculty member (and during which Professor Woodrow Wilson also spoke), and another at a church. Cleveland lauded McKinley's character.[23]

At 3:30 P.M. on the day of the funeral all business throughout the United States stopped for five minutes. All trains and carriages came to a halt, and even ferry boats stopped their motors. Pedestrians stood in place, hats off and heads bowed. The entire national telegraph system was shut down. Government buildings, banks, schools and most businesses closed for the entire day, or at least for the afternoon, including the stock exchanges. Church bells tolled all day long, and cannons were fired at intervals at military bases. Most games and amusements were postponed or cancelled, including major league baseball.

In Buffalo, the Pan-American Exposition had been closed the previous Saturday and Sunday. It reopened on Monday but shut down on Thursday, the day of the funeral. The exposition resumed its full schedule on Friday, and the Temple of Music continued to be used for some concerts and speeches, though most were moved elsewhere. A railing was put in place around the spot on which McKinley had been standing when he was shot, to prevent souvenir hunters from taking the floorboards. Guards had been posted near the spot a few minutes after the shooting. The configurations formed for the president's reception remained in place, and visitors were allowed to walk down the makeshift aisle just as the assailant had. Performers at the halls usually made mention of the tragedy in their remarks and paid tribute to the late president. The exposition closed down in November, and most of the buildings, including the Temple, were torn down, having been only temporary structures of wood and plaster. Today a plaque marks the spot near where the Temple of Music once stood. The house in which McKinley died was torn down in 1956 to make way for a high school parking lot. The gun used to kill McKinley and the floorboards on which he stood when he was shot are in the collection of the Buffalo and Erie County Historical Museum, which is housed in the only permanently constructed building at the Pan-American Exposition, though it was outside the actual fairgrounds. Czolgosz's handkerchief is at the Theodore Roosevelt Inaugural National Historic Site in Buffalo.

In 1907 the state of New York completed construction of a McKinley

Monument in downtown Buffalo. In the shape of an eighty-foot obelisk, it occupies the center of a large square in front of the new city hall.

Improved, round-the-clock Secret Service protection for the president was ordered by the secretary of the treasury shortly after McKinley's death. It was not until 1907 that this was mandated by law, and was not made permanent officially until 1951.

Although the assassin Czolgosz was a native-born American of Polish descent, he was generally considered to be a foreign immigrant who had brought his anarchist beliefs with him from Europe. Overt incidents of violence and discrimination against European, and particularly Polish, immigrants did not increase greatly after the attack on the president, except for wholesale arrests of anarchists, including the controversial leader of the movement in America, Emma Goldman. But insidious forms of prejudice probably worsened. The crime led to the passage of a law that barred from entering the United States anarchists or persons who advocated the overthrow by force or violence the government, or the assassination of public officials, allowing authorities for the first time to bar entry based on political views.[24]

Czolgosz's crime was connected to the attempted assassination of Theodore Roosevelt years later. When Roosevelt was running for president in 1912, John Schrank tried to kill him. Schrank said the ghost of William McKinley told him to kill Roosevelt, and that he had had a dream in which McKinley sat up in his coffin and accused Roosevelt of being responsible for his murder.[25]

Immediately following President McKinley's death, people began questioning the efficacy of the care given by the doctors, especially in light of the Garfield case. Though the principal attending physicians signed a statement that said they concurred in the treatment given to the patient, stories circulated that disagreements existed among them.

Some of the controversies that surrounded the case:

- Dr. Mann, a gynecologist who had no experience treating gunshot wounds, was chosen by the layman John Milburn to operate, even though Dr. Mynter was the most experienced in that field.
- The doctors chose to operate immediately rather than wait for Dr. Roswell Park, the preeminent surgeon in the Buffalo area. They also chose not to transfer the patient to the well equipped Buffalo General Hospital, but to operate at the small exposition hospital. They feared internal bleeding could have killed McKinley if they had delayed.
- The bullet was not found but left in the body because the patient reacted badly to the probing. An x-ray machine was available but not used to locate it. As it was, leaving the bullet did no harm. It was not poisoned, as one of the doctors thought.

- The wound was not allowed to drain after the operation, causing a build-up of poisons in the system. Drs. Mynter and Park apparently were in favor of draining.
- The doctors overlooked the seriousness of a possible infection on Tuesday, and Dr. McBurney's miscalculation, calling the crisis past, may have put everyone off his guard because he was one of the leading surgeons in the world.
- From the aspect of modern science, too many enemas and cathartics caused a loss of fluid and a possible electrolyte imbalance, but these were standard treatments at the time.

Dr. Park thought the wound to the pancreas caused the death, as pancreatic juices escaped into the peritoneum, were absorbed into the blood stream, and caused toxemia and the gangrene along the bullet's path. Dr. Mann said the general weak condition of the body, due to a sedentary life, retarded recovery and led to the death.

It may be accurate to say that there were multiple causes of McKinley's death due to the gunshot wound: infection, toxemia, dehydration, poor nutrition and electrolyte imbalance, all taxing a body that was in an unhealthy condition to begin with.[26]

A total of $45,000 was appropriated by the federal government for medical services rendered to McKinley, most of which was disbursed in different amounts to the attending physicians. None of their reputations suffered as a result of their involvement in the treatment of McKinley.[27]

President McKinley's widow, Ida Saxton McKinley, died on May 26, 1907, at the age of 59. She was an

The sarcophagi of President and Mrs. McKinley under the dome of the McKinley Memorial in Canton, Ohio. (M. Nowak)

epileptic who suffered from phlebitis and depression. She died peacefully in her Canton home, and was interred in the receiving vault in West Lawn Cemetery next to her husband.

A memorial committee purchased twenty-six acres next to the cemetery, and a memorial mausoleum was completed on the land in 1907. On September 18, Mrs. McKinley's body was moved from the vault to the mausoleum.[28] The late president's body was moved the following day, exactly six years to the hour since his funeral.[29] Sightseers were kept from the cemetery and mausoleum grounds by soldiers, and no ceremony was held. The couple had been placed in duplicate bronze caskets. The bodies of their two daughters were transferred later.

On September 30 the formal dedication of the memorial took place. President Roosevelt was the principal speaker, and James Whitcomb Riley read a poem. Vice President Charles W. Fairbanks was also present. About 50,000 citizens attended.[30] The mausoleum is a hundred-foot-tall circular building with a bronze statue of McKinley standing in the center of a grand stairway at the entrance. The dark marble sarcophagi of Mr. and Mrs. McKinley stand in the interior rotunda, rising high above the floor.

In his will, William McKinley left to his wife the bulk of his estate, worth an estimated $215,000. Upon her death, anything remaining was to go to his siblings. It also provided for a $1,000 per year payment for life to his mother. Since his mother died before McKinley, his sister Helen received the $1,000 per year stipend.[31]

Leon F. Czolgosz

Leon F. Czolgosz was born in Detroit. He became a factory worker in Cleveland. He was apparently normal in every way until his behavior changed in 1898. He quit his job and became alienated from his family. He fancied himself an anarchist and sometimes attended meetings of anarchist organizations.

He was put on trial for the murder of William McKinley on September 23, 1901. The trial lasted just two days, and a guilty verdict was reached by the jury in

Police mug shot of Leon F. Czolgosz, assassin of President William McKinley. (Collection of Buffalo and Erie County Historical Society; used by permission)

only thirty-four minutes. Two retired judges were appointed to represent Czolgosz. Their defense consisted of a eulogy to the late president and an apology to the court for having to represent the defendant. No attempt at an insanity defense was made. No appeal was filed.[32]

Two days after the verdict, Czolgosz was sentenced to die in the electric chair, and the sentence was carried out on October 29, 1901, at Auburn State Prison. The prisoner made one last statement before his death: "I killed the president because he was the enemy of the good people, the good working people. I am not sorry for my crime but I am awfully sorry I could not see my father." Czolgosz's family was tricked into not claiming the body.[33] Requests from medical schools for the remains were denied. After being autopsied by Edward A. Spitzka, son of the psychiatrist who had examined Charles J. Guiteau, assassin of President James A. Garfield, the body was said to have been buried in the prison cemetery. But another story says the body was dumped into a grave in Auburn's Fort Hill Cemetery. Six barrels of quicklime and a carboy of sulfuric acid were then poured in to dissolve the remains. Mere death was not enough vengeance for American society.[34]

Following these events, many medical and legal experts were critical of the trial, calling it a travesty of justice. Czolgosz was mentally ill, they claimed, and they conducted studies to attempt to show it. The prisoner had been inadequately and hastily examined for sanity before going to court and declared fit to stand trial.[35]

CHAPTER 7

Warren Gamaliel Harding

29TH PRESIDENT OF THE UNITED STATES
TERM OF OFFICE: MARCH 4, 1921, TO AUGUST 2, 1923
BORN: NOVEMBER 2, 1865; DIED: AUGUST 2, 1923
AGE AT DEATH: 57 YEARS, 273 DAYS
PLACE OF DEATH: SAN FRANCISCO, CALIFORNIA
CAUSE OF DEATH: APOPLECTIC STROKE
BURIAL PLACE: MARION, OHIO

The personal and political scandals that surrounded Warren G. Harding make his death very intriguing. A small-town newspaper owner and editor in Marion, Ohio, Harding did not pursue politics; politics pursued him. His inoffensive homespun style of speaking and writing caught the attention of state Republican politicians who used him to further their own careers. Harding himself had no illusions about his limited executive abilities. He always considered himself a simple man, just "one of the boys" who enjoyed nothing better than getting together with friends over a game of cards and a few drinks.

Harding's wife Florence, called "the Duchess," was a domineering, rather unattractive woman whose main concern seemed to be the attainment of social status through her husband. She and the "Ohio Gang" of politicians were the main thrust behind Harding's political career. They eventually succeeded in getting him elected president of the United States.

Scandals surrounded Harding, and were of two types—personal and political. He was involved in extramarital affairs both before and during his presidency. With one woman, Nan Britton, he probably fathered an illegitimate child in 1919. He continued to see Nan even in the White House. Politically, Harding placed his Ohio political friends of dubious character in high federal positions, where they proceeded to fleece the government. Their misdeeds were just becoming known to President Harding and the public when Harding died in the middle of his term.

Harding's health had not been good even before becoming president, though this was not public knowledge. A rumor circulated around Washington that Mrs. Harding consulted a soothsayer shortly after the inauguration who told her that the president would not see the end of his term.[1] As a young man he suffered from bouts of nervous depression. He had an enlarged heart and high blood pressure, was overweight, and smoked and drank too much. By 1919 he suspected that he had a heart ailment. In early 1922 President Harding experienced an attack of influenza that may have been accompanied by a coronary thrombosis. After this he became tired easily, began having chest pains, had difficulty sleeping, and could not breathe while lying down — all signs of heart disease. When Harding met a heart specialist at a party in late 1922, the doctor privately opined that the president would be dead of coronary complications within six months. While Harding's heart problems were not directly caused by the burdens of the presidency, the mental and emotional strain of the office must have had some effect. After the suspected thrombosis, on appearance alone it became clear to those around him that the president was a sick man, weary and depressed.[2]

In June 1923 Harding began a two-month journey across the country that was to take him to Alaska, Canada, the Panama Canal and Puerto Rico. He was accompanied by several aides and administration officials, including cabinet secretaries Herbert Hoover, Hubert Work and Henry Wallace, and more than a score of newspaper reporters. It was to be a combination political and vacation excursion, but the president's appearance schedule was arduous. Many of those close to him worried about how the crushing itinerary would affect his declining health. On a similar railroad trip to the west only four years earlier, President Woodrow Wilson suffered a stroke that almost killed him. Despite this, Harding's trip went on as scheduled.

As the train with its presidential car "Superb" moved westward, Harding made several speeches and appearances per day, often waking before dawn and not getting to sleep until after midnight. The weather alternated between intense heat and cold. Adding to the strain were new revelations about the scandals committed by his "friends" in high office. "I can take care of my enemies all right, but my damn friends ... they're the ones that keep me walking the floor nights," confided Harding.[3]

It was not until the Alaska leg of the journey that the president was able to get some rest. He truly seemed to enjoy himself, but when his ship sailed south for Seattle he became nervous and worried again. When his vessel had a slight collision with a destroyer, Harding did not move from his bed. With his hands covering his face, he said, "I hope the boat sinks."[4] In a Seattle stadium on July 27, Harding gave a speech to an audience of 60,000 under a searing sun. During the address the president physically faltered, dropping the pages of his speech and grabbing the lectern in front of him with both hands to steady himself. That evening he addressed the press club and sat down afterward in a state of collapse.[5]

Harding was hustled back to the presidential train and immediately put to bed in his car. He complained to doctors of nausea and upper abdominal pain. The doctors, who had been on board since the journey began, were Harding's personal physician, Charles Sawyer; Joel T. Boone, of the White House physician's office; and secretary of the interior work. Dr. Sawyer said the ailment was an attack of ptomaine due to bad crabmeat and released a bulletin to that effect, though the president had apparently not eaten any crabmeat recently. Doctors Work and Boone suspected that Harding had had a heart attack.

As the train moved southward that night, the physicians took Secretary of Commerce Hoover aside and told him of their diagnosis. He agreed that all stops between Seattle and San Francisco should be cancelled. It was arranged for the train to travel straight to San Francisco where two noted doctors would meet the train, Dr. Ray Lyman Wilbur (later secretary of the interior) and Dr. Charles M. Cooper.

On Sunday morning, July 29, the train arrived in San Francisco. Because Harding felt better, he was allowed to dress himself and walk to a waiting automobile. He was driven to the Palace Hotel and went to bed immediately in his eighth floor suite, room 8064, overlooking Market Street.[6] Other members of the party had rooms near him, and his wife stayed across the hall. Doctors Wilbur and Cooper diagnosed his condition as a coronary attack with bronchial pneumonia. His condition worsened on Monday, and the doctors treated him with digitalis and caffeine. Visitors were strictly limited, and the president transacted no official business during this time. He was allowed to get up only to use the bathroom, a supposedly unwise decision that put further strain on his heart.

News of the illness was first reported on Sunday, but the seriousness of it was not revealed for two more days. Regular bulletins on the president's condition were issued, signed by the five doctors. They cited his various symptoms but did not explicitly mention a heart attack, referring to a circulatory collapse, pneumonia, acute indigestion and exhaustion. The doctors also answered questions from the many reporters who had gathered at the hotel. They were allowed into the eighth floor corridor, where they maintained a twenty-four-hour watch on the sick room. The Associated Press had installed a direct telephone and telegraph line from the corridor to its office across the street. The hotel was the focal point of the nation's attention, and the president's illness was headline news for days in the U.S. and in many places abroad.

Harding was improved on Tuesday and was more cheerful. The doctors became more optimistic as the president showed further improvement on

Wednesday and Thursday, August 2, when he was allowed to sit up in bed. That evening, at about 7:30, the Duchess was seated at the president's bedside reading a magazine article to him entitled "A Calm Review of a Calm Man," which was a favorable account of his presidency.[7] His nurse, Ruth Powderly, who had also attended Woodrow Wilson during his serious illness, was also in the room. Harding was in a half-sitting position, with his head resting on a couple of pillows. Mrs. Harding stopped reading to fluff up the pillows, and the president remarked, "That's good. Go on, read some more."

As the Duchess began to read again and the nurse emerged from the bathroom across from the bed, Harding's frame shuddered, his face convulsed, and his mouth dropped open. Mrs. Harding ran into the corridor, shrieking, "Doctor Boone! Doctor Boone!" Two doctors reached the room in a few seconds and found the president apparently dead. They administered stimulants, to no avail.

That is the most commonly accepted version of President Harding's death. But there are conflicting versions of the scene, which led to rumors that the Duchess or the doctors poisoned the president, or that he committed suicide because of the emerging administration scandals. One story has Mrs. Harding leaving the room before her husband's fatal attack. Another has the nurse at a desk or speaking to the Duchess. Another puts two nurses or a doctor in the room. It is not clear who reached the room first after Mrs. Harding's calls—either Doctors Work and Wilbur, Boone and Sawyer, or Work and Secretary Hoover.

An Associated Press reporter in the hall at the time of the fatal attack, Stephen T. Early (who later became press secretary to President Franklin D. Roosevelt), called his office and relayed the news of the president's death, giving the AP a news scoop of some thirty minutes.[8] Other reporters began to gather on the eighth floor for a scheduled interview with Dr. Sawyer. Instead, they were handed copies of a bulletin that informed them of Harding's death a few minutes earlier: "The President died at 7:30 P.M.... Without warning a slight shudder passed through his frame; he collapsed, and all recognized that the end had come. A stroke of apoplexy was the cause of his death."

The news spread rapidly throughout the hotel, San Francisco and the nation. Hotel officials interrupted a dinner dance to announce the news. Reporters and some hotel guests gathered in groups at the end of corridors that led to the presidential rooms. Secret Service men and screens cordoned off that area of the eighth floor, which became jammed with officials of the city and state, and the presidential party. Everyone who emerged from the corridor was bombarded with questions. Police were soon stationed at the hotel entrance to prevent anyone from entering except guests and reporters.

News spread nationwide by telegraph and telephone. The following telegram was sent to Vice President Calvin Coolidge, Chief Justice William Howard Taft, and members of the cabinet who were not in San Francisco: "The President died at 7:30 P.M. from a stroke of cerebral apoplexy. The end came peacefully and without warning." It was signed by Herbert Hoover and three other cabinet members.[9]

Within a couple of hours of President Harding's passing, newsboys were on the streets of most major cities with "extras," shouting the news. The offices of the *Marion Star*, Harding's old newspaper in Ohio, received the news a few minutes after his death. The paper's general manager and Dr. Sawyer's son, a resident of Marion, went to the home of the late president's father, Dr. George T. Harding, 80, and broke the news to him.[10] Bells throughout the city began tolling, and people gathered in the streets as newsboys peddled their extras.

Harding had been the first person to have the results of his presidential election victory broadcast on the radio, and the first president to have a speech broadcast on the radio. He now became the first president whose death was announced over the radio. Station WOR in the New York City area went on the air at 1:30 A.M., August 3, announcing the death. The broadcast gave a short history of his illness, the time of death, and a statement by Dr. Sawyer. Most radio stations suspended broadcasting on August 3 and on the day of the burial, but in between featured funeral music and talks by prominent men on Harding's life.[11]

In the White House an executive clerk received the news from San Francisco minutes after the death. Secretary of State Charles Evans Hughes, ranking executive officer in Washington at the time, was contacted. Vice President Coolidge had been vacationing at his father's farm in Plymouth Notch, Vermont. News of Harding's death reached him early on the morning of August 3, when telegrams from San Francisco, and the *New York Times*, reached him at the same time. He had retired for the evening but was awakened, dressed and took the presidential oath of office in the living room of his father's home at 2:47 A.M. It was administered by his father, John Coolidge, a notary public, by the light of a kerosene lamp, and was witnessed by Calvin Coolidge's wife, his chauffeur Joseph McInerney, his stenographer Ewin Geisser, newsman William H. Crawford (who was staying nearby and was alerted by McInerney and Geisser), and Joseph H. Fountain of the *Springfield* (Mass.) *Reporter* and L.L. Lane of the Railway Mail Association, both of whom accompanied Senator Porter H. Dale, who happened to be in the area and was summoned to the house.[12] Later that morning the new president and his wife left for Washington, arriving there that night.

Because the legality of this oath-taking was called into question, Coolidge re-took the oath of office on August 17 in his suite at the Willard Hotel in Washington, where he had been staying before moving into the White

House. It was administered by Justice A.A. Hoehling of the Supreme Court of the District of Columbia. Some had contended that John Coolidge could only administer oaths to Vermont state officials, and had no authority to do so for federal offices. This second ceremony was kept secret and not revealed for many years.[13]

In San Francisco, later on the night of Harding's death, the five attending physicians issued a more lengthy statement concerning his demise. In it they stated that the cause of death was apparently an apoplexy, which is a rupture of a blood vessel in the brain, near the respiratory center. Apparently there was some disagreement among the doctors, but the diagnosis of Dr. Sawyer, Harding's personal and official physician, won out. It is possible that the death was caused by a cardiac attack, quite possibly a rupture in the wall of the heart. The cause of death could not be absolutely determined because Mrs. Harding refused to allow an autopsy, despite the pleadings of the doctors.[14]

The Duchess did not break down. She was ordered to retire to her room, and she remained there throughout the night, spending time talking to the wives of the men who had accompanied the president on his trip and to the late president's sister, who had arrived in San Francisco to visit her sick brother. Mrs. Harding decided that evening on the general plans for her husband's funeral, and an official announcement was made. The body would leave San Francisco on the presidential train, go straight to Washington, D.C., for a funeral service, and then to Marion for final ceremonies and burial. As more specific plans were decided upon in the days that followed, they were made public. President Harding's personal secretary, George Christian, took charge of coordinating the plans.

Orders went out to the military informing them of the death of their commander in chief and calling for appropriate displays of respect and mourning by the different service branches.

Late in the evening two undertakers and an embalmer from N. Gray and Company arrived at the hotel with a brown metal coffin. Harding's body was embalmed by Engel T. Mayne and prepared for burial in the room in which he had died. The work was finished in the early morning as the body was dressed in a black morning coat and striped trousers, and placed in the coffin. It was moved to the adjoining drawing room.

By mid-morning the large room was filled with flowers sent by officials, organizations, governments and citizens. The floral pieces were set along the walls and in the corners, on a mantel, and on a baby grand piano. With light streaming through the windows, and the presence of rose-colored damask furniture, the room looked almost cheerful. The open casket was placed against one wall between two windows. The interior of the coffin was lined with white silk. Harding's face looked peaceful and unworried. On the outside of the casket was fastened a silver plate engraved with "Warren Gamaliel Harding."

Mrs. Harding arose late that morning. She bore up well under the strain. She would enter the drawing room from time to time, particularly to accompany those who had come to call on her. She was dressed in a simple black gown with a brimmed black hat. She busied herself during the day approving plans for the train trip to Washington.

Thousands of San Franciscans gathered around the hotel, either out of curiosity or respect. Thirty-two years earlier another head of state had died at the Palace Hotel. That was King David Kalakaua of Hawaii.[15] Former President Grant was a guest there during his world tour, and President Rutherford B. Hayes stayed there on his visit to San Francisco.

Messages of condolence poured in from around the world. They came from diplomats, foreign governments, governors, mayors, social organizations and friends. One came from President and Mrs. Coolidge. Former President and Mrs. Wilson paid a personal call at the White House to leave sympathy cards.

Throughout the country many buildings were draped in black and white mourning bunting. Flags flew at half mast. On August 3 all the major stock and commodity exchanges closed. Most professional and amateur sporting events were postponed. Celebrations, festivals and carnivals across the United States were cancelled or postponed until after the day of burial. In the capital, President Coolidge met with cabinet members, legislators and aides. Tentative plans for the Washington part of the funeral were formulated by the new president's military aide. Coolidge proclaimed Friday, August 10, the day of Harding's burial, a national day of mourning.

In what had come to be almost a standard reaction to an incumbent president's death, Harding was compared favorably to Abraham Lincoln by many people, just as Garfield and McKinley had been. With the benefit of many years of hindsight, we know that Harding does not measure up to the legend of Lincoln. But, like McKinley, he was extremely well liked as a person by almost everyone, and the sorrow at his passing was great, especially in the rural areas, where he was particularly well respected. He was probably the most deeply mourned president since Lincoln.

Shortly before 6 P.M. on August 3, at the hotel in San Francisco, a short religious service was held over the body in the drawing room of the presidential suite. It was conducted by the Rev. James S. West, the pastor of the First Baptist Church of San Francisco. The attendees included the members of the presidential party; the newsmen who were on the western trip; one reporter from each of the local newspapers; the late president's sister, Mrs. Charity Remsberg, and her two daughters; General John J. (Blackjack) Pershing; and Attorney General Harry Daugherty, who joined fellow cabinet officers Hoover, Work and Wallace.

Lamps with rose-colored shades cast a soft glow throughout the room. All except Mrs. Remsberg and Mr. Daugherty stood during the service. Mrs. Harding was the last to enter the room, arm in arm with the late president's personal secretary, George Christian. They took a place in the center of the room directly in front of the open coffin. The Duchess wore a long black cape and a veil over her face. The service consisted of a simple prayer read by the pastor, and lasted but a few minutes. When the reverend finished, General Pershing led the group out of the room as Mrs. Harding spoke to the pastor.

The coffin was closed and covered with an American flag and a wreath of flowers. Two soldiers, sailors, Marines and California National Guardsmen carried it down the corridor to the freight elevator. On the ground floor the body was carried through lines of military officers to the hotel entrance. The corridors thronged with people. The body bearers paused at the entrance as a military band played the national anthem. Then they moved through the courtyard to a motor hearse, and the coffin was placed inside.

Chopin's "Funeral March" played, and before tens of thousands of spectators the procession began for the Third and Townsend Street railroad station three-quarters of a mile away. Airplanes from nearby army fields circled overhead in tribute, dropping clusters of roses. A nearby church's chimes played "Nearer, My God, to Thee." Leading the procession were detachments of soldiers, sailors and Marines in the colors of their dress uniforms. Behind a troop of cavalry followed the hearse, then the group of mourners from the hotel on foot. Attorney General Daugherty, too ill to walk, was the only participant to ride in a limousine. Mrs. Harding remained at the hotel until after the procession reached its destination.

The crowds of people lining the route were silent as the horses' hooves clattered by and the army band pounded out a mournful marching beat. The hotel, the railroad station and many other buildings were decked in mourning bunting. At the railroad station the body was carried from the hearse to the Superb, now the funeral car. The coffin was passed through a specially cut window of the car and placed upon a bier above window level to allow viewing by the public. The interior of the car was decorated with purple asters and green ferns.

A telephone call went out to the hotel, and Mrs. Harding started for the station in a limousine with drawn curtains. She was accompanied by Mr. Christian as she walked through the gates and boarded the Superb. The rear platform of the car, from which the president had addressed many crowds on the westward journey, was banked with flowers and ferns, and hung with crepe. The locomotive, adorned with black and white bunting, chugged out of the station at 7:15 P.M., while the crowd gathered there sang Harding's favorite hymn, "Lead, Kindly Light." There was no definite schedule set for the train, but it would go through Ogden, Omaha and Chicago to Washington, taking about four days, during which the only stops would be to change engines and service the train.

It passed through Stockton and Sacramento in California, and Reno and Sparks in Nevada. People gathered at railway stations and along the tracks to watch the train pass by. They came from ranches, cities and towns for miles around, in the middle of the night and in the searing desert heat of the day. At some stations the mostly silent and reverent crowds would sing a hymn. Some towns tolled their church bells and closed businesses as the train passed. Many veterans in their old uniforms saluted the late president. In the lighted observation end of the Superb the flag-draped coffin could be seen clearly, guarded by two soldiers, a sailor and a Marine, one standing at each corner of the bier. The guard changed every two hours.

In the early daylight at Sparks the train stopped to change engines, and the governor and other state and local officials presented a wreath, which was placed near the coffin. This was a ritual repeated each time the train made a stop. Local government officials were present at nearly every town along the route. The train rolled on across Utah, through Ogden and into Wyoming, where it made a stop in Cheyenne. In that city a cavalry squadron, with its band playing hymns, was assembled. They had come from nearby Fort Russell, where minute guns boomed in salute. A rainstorm blew in during the brief stop, but none of the thousands of spectators fled for shelter during the ceremonies.

Moving slowly through Chappell, Nebraska, one of the wheels of the locomotive slipped, which caused an unscheduled delay while a new engine was hitched up. The train continued on across Nebraska. It passed cowboys on horseback, farmers in their fields, and cars parked at highway crossings to let their passengers catch a glimpse of the coffin. At 3 A.M. on August 6 the train reached Omaha, where 40,000 stood along the tracks and at the railroad station. More flowers were placed aboard, and the funeral and baggage cars were by now filled with them. Iowa was crossed, and then the train entered Illinois. Airplanes escorted the train and showered flowers down upon it.

At Dixon, President Harding's brother and Dr. Sawyer's son boarded the train. The Duchess gave her detailed instructions for a simple funeral to the young Sawyer, who carried them to Marion. The old Marion Civic Association, which had headed arrangements during Harding's presidential campaign, had been revived to take charge of funeral plans in the city. President Harding's father and other family members wished to have Mrs. Harding's wishes carried out as closely as possible. Military officers from Washington also had to be conferred with. On August 7 in Marion, detailed funeral plans were announced by a military representative of President Coolidge and a representative of the Marion Civic Association.

At the outskirts of Chicago in the late afternoon the crowds grew thicker along the route of the train. From Geneva, about thirty miles away, to Chicago the tracks were lined solidly with spectators. Every station was filled and every crossroad jammed with cars. In the city the crowds along the tracks were so dense that the train could move no faster than a man could walk. People surged onto the tracks, and a flagman had to walk ahead of the engine to warn back the crowds. The train made two brief stops in the city. It was estimated that 300,000 people had turned out in Chicago.

The train proceeded across Indiana and into the Hardings' home state of Ohio, where Mrs. Harding ordered it to move more slowly. Some people waited all night to catch a glimpse, sleeping in stations, automobiles, or on lawns. The train did not pass through Marion. It rolled across Pennsylvania and into Maryland with no let-up in the outpouring of citizens to view it. Finally, at 10:30 Tuesday night, August 7, nine hours behind schedule, the train reached Union Station in Washington.

The train backed into the station so that the funeral car would be close to the exit. Mrs. Harding, accompanied by Mr. Christian and Dr. Sawyer, and dressed in a long black cloak, left the train immediately and was driven directly to the White House. The Marine band at the station began playing "Nearer, My God, to Thee" as the flag-draped coffin was carried off the Superb by military bearers for its trip to the White House. It was followed by an entourage from the train. The casket was carried between a cordon of soldiers through the concourse of the station, where a large crowd had assembled, and out the east entrance. President Coolidge, other officials, and friends of the Hardings were also present at the station. Outside, a huge throng had gathered in front of the building, and all along Pennsylvania Avenue to the White House the people stood twenty deep and more behind steel cables. They perspired freely in the oppressive heat of the summer night.

The coffin was placed upon a military caisson, the same one used in 1921 for the Unknown Soldier. At 11 P.M. the caisson, drawn by six horses wearing red cloths beneath their saddles, pulled away from the station. It was preceded by mounted cavalry troops and an artillery unit. The first car behind the caisson was occupied by President Coolidge and Speaker of the House Frederick Gillett. In three other cars were former president and then chief justice William Howard Taft and various senators, House members, and cabinet officers. Following behind was another formation of cavalry and artillery troops.

In thirty minutes the procession arrived at the White House. The soldiers carried the casket into the East room where it was placed on a catafalque in the center of the room beneath the huge crystal chandelier. President Coolidge and the other dignitaries who had ridden in the procession entered shortly thereafter. Hundreds of floral pieces banked the walls, and a few lay near the bier. A wreath from Mrs. Harding lay atop the flag-draped coffin.

President Harding's flag-draped coffin lying in state in the White House East Room. (Library of Congress)

There was no ceremony, but each person bowed briefly at the coffin and then departed.

After the East Room was cleared of everyone except the military guard, the Duchess entered the room at about 1 A.M. She was accompanied by her friend Evalyn McLean, who was the wife of a newspaper owner, and Mr. Christian. She had him open the coffin and then sat down on a chair. She reportedly talked to her husband for over an hour, assuring him that no one could hurt him now. She picked some blossoms from the many floral arrangements and made a small bouquet. After ordering the coffin closed, she placed the bouquet on top of the casket.[16]

Meanwhile, in the Capitol building, arrangements were being made for the ceremonies to take place there later that morning. The black catafalque on which the remains of Lincoln, Garfield and McKinley had lain was brought up from the crypt in the basement and placed under the dome. Chairs were put in place, and flowers, over a thousand arrangements, were placed along the walls of the Rotunda.

By 7 A.M. 10,000 people had already gathered near the Capitol. Within an hour, military troops began arriving at their points of formation near the White House for the march to the Capitol. The colors of each military unit were hung with black ribbons, and officers wore black arm bands. The casket in the East Room was opened to allow friends and relatives a last look at Mr. Harding in the White House. At 9 A.M. invited mourners began arriving at the Executive Mansion. They gathered in different rooms on the ground floor: Presidents Coolidge, Taft and the cabinet; the diplomatic corps; state governors, U.S. senators and representatives; and family members and friends. An open touring car arrived and parked in the White House driveway. In it were former president Woodrow Wilson, his wife and his physician. In frail health, Wilson did not leave the automobile.[17]

Shortly after 10 A.M. the guests and Mrs. Harding entered the East Room, where a brief prayer was recited by the pastor of a local Baptist church, with others in the room joining in the reading. Dressed in black and veiled, the widow led the mourners out of the White House and into their cars. The flag-draped coffin, a single wreath of flowers on its top, was carried out of the room by twelve soldiers and sailors and strapped to the crepe-draped caisson.

The one-mile procession down Pennsylvania Avenue to the Capitol got under way as the Marine and army bands played hymns. Preceded by an escort of mounted police, General Pershing led the way on horseback, followed by the army band, a cavalry unit, artillery, infantry troops, the army engineers band, the Marine band, Marines, the navy band and a navy unit. Then came the caisson, preceded by the president's flag. Following on foot were two clergymen, doctors Sawyer and Boone, and an honor guard of infantry and sailors with fixed bayonets.

Flanking the caisson were six admirals. Behind marched the body bearers, Secret Service men, newspaper reporters from the western tour, and automobiles containing the honorary pallbearers. All during the week, cabinet members, congressmen, and military officers rotated as pallbearers, more than three dozen in all. Following behind them were automobiles containing Mrs. Harding and the family, President Coolidge, former presidents Taft and Wilson, foreign diplomats, associates justices of the Supreme Court, cabinet members, congressmen, state government officials, and representatives of many federal departments.

Then came veterans and their organizations, including the Grand Army of the Republic Civil War group (twenty-two of whose members marched, some in their old worn uniforms). Three Confederate veterans marched alongside their Union brothers, one in his old battle-gray uniform. Other groups marching were the Knights Templar and Knights of Pythias, both organizations to which the late president belonged, as well as the Salvation

Army, the Daughters of the American Revolution (and other women's groups), and dozens of other organizations.

The heat and humidity were oppressive during the march. Perspiration soaked the heavy military uniforms. Scores of marchers and spectators were prostrated by the heat and subsequently aided by volunteer nurses. Many had to be taken to hospitals. The temperature eventually reached a high of 95 degrees Fahrenheit that afternoon.[18]

Steel cables stretched along the curbs to keep back the crowd of tens of thousands. Every few feet in front of them was stationed a policeman or boy scout. Except for some applause for the elder statesman President Wilson, the spectators remained quiet. When the caisson rolled by, men removed their hats. Some veterans in their old uniforms saluted as the casket passed. Minute guns from nearby Fort Myer boomed for the duration of the procession, to the accompaniment of the funeral music and muffled drums.

At about the same time the procession from the White House began, guests who were not taking part in the march were allowed to enter the Capitol Rotunda. Among the distinguished invitees was First Lady Grace Coolidge, who took her seat to await the arrival of her husband. Shortly after 11 A.M. could be heard the muffled drums, bugles and sharp commands of the military as the caisson arrived at the east front of the building. The strains of "Lead, Kindly Light" could be heard as the coffin was taken from the carriage and carried up the stairs into the Rotunda, there to be placed upon the Lincoln catafalque. Mrs. Harding, again accompanied by George Christian, had entered the Rotunda by elevator and already taken her place near Mrs. Coolidge. President Coolidge and all the other mourners from the procession followed the casket into the building.

When everyone had taken his place, the ceremonies began. President Coolidge, Chief Justice Taft and House Speaker Gillett each placed a wreath at the catafalque. A Baptist minister opened with a prayer at the head of the coffin. A male church quartet sang "Lead, Kindly Light." The minister recited some Bible verses, after which the chaplain of the House of Representatives read a short prayer. The quartet sang "Nearer, My God, to Thee." A brief benediction ended the twenty-minute service just as a distant bell tolled noon.

The guests began to depart from the Rotunda, and preparations were made to begin admitting the public. The body had lain with its head to the east, and the coffin was now turned around to allow proper viewing. The flag was folded down to the bottom half of the casket, and the top half was opened to allow the face to be seen under the glass cover. The guest chairs were put aside. Two soldiers, a sailor and a Marine were stationed, with fixed bayonets, at each corner of the bier. Some of the official guests at the ceremony were the first to file by the casket. They were followed by contingents of military officers, disabled veterans and others who had marched in the procession from the White House. Then the general public was admitted. The mourners entered the east door in two lines, passing by on either side of the coffin, and left through the west door. Ropes were stretched between the two doors, and on each side of this flowers were placed so that the entire passage between exit and entrance was banked with the blossoms. The scent of the flowers in the Rotunda was overpowering.

The stream of people in civilian dress was punctuated periodically by uniformed members of such groups as the Masons, veterans and soldiers. Some shed tears as they walked by. Some brought bouquets or wreaths and handed them to attendants. After about an hour the lines were briefly halted as a group of cameramen took movies and photographs of the scene. The films were immediately flown to New York and Chicago. Two long lines stretched from the east entrance around each side of the capitol to a point where they almost met on the opposite side of the building. At about 4 P.M. the lines were cut off and the viewing stopped at 4:30. Approximately 30,000 people had passed by Harding's casket in the four hours the Rotunda was open.

Preparations were made to move the body for its final train ride to Marion, Ohio. Attendants placed the lid back on the coffin, then covered it with the American flag and Mrs. Harding's wreath of gladioli. This was done in the presence of a few newspapermen. The four military men guarding the coffin moved behind it. At 5 P.M. President Coolidge, his aides, and the cabinet entered the Rotunda. They were followed by congressmen and military officers. Military pallbearers carried the casket out of the east door and down the steps to the waiting caisson. The army band among the troops assembled played "Nearer, My God, to Thee." President Coolidge and his entourage entered automobiles. Led by the cavalry, Marines, sailors and the presidential flag, the horse-drawn caisson moved out to Union Station, followed by the autos and artillery and cavalry units. The body moved down Delaware Avenue through a lane of enlisted men from the three branches of service, with their rifles at salute. Behind them once again stood reverent crowds of people.

Upon reaching the railroad depot, another hymn was played. President Coolidge and the cabinet took places inside as the coffin was carried from the caisson through the station and placed aboard the Superb in the same spot it had occupied on its journey from San Francisco. Most of the invited passengers were already onboard. For this trip they included some of the cabinet members and their wives, congressional leaders, the brother and sisters of President Harding, and other family members and friends. Most of those who had accompanied the president on his western trip were also aboard. Mrs. Harding, with her escort Mr. Christian, was among the last to board. A minute later, at about 6 P.M., the train pulled out of the station. Another train, carrying President Coolidge and other officials, would leave the next day for Marion.

The funeral train, its engine decked in black and with a photograph of Harding below the headlight, passed through Baltimore, Pittsburgh and on to Marion in central Ohio. Passing through Canton, the late president William McKinley's home town, the train stopped for a moment in his memory. The trip was largely a repeat of the San Francisco to Washington run of a few days earlier, with thousands turning out along the route to pay their respects.

The train arrived in Marion shortly after noon on Thursday, August 9. It was met by old hometown friends and associates of Harding, as well as a huge crowd of citizens. The body was carried by the honor guard to an automobile hearse. Other members of the funeral party, including Mrs. Harding, entered cars for a slow motorcade to the home of President Harding's father, where the body would lie for twenty-four hours before burial. The route of just over a mile was lined with thousands of people, and many watched from their front porches. Church bells tolled. Hundreds of National Guardsmen were stationed along the curbs to keep back the crowd. The procession and all the ceremonies in Marion were without military pomp except for the sixteen-member honor guard charged with carrying and guarding the body. During the motorcade the men walked alongside the hearse. He had been commander in chief, but these funeral ceremonies were for Warren G. Harding, citizen.

Marion fondly recalled Harding as the editor of the *Star*, the embodiment of the American dream of the small-town boy who grew up to become president of the United States. Now the city was in deep mourning for its son. Huge drapings of black and white cloth hung from the fronts of buildings. American flags flew with black and white streamers, and nearly every business displayed a photograph of the late president. His old office at the *Star* was opened to some visitors who passed through to get a look at his old desk and chair, draped in mourning.[19]

Visiting motorists were ordered to park their cars on the outskirts of town, and Marionites were asked not to drive during the two days of obsequies to avoid congestion. The railroads serving the city ran a great number of special trains to handle the influx of thousands of visitors into Marion. Hundreds of residents opened their homes to these people, as hotels were filled to capacity. Also, many visiting motorists brought camping gear. More than a hundred newspapermen from around the country arrived in Marion to cover the funeral. Several extra wires were installed to handle the dissemination of the news.

The funeral cortege from the railroad station stopped at Dr. Harding's home, where he waited at the front door in his Grand Army of the Republic veterans uniform.[20] The coffin was carried into the house, followed by Mrs. Harding, and placed in the living room. The honor guard took up their posts beside the coffin, and the half-lid was opened.

The public was then admitted to view the body. Old friends and neigh-

A portion of the funeral procession for President Harding in his hometown of Marion, Ohio. (Library of Congress)

bors were the first to enter. A mass of people six blocks long formed into a line on this splendid summer afternoon to pay their respects. They stood two and three abreast in a neat line down the beautiful tree-lined, shaded residential street. The mourners entered the house through the rear kitchen door and left out the front. A few National Guard troops helped keep things orderly. Persons of every walk of life and of every age stood in line to honor their neighbor, a large number dressed unpretentiously in their everyday clothes. Many who could not wait in line paused across the street from the house and bowed their heads for a moment of silence. Flowers filled the front, side and back yards, as well as every downstairs room.

The people kept coming all night long. At one point the line stretched for fifteen blocks. On Friday, August 10, the day of the burial, a car containing a relative, government official, or celebrity would pull up at the house every so often. Three such visitors were Henry Ford, Thomas Edison and Harvey Firestone, all acquaintances of President Harding. They were besieged by a crowd of photographers as they arrived together. The three were allowed to cut in line to view the body, then they spoke to Mrs. Harding.[21] She had spent the night at the house.

In the morning, funeral organizers went over final plans with the widow. At 1 P.M. the doors to Dr. Harding's home were closed; thousands still waiting in an eight-block line were turned away. An estimated 40,000 people had passed by the coffin in the twenty-three hours the house was opened. At 2 P.M. a Baptist minister read brief prayers in the living room in the presence of the widow and several others, including President Coolidge, who had arrived in Marion a short time earlier. The casket was closed and covered with the flag. The military guard carried the coffin to the gray hearse and placed it inside. This same group of sixteen soldiers and sailors had guarded the body ever since San Francisco and would now carry it into the burial vault. These men marched beside the hearse on its way to the cemetery. Following in cars were the invited guests to the private interment, all attending as friends of the late President. Included among them were President Coolidge, Chief Justice Taft, House Speaker Gillett, the Harding cabinet as honorary pallbearers, Mrs. Coolidge and the cabinet wives, a few U.S. senators and representatives, people from the western trip, four clergymen, Mrs. Harding, the late president's father and stepmother, his brother and sisters, and several other relatives and close friends. A body of employees of the *Marion Star* was the only group allowed to march in the cortege. A unit of the Ku Klux Klan had announced its intention to march in the procession, but officials made it clear that they were not welcome. The Klan, a strong and influential organization in the 1920s, had previously sent flowers and messages of condolence upon Harding's death.[22]

Tens of thousands of people lined the one-and-a-half-mile route to the Marion Cemetery. People who had been sitting on shaded lawns while waiting for the procession on this hot summer afternoon rose in respect as it approached. Church bells tolled and cannons boomed in the distance.

Already in the cemetery were many other invitees, including General Pershing, a large group of U.S. senators, Edison, Ford and Firestone. The cemetery gates were open to the public, but the area near the burial vault was roped off. Thousands were present in the graveyard, and some managed to get past the National Guard and into the restricted area.

The cemetery's receiving vault, in which President Harding's coffin would be placed, was of gray-brown stone with a peaked roof, located in a large semicircular grassy area and set into a hillside. A short stone walkway led to an ivy-covered porch entrance. It was decorated with black and white streamers. The iron gates were open. A large number of floral pieces were in place around the sides of the vault. On a small rise to one side was assembled a girls' choir from the late president's Trinity Baptist Church. As the funeral procession arrived at the cemetery, the assembled guests took their places just to the left of the vault entrance. At 3 P.M. the hearse drove up the roadway to the roped off area. The casket was removed and carried fifty yards to the vault entrance. The coffin was preceded by the four clergymen and a white-uniformed soldier carrying the flag of the president of the United States. Following behind came President Coolidge, Chief Justice Taft, the honorary pallbearers, a group of white-clad admirals and khaki-clad generals, and the rest of the mourners from their automobiles.

The admirals and generals formed two lines to the left and right just before the stone walk in front of the vault. In between them the military honor guard carried the coffin and placed it on a brown velvet catafalque. Coolidge, Taft and the honorary pallbearers took places between the two lines of officers. On the grass to the right of the coffin came the veiled figure of Mrs. Harding, escorted by George Christian. Near her stood the father of the late president, in tears, and behind them were other family members and friends. Off to one side were reporters and other members of the western trip. A little dog wandered among the feet of those gathered near the vault, finally lying down just inside the door during the ceremonies.[23]

When all had taken their places, the choir sang "Lead, Kindly Light." Two of the ministers each recited a prayer, after which the choir sang "Nearer, My God, to Thee." A Methodist minister went to the head of the casket and pronounced a benediction. The honor guard then stepped forward, lifted the coffin and carried it into the vault. An army bugler stood at the entrance of the burial vault and played "Taps," which was followed by a twenty-one-gun salute. Then the widow entered the vault for a minute, reemerged and headed for her car. The entire ceremony at the cemetery had taken just twenty minutes.

The rest of the country also mourned on that day. Houses of worship everywhere held memorial services. Most businesses and government offices closed for the day. The stock exchanges closed. Most sporting events were postponed and theater shows cancelled. In the nation's capital, at the hour of the burial, traffic came to a standstill and pedestrians stopped, the gentlemen removing their hats. The city was motionless for two or three minutes while "Taps" sounded from the steps of the Capitol and several other points in the city. Even telephone and telegraph service was halted. There was no draping of federal buildings in Washington due to the law, but government offices closed for the day. Post offices and federal offices throughout the country were closed at the hour of the funeral. At noon, a twenty-one-gun salute was fired at all military installations and on all naval vessels of the United States. Almost all cities observed some form of final tribute to President Harding.

In the months following Harding's death, the scandals and mismanagement of his administration started to come to light. His personal life was also revealed as being tainted, especially inasmuch as it involved the probable fathering of an illegitimate daughter and philanderings in the White House. The unclear circumstances surrounding his death, and the lack of an autopsy, fuelled rumors that Harding had been poisoned by his wife and/or doctors, or had committed suicide. The reasoning was that the president was murdered to save him from the anguish of facing the emerging scandals, or that his wife killed him to avenge his extramarital affairs.

In 1930 a man named Gaston B. Means, peripherally associated with Harding's "Ohio Gang," wrote a best-selling sensational book, later discredited, that alleged the president had been murdered by Mrs. Harding and Dr. Sawyer. Means was a con man continually in trouble with the law; he eventually died in prison. He even repudiated his own book, apparently ghost-written for him, entitled *The Strange Death of President Harding*.[24]

Harding's body was expected to remain in the vault only temporarily, until a memorial tomb could be built. The Harding Memorial Association and Mrs. Harding chose a site adjoining Marion Cemetery in June 1924.[25] She died on November 21, 1924, just fifteen months after her husband. Florence Mabel Kling DeWolfe Harding was sixty-four years old. She had been ill for a month, and her death was due to chronic kidney disease and a heart ail-

The beautiful Warren G. Harding Memorial in Marion, Ohio. The graves of President and Mrs. Harding lie in the center of the circle of columns. (M. Nowak)

ment. Three days later her body was placed in the vault next to that of the late president. Their bodies rested there until the memorial was completed.

A design was chosen in the summer of 1925, and ground was broken the following spring.[26] The cornerstone was laid by Vice President Charles G. Dawes in May 1926.[27] On December 20, 1927, the bodies of President and Mrs. Harding were removed from the guarded vault and transported to the completed memorial,[28] a beautiful circle of Tuscan columns of white marble, with graves in the center and the entire area landscaped to perfection. The following day, brief interment rites were held at the tomb, attended by a few relatives and close friends.[29] Not wishing to be connected in any way to the scandalous Harding administration, Presidents Coolidge and Hoover put off dedicating the memorial. Finally, on June 16, 1931, President Hoover and former President Coolidge attended dedication ceremonies. In his address delivered there, Hoover cited the betrayal of Harding by his friends as the tragedy of the late president's life.[30]

The Palace Hotel in which President Harding died still operates as a hotel but has undergone extensive renovations since then. The hotel does not memorialize his passing with a sign or plaque, but does reference the event in its hotel history.[31]

In his will, Warren G. Harding left the income from a trust of $100,000 in stocks and bonds to his wife. The widow also was left real estate and all of her husband's personal effects. Sadly, she was allowed to destroy much of her husband's correspondence and files. These materials probably would have shed additional light on his troubled life and administration. To his father, Harding left the income from a $50,000 trust and the house in which he was then living. Various relatives and friends, and two churches, were left a few thousand dollars each. The Marion Park Commission received $25,000. The remainder of the $900,000 estate was bequeathed equally to his brother and three sisters.[32]

CHAPTER 8

Franklin Delano Roosevelt

32ND PRESIDENT OF THE UNITED STATES
TERM OF OFFICE: MARCH 4, 1933, TO APRIL 12, 1945
BORN: JANUARY 30, 1882; DIED: APRIL 12, 1945
AGE AT DEATH: 63 YEARS, 72 DAYS
CAUSE OF DEATH: CEREBRAL HEMORRHAGE
BURIAL PLACE: HYDE PARK, NEW YORK

When Franklin D. Roosevelt died he had been president for more than twelve years, longer than any other person. To a whole generation of young people he was the only president they had known, and he was greatly admired. He was the rich man who sympathized with the poor and brought millions out of poverty and depression. He was the crippled man who stood up to lead the country through a tough war.

FDR is consistently ranked by historians as one of our four or five greatest presidents. He was certainly one of the most influential. Under his leadership this country liberalized its basic social policies and greatly expanded the government's role in people's lives, so much so that the federal government today is fully expected to provide minimum levels of support to its citizens.

Roosevelt's life began rather inauspiciously. At birth, mother and son almost died of an overdose of chloroform given to relieve labor pains. The baby was born blue and limp, and was given mouth-to-mouth resuscitation to revive him. But young Franklin enjoyed a healthy childhood. An only child, he was raised by nurses, nannies and tutors in an atmosphere of wealth and privilege. He developed a strong attachment to his mother, who was a domineering, overprotective woman.[1]

In 1905, at 23, he married his distant cousin Eleanor Roosevelt but did not remain faithful to her. In 1918 she discovered that he was having a love affair with her secretary. Eleanor and Franklin agreed to stay together to protect his political career, which had already advanced to assistant secretary of the Navy, but the marriage was not the same after this.

Roosevelt loved to spend time at his vacation home at Campobello in New Brunswick, Canada. While there in the summer of 1921, he caught a chill and developed poliomyelitis. It was misdiagnosed, and the daily massages administered during the first few days probably worsened the condition of his stricken legs. FDR became paralyzed from the hips down and was never really able to walk again on his own. With the help of heavy leg braces, a cane, and a strong man to support him, he could move forward slowly and with great difficulty, but for all practical purposes he had to use a wheelchair for the rest of his life, a fact that was very successfully concealed from the general public. At first his condition devastated him emotionally because he was a young, physically active man of only thirty-nine.

For several months after the onset of his polio, Roosevelt stayed out of politics, but he was soon convinced to get back into the fray by his wife and his good friend and political aide Louis Howe. FDR was already a known politician on the national scene, having been the Democrats' nominee for vice president in 1920, and now he worked to extend his influence. In 1928 he was elected governor of New York. His star continued to rise, and four years later he was the choice of his party — and the nation — to be the thirty-second president.

The state of the president's health, especially during the last couple of years of his life, has been a matter of debate for decades. What effect the presidency had on his well-being cannot be known for certain, but the mental stress and strain of the twelve years probably affected his physical health for the worse.

By March of 1944 Navy admiral Dr. Ross McIntire, Roosevelt's personal physician, knew that the president was very sick. McIntire retained heart specialist Dr. Howard Bruenn as his assistant in treating the patient. Dr. Bruenn conducted a thorough physical on FDR and, in consultation with Dr. McIntire and three other doctors, revealed his findings: congestive heart failure, enlarged heart, left ventricle problem, hypertension, arteriosclerosis, bronchitis, fluid in both lungs, a soft and persistent cough, decreased lung capacity, and difficulty breathing while lying in bed. Roosevelt had a grayish pallor, and his lips and fingernails were bluish. The five physicians were the only ones who knew the medical truth about FDR, and they vowed to keep it secret. The doctors knew the president would not accept a stringent program that would severely restrict his activities, so they put him on a more moderate program, with plenty of rest, to deal with these serious problems. They did not tell Roosevelt what they had diagnosed, nor did he even ask what the matter was, though there can be little doubt that he knew he was seriously ill.[2] He just chose not to confront it, probably because he did not want to become a complete invalid following doctors' orders to rest and do nothing. He had always been active and involved, even after his legs became paralyzed. If he was going to die shortly anyway, he was going to do it while staying as active as possible.

In 1944 it was painfully obvious to people around him that Roosevelt was a sick man. Those who saw him daily became concerned as his health deteriorated. Visitors were shocked at his appearance. Among the things they noticed were a persistent cough, a gray complexion, sunken eyes, mouth sometimes hung open, a slight droop at the corner of the mouth, trembling hands, loss of weight and appetite, and a general appearance of physical and mental exhaustion. In addition, FDR sometimes lapsed into depression, became easily irritable, would sometimes lose his train of thought and even nod off at his desk. Impaired mental functioning is one of the signs of hardening of the brain arteries, which can lead to a stroke.

Those who saw the president close up could tell he was very ill, even a dying man, some surmised. But the public at large had no way of knowing this. The reporters who saw Roosevelt speculated on his health in the papers, and the Republicans played up the health issue as he announced his candidacy for a fourth term in 1944. But Dr. McIntire never told anyone the truth, not even the family or the patient, and FDR managed to stage brilliantly grand appearances in public. McIntire always painted a rosy picture of the president's overall condition.

President Roosevelt suffered from his share of minor maladies, such as chronic sinusitis, intestinal discomforts and high blood pressure. He had a fainting spell in 1938 from which he quickly recovered, a bout of severe anemia in 1941 and a gall bladder attack three years later. More seriously, speculations that he had cancer or suffered a series of "little strokes" have never been proved. However, FDR did have two mysterious seizures during his presidency in the presence of his son James. The first occurred in July 1944 in his train in San Diego. For ten minutes intense waves of pain struck his body. On Inauguration Day, 1945, he was hit with the same hard pains across his chest, probably first while giving his inaugural speech but also afterward in the White House. James brought him some whiskey, and after a few minutes the pains subsided. Both father and son kept these attacks secret from everyone — at FDR's insistence.[3]

This was Roosevelt's fourth inauguration, and, at his request, it was a smaller, simpler one held on the south portico of the White House instead of the traditional site at the Capitol. He said it was due to wartime conditions, but no doubt it was mostly because he could not stand the strain of a long, drawn out public celebration. Shortly after the inauguration, extra Secret Service guards were assigned to Vice President Harry S Truman due to the precarious state of the president's health.

In January and February FDR took a grueling trip to attend difficult negotiations with Winston Churchill and Josef Stalin in Yalta in the USSR.

He pushed himself beyond his deteriorating physical limits. This further taxed his ebbing strength. Not at his sharpest mentally, he agreed to Stalin's plans for the Soviets to control east central Europe and annex huge areas of land, mainly from Poland, and to move the USSR's borders westward.

He delivered his final speech to Congress in March while sitting down, no longer able to bear the strain of the leg braces that made him stand. He could hardly sign his name. He could not bathe nor shave himself. He was hit with depression and melancholy more often. During these moods he often voiced morbid thoughts, such as his wish for a small memorial in Washington, or who should get his dog after his death, or his request to be buried at sea if he should die on board a ship.

His mood was not helped by the deaths of his secretary Missy LeHand, his mentor Al Smith, his friend and rival Wendell Willkie, and his aide Edwin Watson, all during his last year. One thing that did brighten his spirits were his visits with Lucy Mercer Rutherford. His affair with Lucy had ruined his marriage in 1918, and although he promised never to see her again, the two maintained a surreptitious correspondence and met secretly. Mrs. Roosevelt knew nothing of the continuing relationship, but a few others did know and kept quiet, most notably the Roosevelts' daughter Anna.

Mr. Roosevelt looked forward to seeing Lucy in April 1945 during a visit to one of his favorite retreats, the Little White House in Warm Springs, Georgia. At the Warm Springs Foundation there, polio victims underwent treatment for their damaged muscles. The president arrived on March 30. Making the trip with him were Grace Tully and Dorothy Brady, his secretaries; William Hassett, his press aide; Dr. Bruenn; Lieutenant Commander George Fox, White House pharmacist; Arthur Prettyman, FDR's valet; Laura "Polly" Delano and Margaret "Daisy" Suckley, the president's distant cousins; correspondent Harold Oliver of the Associated Press; Merriman Smith of United Press; Robert Nixon of International News; a Secret Service contingent; a few others; and FDR's little terrier Fala. Staying in the Little White House with the president were Polly, Daisy and Prettyman. The others were put up at the nearby hotel or in nearby cottages on the foundation grounds. Due to the war, this trip was officially a secret, and the reporters were ordered not to divulge FDR's whereabouts. Of course, many Warm Springs residents knew that the president was in town.

The Little White House was a six-room clapboard cottage with a columned front portico and back porch with table and chairs. One entered the front door into a foyer, then the central living room that included a dining area to the left that sat six at a wooden table. The room had pine paneling and bluish-green Venetian blinds on the windows. On the right wall were several bookshelves and a stone fireplace with a ship on its mantel. Naval prints adorned the other walls. A sofa, chairs and hardwood furniture graced the room. FDR's bedroom was to the left rear as one entered the cottage; Mrs. Roosevelt's, when she stayed, was to the left front. Another bedroom was to the right rear. In the glen behind the house was stationed a platoon of armed Marines, and the immediate area around the cottage was guarded by the Secret Service, which had installed a telephone near some shrubs under the president's bedroom window.

The Little White House, President Roosevelt's cozy clapboard cottage in Warm Springs, Georgia, where he died on April 12, 1945. (M. Nowak)

Each day Roosevelt did a little work and rested. His health remained stable. On Monday, April 9, Lucy Rutherford, artist Elizabeth Shoumatoff, and her assistant Nicholas Robbins arrived in Warm Springs. Shoumatoff was to paint a portrait of the president for Lucy's daughter.

On Thursday, April 12, the official mail pouch from Washington would be late, so the president was allowed to sleep later than usual. He awoke in late morning, was served breakfast and read a newspaper. Among the other war news, the paper reported a rumor that Hitler was very sick and dying. FDR had a friendly conversation with Lizzie McDuffie, the black maid, during which he complained that he did not feel very well and rubbed the back of his head as if he had a headache. Valet Prettyman helped him out of bed shortly after eleven.

It was about one o'clock as the president sat in the living room in a cushioned wooden arm chair. He was working on his official papers on a card table in front of him. His back was to the bookshelves and the spare bedroom. Some six feet straight ahead was Madame Shoumatoff at her easel. She was working on a watercolor portrait of Roosevelt. For this sitting he wore a dark gray suit with a red tie and a blue navy cape over his shoulders. To his right, sitting in an easy chair, was Lucy, her back to the windows at the rear of the room. Directly across from her on a sofa sat Daisy Suckley, crocheting. Polly Delano was filling vases throughout the cottage with fresh flowers.

Daisy Bonner, the black cook, brought Mr. Roosevelt a cup of gruel from the kitchen. He had a spoonful and left the rest. Filipino houseboy Joe Esperancilla and Prettyman came in from the kitchen to set the table for lunch. The president looked at his watch and said to Madame Shoumatoff, "We've got just fifteen minutes more."

A few minutes later Lizzie the maid left the cottage through the front door. It was now 1:15 P.M., Central War Time. FDR put a cigarette in his holder and lit it, then set it down in an ash tray. He raised his left hand to his temple and pressed it, then brought the hand to his forehead and squeezed. In an awkward, fumbling motion the hand dropped down. Noticing this, Miss Suckley rose from the couch, approached the president and asked, "Did you drop something?" Leaning forward, he put his left hand to the back of his neck. His eyes were closed. He said quietly, "I have a terrific pain in the back of my head."[4] Then the arm dropped down and he slumped to his left against the arm of the chair. Polly, emerging from the bedroom behind FDR, asked, "Franklin, are you all right?"

Madame Shoumatoff screamed. Polly on the right and Daisy on the left each grabbed a shoulder of the president to hold him up in the chair. Prettyman and Esperancilla ran in from the kitchen. Shoumatoff dashed out the front door and shouted to Secret Service agent James Beary, "Call a doctor, something terrible has happened to the president." Beary rushed for his car radiophone. Meanwhile, Daisy called the operator on the living room telephone and asked her to get Dr. Bruenn up to the cottage right away. Lucy was horrified.

Prettyman and Esperancilla locked arms behind the President's back and knees and carried the limp body across the room to FDR's bedroom, his cape sweeping the floor behind them. They laid him on his bed. Lucy and Madame Shoumatoff left the house and went to their guest cottage where they hurriedly started packing. They were gone from Warm Springs in a few minutes.

One of the last photographs taken of President Roosevelt, during the last week of his life in April 1945. It was snapped by his cousin Margaret Suckley in FDR's cottage in Warm Springs. The president is seated in the same spot, working on papers, as when he suffered his fatal stroke on April 12. (Franklin D. Roosevelt Presidential Library)

It was about fifteen minutes after FDR collapsed that Dr. Bruenn arrived, just as Commander Fox showed up with the doctor's medical bag. Shortly thereafter Grace Tully and Dorothy Brady came in. Bruenn barked out an order to get Dr. McIntire on the telephone from Washington. The president was making a snoring sound that could be heard throughout the cottage. Bruenn cut off his clothing and examined the nude body. He immediately suspected a cerebral hemorrhage or stroke. He injected aminophylline and nitroglycerine into one arm. He talked to Dr. McIntire on the phone, who said he would call heart specialist Dr. James Paullin in Atlanta to hurry to Warm Springs, a distance of seventy miles.

William Hassett and Secret Service agent Michael Reilly arrived at the cottage. In the kitchen sat the servants, Daisy and Lizzie. The others waited in the living room silently, concerned and frightened. In the bedroom Fox dressed the president in pajamas. Dr. Bruenn checked FDR's vital signs and gave injections of papaverine and amyl nitrite. Hot water bottles and blankets were applied to the hands and legs, as he was cold but sweating profusely. The navy cape was placed over him. Bruenn kept in touch with McIntire on the telephone.

Polly Delano telephoned Eleanor Roosevelt at the White House and told her that the president had passed out. Eleanor talked to Dr. McIntire on the phone; incredibly, he downplayed the seriousness of the attack, even though he knew FDR was probably on his deathbed. He urged Mrs. Roosevelt to keep her schedule, lest rumors start circulating.

There was little anyone could do except wait. The minutes turned into hours. It was now more than two hours after the collapse. In the cottage, the heavy breathing stopped and Dr. Bruenn, on the phone to McIntire, dropped it to rush back into the bedroom. He made an injection of caffeine. Fox started artificial respiration. Roosevelt, lying in a propped up position, looked ashen. His lips and fingernails were blue, his pupils dilated. At 3:28 Dr. Paullin arrived. After a fast examination he took a syringe and injected adrenalin directly into the heart. He heard two or three beats, then nothing. Blood pressure was zero. "This man is dead," Dr. Paullin said. It was 3:35 P.M. The body was covered with the bedspread.

The three men emerged from the room. Dr. Bruenn got back on the telephone to McIntire and told him the news. The little dog Fala began barking, crashed open the screen door and ran outside. The others in the room sat silently. Agent Reilly took samples of FDR's breakfast to have them analyzed by chemists, a routine procedure that would uncover no foul play.

In Washington, Mrs. Roosevelt was attending a luncheon at the Sulgrave Club when she was called back to the White House. When she arrived there she was met by Dr. McIntire and White House Press Secretary Stephen T. Early, a former Associated Press reporter who had been the first person to report the death of President Warren G. Harding in 1923. Early said to the First Lady, "The president slipped away this afternoon." Mrs. Roosevelt remained calm and unemotional. After all, she was aware of his precarious health and knew that the end could come at any time. She thanked Early and McIntire, then asked the press secretary to call Vice President Truman to the

White House. She composed a short telegram to her four sons who were serving in the war and gave a few general instructions for the funeral. She decided that Early, McIntire and she should fly to Warm Springs that afternoon and accompany the body back to Washington via railroad. One thing Mrs. Roosevelt was certain she did not say was the following, reported by Early to the press and widely circulated: "I am more sorry for the people of this country and of the world than I am for ourselves."

Harry Truman was on Capitol Hill at a meeting in the office of the speaker of the House when he was summoned to the White House. Upon his arrival there at 5:30 (4:30 Warm Springs time), he was shown to Mrs. Roosevelt's study. She greeted him by putting a hand on his shoulder and matter-of-factly stating, "Harry, the president is dead." Truman stood there stunned for a few seconds, then asked, "Is there anything I can do for you?" Mrs. Roosevelt, referring to the awful burdens of the presidency suddenly thrown upon the man, replied, "Is there anything we can do for you? You are the one in trouble now."

At 4:45 in Warm Springs, Hassett met with the three press reporters in his cottage. Simultaneously in Washington, at 5:45 Stephen Early made a conference call to the three major wire services. The message was the same: The president is dead. In a minute or two the news was flashed by teletype to newsrooms around the country. In another minute the radio networks were interrupting their programs to make the shocking announcement.

Truman called for the cabinet and chief justice to meet him in the Cabinet Room of the White House. There, a few minutes past 7 P.M., some two and a half hours after FDR's death, Chief Justice Harlan F. Stone swore in Harry S Truman as the thirty-fourth president of the United States.

Though the new president had been kept in the dark by FDR about most major developments, the late president's aides and cabinet quickly brought him up to speed, and Truman proved to be competent as Americans closed ranks behind him while he provided the leadership needed to prosecute the war to its end.

The leading politicians of all persuasions throughout the country expressed their sorrow at President Roosevelt's passing and greatly praised him. Tributes and messages of sympathy began coming in from abroad as the word spread throughout the world that evening. England was especially sorry to lose its great wartime ally. Winston Churchill called it a terrible blow. He sent a radiogram to Mrs. Roosevelt and called King George to tell him the news. In allied Russia, Premier Josef Stalin was saddened and conveyed his sorrow in person to the American ambassador in Moscow. The premier declared two days of mourning in the USSR, with flags flown at half-staff, tributes never before or since paid to an American leader by that country. Surprisingly, even the enemy nation of Japan broadcast a message of condolence over Radio Tokyo and played special music. The Japanese premier Tojo expressed his sympathy to the American people on the air. But in Germany, the Nazis rejoiced at the news of the death of their adversary.[5]

American fighting men throughout the world, getting the news through their commands or over the radio, were deeply affected. Our great generals in Europe — Eisenhower, Bradley and Patton — were depressed. In this country, as news spread by radio and from person to person, people gathered around radios for more details or for a confirmation of this shocking, unbelievable announcement. There was extremely heavy telephone usage during the six o'clock hour. Many newspapers printed extras that evening. In Washington, people began to gather in Lafayette Park across from the White House. To be sure, the sadness was not universal, because even at this tragic time there were Roosevelt haters, but they were few and far between.

At 6 P.M. in the White House, Dr. McIntire and Stephen Early met with reporters. They gave more details about the death, the circumstances, Mrs. Roosevelt's reaction, and the cause, which was specifically "massive intracerebral hemorrhage which in all probability had ruptured into the subarachnoid space."

The perimeter of the Warm Springs Foundation, upon whose land the Little White House was located, was ringed with soldiers. Georgia state police were also on duty. Closer to the cottage the Secret Service stood guard. At the little Warm Springs railroad station a crowd of hundreds had gathered. Newspapers and radio networks set up, awaiting Mrs. Roosevelt, who would not appear there but arrive by automobile from Columbia airport. The nearby Warm Springs Hotel lobby also became crowded with the curious.

At Dr. Paullin's suggestion, the Atlanta undertaking firm H.M. Patterson and Son was called. Mr. Patterson and his assistants arrived at the cottage before 11 P.M. with two caskets and embalming equipment. They were instructed to wait inside with cousins Polly and Daisy, Grace Tully, Hassett, Paullin, Bruenn and Prettyman, for the arrival of the widow.

At 11:25 Eleanor Roosevelt walked into the cottage with Dr. McIntire and Early. She wore a black dress and hat, and appeared calm but somber. Weeping, the cousins and Tully each embraced and kissed her. Tully remarked, "You know how deeply sorry I am for you and the children."

Mrs. Roosevelt put a hand on the secretary's shoulder and said, "Tully dear, I am so very sorry for all of you."

The widow sat down on the sofa and asked each of the ladies to tell her what had happened. Then she entered her husband's bedroom and closed the door. When she came out after five minutes she was still composed and wore a grave expression on her face. She was asked by the men for her choice of a casket. Dr. McIntire suggested the bronze-colored copper one. Mrs. Roosevelt nodded her assent. Since the cause of death was so obvious, none of the three doctors saw the need for an autopsy. The undertakers were given permission to begin their work.

Patterson and two embalmers brought their equipment into the bedroom. Prettyman went in to help in whatever way he could, and a Marine guard was posted inside the doorway. Being nine hours after death, the embalmers were concerned because rigor mortis had set in. Also, the severe arteriosclerosis made the process very difficult. They did the best they could, and when they were done, the body was dressed in a double-breasted blue suit, white shirt, blue and white tie, and black socks. No shoes were put on the feet. The body was laid out on the bed. Mrs. Roosevelt was called inside. She looked at the body, nodded her approval and thanked the men.

The coffin was carried into the bedroom and the body placed in it. It was then taken into the living room and placed on the floor on a hooked rug near FDR's bedroom. The bottom of the inner glass lid was closed, but the outer lid was left half open. Prettyman sat up with the body all night. Mrs. Roosevelt retired to her bedroom. The others tried to rest, perhaps catching some sleep lying across a bed, but more likely staying awake and thinking, remembering what FDR had meant to them and the nation, and wondering what would happen now.

All during the night the sound of trucks could be heard carrying soldiers from Fort Benning into Warm Springs. They were to take part in ceremonies when the body would be removed to the train. At 2 A.M. that eleven-car train known as POTUS, for "President of the United States," was backed into the Warm Springs station. The rear compartment of the last car, named Conneaught, was empty of everything except a small mirror. A bier was constructed and placed in the center of the compartment, then covered with brown-green army blankets. The rear window on one side of the Conneaught was removed, as the casket would have to be lifted in through there. A ramp to the window was also being built at the station. A special schedule for the train's return to Washington was worked out by the Secret Service and FDR aides, as well as plans for the removal of the body from the cottage to POTUS.

As 9 A.M. neared, those gathered in the Little White House prepared for the four-mile ride to the station. Lizzie the cook was remarking how handsome the president looked in the casket. Mrs. Roosevelt, Polly and Daisy were there, and Early, Hassett, Bruenn, McIntire and Tully. Patterson closed the casket, and it was lifted onto a roller table. A flag for the coffin could not be located, so the one on the flagpole outside the cottage was lowered, dusted off and placed on it. The pallbearers were then called in. Four soldiers, four Marines and two sailors carried the eight-hundred-pound coffin outside and slid it into the back of a black Cadillac hearse.

Mrs. Roosevelt and the others emerged from the Little White House and got into two limousines. The undertakers got into another car and sped ahead to the railway station. Led by the army band from Fort Benning, followed by a thousand infantrymen, the hearse and the other cars, the procession got under way at 9:25. The muffled drums boomed out a sad cadence as the cortege headed down the rough, partially unpaved road. On each side of the road stood two thousand paratroopers at present arms, spaced twenty feet apart. Tears rolled down the faces of some of the young men. One fainted. The morning was sunny and hot, as the day before had been. The procession turned in to the semi-circular drive in front of Georgia Hall, the patients' residence at the foundation. On crutches and in wheelchairs, even in beds, the patients had gathered out front, along with staff, for a tearful goodbye to their friend and fellow patient. From the crowd, out stepped the uniformed figure of Navy Chief Petty Officer Graham Jackson, who began to play the sad strains of "Going Home" on his accordion. He was one of FDR's favorite musicians, always called on to perform for him when he was in Warm Springs. As he played and a vocalist sang, tears streamed down his face. As he finished, the formation resumed its mournful beat and marched on toward the train, past sobbing, sorrowful townspeople, until it halted at the small railroad station.

There, another crowd had assembled. The front porch of the nearby hotel was also packed with onlookers. The flag-draped coffin was removed from the hearse by ten military men, carried up the ramp and handed to ten more men inside the Conneaught, who placed it on the bier. An honor guard of a soldier, sailor, Marine and Coast Guardsman took places at each corner of the casket. Patterson the undertaker placed some embalming equipment under the covered bier, should it be needed in Washington by the funeral director there. Mrs. Roosevelt left her sedan and boarded FDR's armor-plated rail car, which was in front of the Conneaught. Others boarding the train were Polly and Daisy, McIntire, Bruenn, Early, Tully, Prettyman, Lizzie the cook, Fala, Secret Service agents and three wire service reporters. The train pulled away from the station as the army band played a dirge.

Preceded by a lead locomotive half a mile ahead, the train went through Atlanta; Greenville, South Carolina; Charlotte, North Carolina; Charlottesville, Virginia; and on to D.C.; where it would arrive after a twenty-four-hour journey. Every few hours stops were made to take on coal or water, or to change engines and crews. At each stop, flowers were presented and placed aboard. The train's speed was kept slow because people were expected to line the rails to watch it go by. And they did. At each town and city, at each crossroad and overhead bridge, people congregated to wish their sad farewells. Some wept, some knelt. The rear coach was lit, and the four servicemen and the top of the flag-draped coffin could be seen clearly, day and night. White farmers and black sharecroppers stopped in the fields to pay their respects as the train chugged by. At Atlanta, the mayor boarded the train to place a basket of flowers on the casket. In Charlotte, boy scouts started to sing "Onward, Christian Soldiers," and the crowd of ten thousand soon joined in. African Americans sang spirituals.

Occasionally airplanes would circle over the funeral train. At many of the crossroads a lone soldier stood with his weapon at present arms. At the cities, larger military formations were present.

Inside the train the passengers got little sleep. Eleanor questioned Tully about any funeral wishes her husband may have mentioned. Mrs. Roosevelt also talked to Daisy Suckley and Polly Delano, who told the widow that Lucy had been present in the room when FDR died. Eleanor must have reacted with anger at finding out about the ongoing secret liaison, but being very private on personal matters and one who kept strict control over her emotions, we shall never know her exact feelings regarding the affair.

Mrs. Roosevelt had entrusted details of the funeral plans to her daughter Anna and a few Roosevelt aides. They worked up a guest list for an East Room religious service for Saturday the fourteenth, with the burial services to be held at the Hyde Park estate on Sunday. They could not find any files on the Harding funeral, the last for a sitting president, because the files had been given to Mrs. Harding.[6] Anna did not wish to go back any further than that time for guidance. An invitation to the Harding funeral was found, and this was used to make up invitations for the East Room services. Roosevelt had put down his funeral instructions in writing in 1937 for his son James, but they were not found until a few days afterward.[7] Drawing from what they could recall FDR saying about funeral wishes (whenever he had the occasion to discuss them), Eleanor and the others did the best they could to follow them.

Friday's newspapers were filled with stories of the president's death and with tributes to him. Of all these tributes the most touching was a rather simple one. During World War II many papers carried a daily list of war dead. On this day, many of them included an entry on this list for the commander-in-chief. Many people considered Roosevelt to be a victim of the war as much as any soldier on the front lines.

Radio stations carried reports of the death and funeral ceremonies, though they were not allowed to broadcast the White House service or the Hyde Park burial services. In between news and eulogies, the stations played somber classical music rather than their usual programs.

Around the country, theaters, restaurants and businesses closed. Baseball spring training came to a halt until after the funeral. While the train was en route to Washington at noon on Friday, the Senate convened. In a thirty-minute session, eulogies to the late president were read and committees appointed to attend the funeral ceremonies. On Saturday, the House met for five minutes and picked its funeral delegation.

In one of his first official acts, President Truman issued a proclamation designating Sunday, April 15, as a national "day of mourning and prayer throughout the United States." He ordered flags flown at half-staff on public buildings for thirty days, and ordered all executive branch agencies to close on Saturday afternoon. At that time, federal offices were on a full Saturday schedule due to the war. Traditional wearing of mourning bands, draping of colors and firing of salutes was dispensed with by the military due to war conditions.

A little before 10 A.M. Saturday, POTUS backed into Union Station in the nation's capital. Assembled on the platform were President Truman, cabinet members, senators and representatives, the entire Supreme Court, and Roosevelt family members. Police cleared a way for daughter Anna and son Elliott, who wore his brigadier general's uniform, and their spouses. Also there were the wives of sons Franklin Jr. and John. Franklin, John and James, serving in the Pacific theater of the war, were unable to make it back for any of their father's funeral ceremonies. Anna led the family in through the rear door of the Conneaught, where they paused before the casket, then continued into the next car to see Mrs. Roosevelt. Truman and a few other officials followed. The casket was removed from the train through the window and carried by the servicemen to a black caisson and strapped on. Mrs. Roosevelt, Mr. Truman, passengers from the train and a few dignitaries got into limousines for the trip to the White House.

Pulled by six white horses, three with riders, and led by another mounted steed, the caisson emerged from the station onto Delaware Avenue, then Constitution. The procession was led by sixteen motorcycle policemen in a single formation across the width of the street, side by side from curb to curb. They were followed by a group of high-ranking military officers, armored troop carriers, infantry trucks, the Marine band playing Chopin's "Funeral March," Annapolis midshipmen, the navy band (playing alternately with the Marines), a detachment of Marines, and companies of military women.

Then came the caisson. Walking behind it was a military officer and two flagbearers carrying the U.S. and presidential flags. Immediately beside the caisson walked eight servicemen, and flanking them far outside were fourteen motorcycle policemen. Slowly following were the cars bearing the widow and her family. Next came Truman's sedan, and those of the cabinet, military brass, diplomats and others. In all, it was a two-mile-long cortege. All along the route on both sides of the street stood helmeted soldiers at present arms, and behind them stretched a mass of four to five hundred thousand silent, grieving citizens, many of them weeping. In the distance, artillery guns pounded out a salute, adding to the mournful marching beat of the bands. At one point a formation of twenty-four bombers thundered overhead; at another came a squadron of P-51 airplanes. Descriptions of the sad parade

The White House in Mourning

FDR's funeral cortege takes his body from Union Station to the White House in Washington, D.C., April 14, 1945. (Franklin D. Roosevelt Presidential Library)

were carried live on all the radio networks by commentators stationed in buildings or on rooftops along the way. The most unforgettable narration on that day was done by CBS radio announcer Arthur Godfrey, who broke down sobbing as he described the sad spectacle.

After an hour and a half the caisson, followed by the cars of the family, friends and Harry Truman, entered the White House grounds through the northeast gate. Another squadron of bombers flew overhead. Those in the cars alighted. A navy band on the lawn played the National Anthem, then eight army honor guards took the coffin from the caisson and carried it inside the mansion to the East Room, followed by the widow, her daughter and Grace Tully. The casket was placed upon a brown cloth–covered bier that had been set up on a small oriental rug at the east end of the flower-filled room, near paintings of George and Martha Washington. An honor guard representing the four military services took up positions at each corner of the casket. Mrs. Roosevelt retired to rest and have lunch upstairs. President Truman had gone straight from his car to his office and met with aides during the afternoon.

In mid-afternoon invited guests began to arrive for the service. White House ushers showed them to their seats in the East Room. There were about two hundred gold, straight-backed chairs set up, but some attendees still had to stand. An overflow of guests gathered in the Blue Room or Green Room to hear the services over a loudspeaker. White House staffers listened over loudspeakers in a lobby. Among the attendees were 1944 Republican presidential candidate Governor Thomas Dewey of New York, Princess Martha of Norway, Philippine president Osmena, members of the Supreme Court, the appointed congressional delegations, present and former cabinet officers, former chief justice Charles Evans Hughes, Mrs. Woodrow Wilson, personal friends and acquaintances, foreign ambassadors, including Andrei Gromyko of the USSR and Anthony Eden of Great Britain, and many top U.S. military officers.

Close to four o'clock President Truman, his wife and daughter entered and took seats in the front row. Then the guests rose as Mrs. Roosevelt, dressed in black, walked in with daughter Anna and her husband, son Elliott and his wife, and the widow's three other daughters-in-law. They also took places in green armchairs in the front row. The room was dimly lit by three great chandeliers. Long red drapes hung from the huge windows, and large, gold-framed mirrors adorned the walls, which were banked high with flowers. The closed, flag-draped casket was flanked by the American and presidential flags. The robed figures of Episcopal Bishop Angus Dun, the Rev. John Magee and the Rev. Howard Wilkinson walked slowly into the room and stood before the coffin.

At this time the United States came to a halt for a minute or two. Church bells throughout the land rang, while fire bells and ships' horns sounded in salute. Radio stations went silent, telephone and telegraph service stopped. Airplanes did not take off or land, trains and trolleys halted. People stopped in their steps and bowed their heads. Memorial services were conducted all over the country.

In the White House, Bishop Dun began the service by saying, "Eternal Father, Strong to Save," and he led the mourners in singing that hymn. He then delivered the invocation. His assistants read from Psalms, there was the singing of "Faith of Our Fathers," then the Bishop read a prayer and quoted from FDR's first inaugural address. He then delivered the benediction and his blessings as the short service ended at 4:23. The mourners filed by the casket and left the room.

Some time during the day, Anna Roosevelt and her brother Elliott went to the East Room and viewed their father's body. They thought his face looked discolored and distorted, no doubt as a result of the delay in the embalming and the effects of the stroke.[8] And Eleanor visited the East Room, where a member of Gawler's, the undertaking firm handling arrangements in Washington, also opened the casket for her. She placed a few flowers at her husband's hands, then the lid was permanently sealed.[9]

The body of Franklin D. Roosevelt lies in state in the East Room of the White House on April 14, 1945. (Franklin D. Roosevelt Presidential Library)

That evening at 9:30 the cortege again formed outside the White House, and the coffin was carried outside. Past grieving onlookers in the dark, a smaller crowd than before, the marchers and the mourners in their cars accompanied the body down Pennsylvania Avenue and returned to Union Station, where the casket was placed back upon the bier in the Conneaught. This time the POTUS was expanded to seventeen cars for the trip to Hyde Park. Boarding that train were Mrs. Roosevelt and her family, President and Mrs. Truman and their daughter, presidential aides, the cabinet, the Supreme Court, congressional leaders, various federal agency chiefs, and eighteen press and radio reporters. In addition, a second train of eleven cars carried members of Congress, foreign diplomats and many others.

With great difficulty, two locomotives were able to pull the heavy POTUS out of the station. Through Baltimore, Philadelphia and New York the train rolled. Thousands of people were collected at the stations at each city and town, and along the tracks at various points. Security was very tight, with army guards placed at intervals along the route. Whenever the trains made a stop, Secret Service agents, soldiers and police guarded them. The second train was allowed to pass POTUS in New York City so that it could arrive in Hyde Park and discharge its passengers first.

The president's train moved up the Hudson River valley and arrived at Hyde Park at 8:40 A.M. on Sunday. It pulled into a private side track at the edge of the Roosevelt estate near the river. Several minutes earlier the other train had arrived and discharged its passengers. Now mourners began stepping out of the POTUS and were shuttled up the hill to the house in limousines, three or four at a time. Meanwhile, guests from the village of Hyde Park, neighbors, and friends of FDR began arriving on the estate. Because they felt a special closeness to him, many Hyde Parkers were disappointed that a funeral procession did not go through the village, which was draped in black and purple mourning.

Soon after 9 A.M. the guests, about three hundred total, began to gather in the rose garden, a peaceful area secluded from the rest of the estate by ten-foot-tall hedges. A small group of reporters was there also. Along the hedges were lined a group of soldiers, sailors and Marines. Ranking officers of the services were also present as part of the funeral party.

Back at the train, the Roosevelts and the Trumans waited in limousines as the coffin was once again lifted out of the train window. An officer fired a signal gun, and an artillery cannon began booming a twenty-one-gun salute at fifteen second intervals. A village church began ringing its bell, and a squadron of bombers thundered overhead. Soldiers placed the casket in a hearse that started up the hill, followed by the few cars carrying the widow, the new president, and their families. About halfway up the hill the hearse stopped, and the coffin was transferred to a black caisson. The West Point band, in light dress blue, led the caisson the rest of the way up the winding, wooded road to the rose garden. Six brown horses pulled it, and behind it followed a seventh, wearing a black hood over its head and body, stirrups backward, with empty boots in them — the traditional symbols of a fallen warrior. A company of West Point cadets and the cars followed behind.

The band drummed out the mournful funeral cadence, and played Chopin's "Funeral March." Up the road the cortege went, through the shade of hedges and blossoming apple trees on a sunny spring morning, past places where young Franklin had frolicked as a boy. All along the way the route was lined with soldiers at present arms.

When the procession reached the outside of the rose garden, the casket was removed from the caisson by eight servicemen. A young man bearing a crucifix on a staff walked into the garden, followed by the Rev. George Anthony of St. James Episcopal Church of Hyde Park, dressed in white surplice and black cassock. The casket was carried in and placed over the grave. The widow, President Truman and other mourners entered. The Roosevelt

Burial ceremonies of President Roosevelt in the rose garden of his Hyde Park estate. The coffin is carried to the grave as Mrs. Roosevelt, to the right, looks on. (Franklin D. Roosevelt Presidential Library)

family and the Trumans took places at the foot of the grave, well back from it but in front of the other guests who now stood behind them, and to the left and right of them. The Reverend Anthony, an elderly man with a goatee, stood at the head of the grave; behind him were the West Point cadets in formation. To the left of the clergyman, next to the grave, was a huge collection of flowers.

A squadron of fighter planes roared overhead, then the Reverend Anthony removed his skullcap and began the burial commitment. "Unto Almighty God, we commend the soul of our brother departed...." The drone of a small plane circling overhead almost drowned out some of his words, but the minister continued with his reading, reciting the Lord's Prayer. The flag was removed by the military pallbearers. The Reverend Anthony then raised his right hand and read a brief intonation as the pallbearers, four each on both sides of the grave, lowered the coffin into the earth and the band played "Now the Laborer's Task Is Done."

A file of West Point cadets came forward and fired three volleys at the command of a lieutenant. At the sound of the first shots, the little dog Fala, held on a leash by Daisy Suckley, howled and rolled over in the grass. After the second volley, a baby in the crowd began to cry. After the third, a cadet sergeant came to the head of the grave and sounded "Taps," and the ceremony was over. The folded flag was presented to Mrs. Roosevelt. The widow and her family left the garden, the cadets marched out, and the rest of the mourners slowly dispersed.

With the garden empty, William Plog, a groundskeeper at the Roosevelt estate for fifty years, who had supervised the digging of the grave, ordered his workmen to shovel the earth into it. After a few minutes, Mrs. Roosevelt appeared in the garden, watched the burial for a moment, then walked away.

Several days after his death, Roosevelt's missing funeral instructions were found in a safe. He had wanted to be buried in a plain pine coffin in an unlined grave and did not want to be embalmed. Those wishes had not been carried out.

A large rectangular granite block was eventually put in place to mark the grave. It was simply engraved with FDR's name and years of birth and death. Seventeen years later the same information was inscribed for former first lady Anna Eleanor Roosevelt. She died on November 7, 1962, at age seventy-eight after suffering a stroke. Known as the First Lady of the World, she was the most accomplished presidential wife in history, and her death was mourned throughout the world. She was buried next to her husband just two days after her death.

Many years after President Roosevelt's death, his son Elliott revealed that Soviet premier Josef Stalin had insisted that the USSR's ambassador in Washington be allowed to view the body. Mrs. Roosevelt refused the request. Stalin had believed that Winston Churchill may have conspired to poison FDR and wanted his representative to check for evidence of that. He also made a request for an autopsy with the State Department to check for poisoning. This was refused too.[10]

President Roosevelt wished that any memorial to him, if one should be erected, should be no bigger than the size of his desk, plain, and placed in a lawn plot in front of the National Archives building at Pennsylvania Avenue and Ninth Street in Washington. This was done in 1965.

Despite his wishes, after decades of debate, a larger FDR memorial was built in the nation's capital and dedicated in 1997. Spread over more than seven acres near the Tidal Basin, it features four outdoor rooms that trace the history of his time in office. Also prominent are trees and waterfalls. There are several statues, including one of a seated, caped FDR, one of him riding in a car, and another of him in a wheelchair that was added in 2001 under pressure from disabled advocacy groups.

President Harry S Truman lays a wreath at the grave of his predecessor, Franklin D. Roosevelt, as Mrs. Roosevelt looks on at Hyde Park on April 12, 1946. (National Park Service Photograph — Abbie Rowe; courtesy Harry S Truman Library)

In a very lengthy and detailed will, FDR bequeathed almost all of his $2,000,000 estate to his wife. He left her all his personal property as well. Five thousand dollars went to St. James Episcopal Church and one hundred dollars to each of his employees. The Little White House and its contents were left to the Warm Springs Foundation, and in 1947 the cottage became the property of the state of Georgia. The house and grounds at Hyde Park, including the FDR Presidential Library, had already been deeded to the federal government and were formally turned over and dedicated to the people of the United States one year after Roosevelt's death. The Warm Springs Foundation was also the beneficiary of $560,000 in insurance policies.[11]

CHAPTER 9

John Fitzgerald Kennedy

35TH PRESIDENT OF THE UNITED STATES
TERM OF OFFICE: JANUARY 20, 1961, TO NOVEMBER 22, 1963
BORN: MAY 29, 1917; DIED: NOVEMBER 22, 1963
AGE AT DEATH: 46 YEARS, 177 DAYS
CAUSE OF DEATH: GUNSHOT WOUND TO THE HEAD
BURIAL PLACE: ARLINGTON, VIRGINIA

It all happened so swiftly. At 12:30 P.M. the smiling president neared the end of the motorcade route in downtown Dallas, Texas. Just thirty minutes later a doctor pronounced him dead. And an hour after that his body was in a casket ready to begin its final journey back to Washington.

The death of John F. Kennedy is one of the most stunning and tragic events in the history of the United States and the world. It was also a puzzling event. How was one of the most well protected, most carefully observed persons in the world murdered in broad daylight, with the identity of the killer remaining uncertain to this day?

Energetic, affable, friendly, handsome, charming, courageous, intelligent; all these adjectives described President Kennedy. Everyone seemed to like him, and it was hard to believe there was anyone who did not.

At age forty-three, Kennedy was the youngest person ever elected president, and the first Roman Catholic. He and his beautiful wife Jacqueline "ruled" America in gracious style, and their time in the White House would come to be known as the "Camelot" years. The Kennedys were millionaires, but their appeal cut across all social levels.

The president was the picture of perfect health, but he did suffer from a chronically painful back, aggravated by service in World War II, and usually wore a back brace corset. In private he often used crutches. In 1954 he underwent a dangerous back operation and almost died afterward from an infection. He was administered the last rites of the Roman Catholic Church, but survived.[1] During the war, he also contracted malaria.[2] Several years after his death it was confirmed that he had suffered from Addison's disease since 1947. Rumors to that effect had circulated for years. Drugs kept the adrenal ailment under control, and it was apparently not life-threatening at the time of his death.

In November 1963 it was announced that President and Mrs. Kennedy would visit five Texas cities later that month. The chief purpose of the trip was to heal a rift in the Democratic Party in that state that was threatening to ruin Kennedy's chance at winning Texas in the 1964 election. Accompanying the Kennedys on their swing through the Lone Star state were Texas governor John Connally and Vice President Lyndon B. Johnson and their wives.

The trip was going well when the president's airplane touched down at Dallas' Love Field airport shortly before noon on Friday, November 22. Several people in and out of government had misgivings about the Dallas stop, and some attempted to warn Kennedy not to go. But he was a man who often joked about assassination. Dallas was feared by many because it was a conservative city noted at the time for its atmosphere of right wing fervor. A few days before the president's visit, scathing anti–Kennedy handbills were handed out in the streets. And on the morning of November 22, the *Dallas Morning News*, the city's conservative daily, carried a right wing group's full page advertisement attacking Kennedy's policies.[3]

The presidential party settled into their automobiles for a motorcade through the streets of the city, their destination being the Dallas Trade Mart where the president was to give a luncheon address. In the president's Lincoln sat Mr. and Mrs. Kennedy in the rear seat, Governor and Mrs. Connally in the middle, and two Secret Service agents in the front. The convertible glass bubble top was down. Two cars behind were the vice president and his wife, and in other cars were Texas congressmen, various aides and reporters. The lead car of the twenty-four vehicle parade was driven by Dallas police chief Jesse Curry. The Lincoln was the second car.

At 12:30 P.M. the motorcade reached the western end of downtown Dallas and made a zig-zag turn through Dealey Plaza, a grassy expanse of land cut by three city streets. The Dallas crowd was friendly, and the Kennedys waved and smiled. Many people snapped photographs. As the president's car made its way down Elm Street toward a railroad underpass, local merchant Abraham Zapruder stood atop a concrete pedestal to the motorcade's right, about forty feet from the street. In his hands a home movie camera began filming the president. The most famous movie in history was being filmed by the sixty-year-old Zapruder, the most important record of the events about to unfold in the next few seconds. As his camera whirred, what sounded like a series of shots rang out.

The president lurched forward and slumped to his left toward his wife,

9. John Fitzgerald Kennedy

The center building is the former Texas School Book Depository at the edge of Dealey Plaza in Dallas, Texas. Lee Harvey Oswald allegedly shot and killed President Kennedy from the far right window of the sixth floor of the seven-story building. Kennedy's limousine was riding down the center of Elm Street in the foreground when he was fatally struck. (M. Nowak)

clutched at his throat and reportedly said, "My God, I have been hit!" "What are they doing to you?" Mrs. Kennedy exclaimed.[4] Governor Connally, seated directly in front of Kennedy, slumped in his seat and cried out, "Oh, no, no, no. My God, they're going to kill us all!"[5] A shot had hit Connally and seriously wounded him. Another shot apparently missed the car completely and nicked a curb near the railroad underpass, spraying the cheek of bystander James T. Tague with grains of either the concrete curb or the bullet. Five seconds later a shot tore a hole through the top of Kennedy's head. The impact of the shot flung his body backward against the seat of the car, bits of blood and bone and brain tissue flying through the air and spraying nearby motorcycle policemen and the other passengers in the car.

Kennedy's limp body fell toward his wife as she cried out, "Oh, my God, they've shot my husband! I've got his brains in my hand!"[6] The back seat of the car was covered with blood. Part of Kennedy's skull was on the rear seat.

Mrs. Kennedy climbed out onto the back of the limousine, apparently an instinctive reaction to flee the ghastly scene of violence. Secret Service agent Clifton Hill, running up from the following car, jumped on the trunk of the Lincoln and pushed Jacqueline Kennedy back into the rear seat and covered the Kennedys with his own body. The agents in the front now realized that someone had been hit, and the cars sped ahead to the nearest hospital. Two cars back, in the vice president's convertible, agent Rufus Youngblood had pushed Lyndon Johnson down in the back seat and shielded him with his body.

Many spectators in Dealey Plaza threw themselves on the ground. Others fled the area. Sirens screamed. Some policemen left their motorcycles turned over in the street and raced to the north side of Elm Street, sensing that the shots had come from that direction.

Parkland Memorial Hospital was four miles away down a freeway, and the president's car reached it in six minutes. During the frantic trip, the first lady hunched over her husband and held her hands over the wound in the rear of his head, trying to hold his head together and keep the brain from extruding. Strange sounds came from his throat. The car came to a halt outside the hospital's emergency room entrance. Kennedy, his eyes staring blankly ahead and bleeding profusely from the head, was put on a stretcher and rushed into emergency room number one. His wife, hair disheveled and blood stains on her dress, followed alongside. The wounded Governor Connally was wheeled into another emergency room. Vice President and Mrs. Johnson were whisked into a nearby room and kept under guard by Secret Service agents. The hospital's emergency area became filled with agents and other persons from the motorcade. All were deeply shocked.

No one was certain what was going on. Was the United States under attack from its enemies, particularly the Soviet Union? Were more government officials targeted? Were they safe in the hospital? What should be done next?

In the emergency room, Kennedy's clothes were

Frame 313 of the home movie made by Abraham Zapruder shows the instant the fatal shot struck President Kennedy in the head. (Zapruder Film © 1967 [Renewed 1995]; The Sixth Floor Museum at Dealey Plaza)

removed, except for his corset and his undershorts. There appeared to be a gunshot wound in the center of his throat. In the back of the head doctors noticed a two-and-a-half-inch round hole that looked like a gunshot exit wound. The right rear portion of the skull was shattered, with skull bone protruding from the scalp. Part of the brain protruded through the hole. The doctors could see into the skull cavity. The wound continued to bleed profusely. A team of fifteen doctors worked to save the mortally wounded president. He had an occasional heartbeat and made a strained effort to breathe. Blood transfusions were started immediately, and chest tubes were inserted to prevent lung collapse. Dr. Malcolm Perry performed a tracheotomy over the bullet wound in the neck. Injections of cortisone and salt solution were given.

Mrs. Kennedy, who had been silently waiting directly outside the small room, now entered. She was determined to be present when her husband died, though for all practical purposes he had died the instant the bullet struck him in the head. The president's eyes continued to stare transfixed, dilated, seeing nothing. He was responding to nothing. In a last ditch effort to save his life, Dr. Perry started closed chest massage of the heart. For ten minutes he pumped down on the president's rib cage, trying to raise a sustained heart-

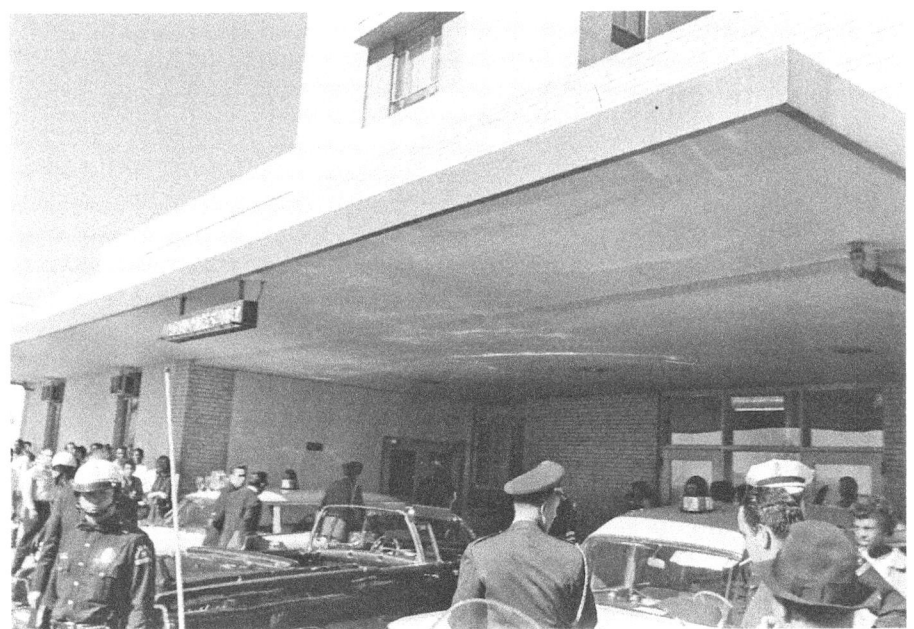

President Kennedy's black limousine stands at the emergency room entrance of Dallas' Parkland Memorial Hospital minutes after the wounded president was carried inside. (John F. Kennedy Presidential Library; Cecil Stoughton/White House)

beat. But there was nothing. No heartbeat, no respiration. Dr. Perry stopped. The body was white from loss of blood. Dr. Kemp Clark, who had been monitoring an electrocardiogram, turned to Mrs. Kennedy and said, "Your husband has sustained a fatal wound." The time of death was officially determined to be 1:00 P.M. Two priests had arrived and administered the last rites of the Roman Catholic Church over the body of John F. Kennedy. The blood was cleaned off the body by nurses and orderlies, then wrapped in bed sheets. Jacqueline Kennedy placed her wedding ring on her husband's finger.[7]

After the last shot rang through Dealey Plaza, police and bystanders' attention centered on the north side of the area, toward the grassy knoll alongside Elm Street, the railroad overpass and the seven-story Texas School Book Depository building. Most of the attention seemed to be directed toward the knoll, which was topped by a five-foot-high wooden fence and several trees. Behind the fence was a parking lot. Several people, including policemen, raced up the knoll and behind the fence or over to the railroad overpass. One police officer came across a man who identified himself as a Secret Service agent, despite the fact that all had left the area with the motorcade. Another policeman smelled gunpowder. Footprints were found in the mud behind the fence. Some people who had been watching the motorcade from the railroad overpass reported seeing smoke near the fence when the shots were fired. Many witnesses thought they heard shots from the area of the knoll, including Abraham Zapruder, who stood a few feet away filming the assassination. Photographs released later showed fuzzy man-like images behind the fence or nearby wall.

The Depository Building was the other focus of attention. A crowd gathered around the building. Some eyewitnesses reported seeing a rifle sticking out of a sixth floor window, and one man was able to identify the person holding the weapon. He told a police officer of his observations as other bystanders also told what they had seen and heard. Another policeman had noticed pigeons scatter from the roof of the building, and he raced inside and up a stairway toward the roof. He confronted an employee, Lee Harvey Oswald, dismissed him, then continued his climb as Oswald left the building. As additional police arrived, the building was sealed off at 12:37 P.M., with no one allowed to leave. Forty minutes later, on the sixth floor, the rifle allegedly used in the murder was found. It was eventually identified as belonging to Lee Harvey Oswald.

After Oswald left the Depository Building, he walked a few blocks and boarded a bus. He left it after it became tied up in traffic and took a taxi from downtown Dallas to his rooming house three miles south of Dealey Plaza. He took a pistol from his room and walked down the streets of south Dallas for a mile, then was stopped by police officer J.D. Tippit. Oswald matched the description of a man wanted in the shooting of the president. Oswald shot and killed Tippit, then ran into a movie theater where he was apprehended by a group of policemen after a brief struggle. He was taken to the city jail in downtown Dallas.

No one knew whether or not the shooting of President Kennedy was a conspiracy or if anyone else was marked for assassination. Secret Service agents were anxious to move new president Lyndon Johnson out of the hospital and out of Dallas. Johnson was whisked away to Air Force One at the Dallas Love Field airport shortly before Kennedy's death was announced to the world. It was decided that the late president's body and Mrs. Kennedy would accompany Johnson on the plane back to Washington, and that Johnson would take the presidential oath of office on board in Dallas.

Communication of the events was relayed to the White House and Secretary of Defense Robert McNamara. Shortly after two o'clock Washington time (1 P.M. in Dallas), McNamara instructed the military joint chiefs of staff to inform all American military installations of the attack on the president. McNamara met with the joint chiefs at the Pentagon to figure out a course of action. Troops all over the world were put on alert.

The electronic news media of 1963 worked swiftly to relay the events from Dallas to the rest of the world. Only four minutes after the first shot, the United Press International wire service flashed the first message across teletypes in newsrooms throughout the country: "Three shots were fired at President Kennedy's motorcade in downtown Dallas." A UPI reporter in the motorcade had radiophoned the statement to his Dallas office. Two minutes later, as the motorcade reached the hospital, ABC Radio read the message over the air. At 12:40 CBS interrupted their programming with the first television newsflash. In Parkland Hospital two wire service reporters commandeered telephones and reported what they had learned to their offices. This was the source of the teletype bulletins, which were then read over radio and television. Meanwhile, Secret Service agents kept a telephone line open from Parkland to the White House, and this was the source of information for government officials there. The United States Senate was in session, with the president's brother Edward presiding, and it adjourned at once when news of the shooting was released.

On this Friday, a workday for most Americans, people on the job learned the news either from radio or television (if they had access to one), or it was relayed to them by those who were listening. Housewives had their radio and television shows interrupted. Schoolteachers and principals informed students. Millions reached for the telephone to call friends and relatives with the startling news, tying up lines all weekend. In some cases phone lines went dead from the overload, especially in Washington, D.C.

At 1:30 P.M. in Parkland Hospital, a White House press secretary announced to the world that John F. Kennedy was dead. People were stunned.

Many cried aloud. Shocked and grieving, they stayed tuned to a radio or television set for further news. The financial exchanges closed down immediately. Schools and businesses closed. Flags were lowered to half staff. The streets of many of our cities became unusually quiet.

Many Americans grieved as though they had lost a close friend or relative. There was disbelief that anyone could carry out such an appalling deed, and that such a thing could happen in America. In the Cold War atmosphere of the time the suspicions of many turned to the communists. A self-styled communist sympathizer, Oswald was later charged with the crime. But others blamed the ultra-conservative demeanor of Dallas for producing a hateful atmosphere in the city. In fact, after Kennedy's death was announced, several acts of disrespect were reported to have occurred in Dallas schools, and many Kennedy haters in the city made no effort to disguise their glee.[8]

Most of the world was shocked and horrified. At the United Nations, U.S. Ambassador Adlai Stevenson made the announcement of the death. Tributes and expressions of sympathy began pouring in from foreign governments. Even Radio Moscow played funeral music. Torchlight processions were held in many western European cities that night. In Vatican City, Pope Paul VI went to his private chapel to pray for the soul of America's first Roman Catholic president.

Back at Parkland Hospital, a local undertaker, Vernon O'Neal, was called to bring a casket, and the sheet-wrapped body was placed inside by him and his assistant. The expensive bronze coffin was closed and ready to move, but now a complication developed. Dr. Earl Rose, the Dallas County medical examiner, informed the Secret Service and Kennedy aides that under Texas law an autopsy had to be conducted in the state before the body could be flown back to Washington. The murder of the president was a violation of state law, and under that law the body was in the custody of the state, pending an autopsy. There was no federal statute at the time relating to the murder of the president.

After an argument lasting several minutes, the Secret Service and Kennedy aides pushed the coffin past Dr. Rose, and thus Kennedy's body started its journey back to Washington illegally. This was probably enough to get murder charges against the president's assailant dismissed in a court of law.

About two hundred spectators looked on as the casket was loaded into a hearse and driven to the airport along with Mrs. Kennedy. The casket was carried aboard Air Force One, and the widow and others followed. With Mrs. Kennedy and more than twenty others present, Lyndon B. Johnson took the oath of office as the thirty-sixth president of the United States, administered by Texas judge Sarah T. Hughes at 2:38 P.M. Ten minutes later the plane was airborne.

The plane arrived at Andrews Air Force Base near Washington in the early evening, and, in an unforgettable scene broadcast on national television, the coffin was lowered from the plane and put into a navy ambulance. Mrs. Kennedy and the late president's brother, Attorney General Robert F. Kennedy, climbed into the vehicle, which left for Bethesda Naval hospital in suburban Maryland where the autopsy would be performed. Three thousand people, including the Supreme Court, Congressional leaders and other officials witnessed the proceedings at the air base. President Johnson stepped off the plane and made a short statement: "This is a sad time for all people. We have suffered a loss that cannot be weighed. For me it is a deep personal tragedy. I know the world shares the sorrow that Mrs. Kennedy and her family bear. I will do my best. That is all I can do. I ask for your help, and God's." Johnson went to the Executive Office Building across from the White House and held a short meeting with Congressional leaders, and telephoned various government officials asking for support. His main concern was for continuity in government.

The new president was well known in Washington as a consummate politician who had been a power in Congress for many years. Well informed by President Kennedy about important issues of the day, he was a take-charge type who instilled confidence in the country at a time of national crisis and sorrow. Though Johnson's tough personality and character served the nation well at first, it would fail him and America as the United States spiraled downward into the abyss of Vietnam, and racial and generational conflict, after his election to the presidency in 1964.

The official navy autopsy began at about 8:00 P.M. It was performed by Navy Commander James J. Humes, assisted by Navy Commander J. Thornton Boswell and Army Lieutenant Colonel Pierce A. Finck of the Armed Forces Institute of Pathology. Dr. Humes and Dr. Boswell were very inexperienced at forensic criminal pathology. Neither had ever performed an autopsy on a gunshot wound victim before. Dr. Finck had training and experience in forensics, but he played only a peripheral role in the autopsy. At one time or another, twenty-four men were present in the autopsy room, including FBI and Secret Service agents, military officers and enlisted men.

Kennedy's body was removed from the casket and placed on the autopsy table by the enlisted men. The wrapping was removed from the corpse. The body was muscular and well developed. The loss of blood left the skin looking white, and there were the beginnings of rigor mortis. After it was measured and weighed, specialists took photographs and x-rayed the nude body. The face was unmarred except for a bruised left eye. The doctors probed and examined the huge head wound and a shallow back wound. A hole in the front of the neck was believed to be only a tracheotomy incision, but the next day it was made clear to the pathologists that the tracheotomy incision was made *over* a bullet wound. Tiny bullet fragments were removed from the brain. The doctors were puzzled by the shallowness of the back wound and the absence of any larger bullet fragments. As is usual in most modern autopsies, the brain was removed from the skull, weighed, and preserved in a container for further study. The standard "Y" incision was made across the front of the body, and the internal organs were removed and weighed, with samples taken. Over the years the brain and tissue samples have mysteriously disappeared. Incredibly, the sampling of body tissues was incomplete and cursory. This was supposedly because the family desired only a minimal examination of the body.[9] Family wishes prevailed over a federal investigation. During the latter stages of the post mortem, skull pieces supposedly found in Dealey Plaza were brought to the autopsy room. The next day a young man found another skull fragment at the assassination site.[10]

After about three hours the autopsy was completed, and the late president's body was sewn closed. Dr. Humes concluded that one bullet entered the rear of the president's head, causing his death, and that another had entered his back and fallen out. When he learned of the nature of the neck wound the next day (a tracheotomy over a bullet hole), he changed his conclusions. The official autopsy report stated that one bullet had entered the back and emerged from the front of the neck, and that Kennedy died from a gunshot wound to the brain — that bullet also entering from the rear.

After the post mortem was completed, the autopsy team left the room. The body was now to be prepared for burial. This normally involved transporting it to a funeral home. However, Mrs. Kennedy expressed her wish to have the preparations done at the hospital by the navy. Bethesda balked at this, and it was eventually arranged to call a private funeral home to embalm, cosmetize and clothe the body at the hospital. The distinguished Gawler's Funeral Home in Washington was chosen for the task, the same firm that had handled FDR's arrangements eighteen years earlier.

Jacqueline and Robert Kennedy, along with family and friends, had been staying in a guest suite at the hospital during the autopsy. They were informed that the Dallas casket was damaged and a new one was needed. Mrs. Kennedy chose three of JFK's aides to select a casket at Gawler's and return with the undertakers. Another aide was sent to the White House to bring back a selection of Kennedy's clothes with which to dress the body. At the funeral home, an expensive mahogany coffin with white rayon interior was chosen. The casket and undertakers arrived at Bethesda at about 1 A.M.

Mrs. Kennedy's wedding ring was removed from JFK's finger and returned to her. Then, in front of an audience of about thirty-five men, the undertaker went to work. The embalming fluid was pumped into the arteries. Makeup was applied to the hands and face. The head wound was repaired, with matching locks of hair attached where hair had been torn away. The body was dressed in a blue suit, blue tie, white shirt and black shoes. The undertakers then lifted the body into the new coffin.

John F. Kennedy looked peacefully asleep. A rosary was laced through his clasped hands in the Roman Catholic tradition, and the lid was snapped shut. The coffin was wheeled out of the autopsy room and an American flag placed over it. Those in the guest suite were notified that all was now ready. Mrs. Kennedy, her brother-in-law and the others were escorted to the dock outside the morgue area. The coffin was placed in a navy ambulance. It was 4 A.M. as the vehicle started a nine-mile drive to the White House, with the others following behind in six limousines. As they moved down the streets, the red light of the ambulance blinking, many people stood along the route, watching mournfully. Some saluted or doffed their hats. Many wept. Hundreds of vehicles fell in line behind the official cars and followed the fallen leader to the Executive Mansion. Across the street in Lafayette Park, and around the White House, hundreds of people stood in silence.

The front portico of the mansion was already draped in black crape when the ambulance arrived. The casket was removed and carried into the East Room by a detachment of Marines. It was placed on a black velvet–draped catafalque, and a tall candle at each corner of the casket was lit. A five-man military honor guard, one from each branch of the armed services, began a three-day watch over the flag-draped coffin, and then a priest gave a brief blessing.

The widow had expressed a desire to have the lying in state and funeral resemble Abraham Lincoln's, and the East Room had been decorated somewhat similarly to its appearance then. The chandeliers and curtains were draped in black. The catafalque was a replica of the one on which Lincoln's coffin had rested.

Robert Kennedy, from the time he learned of his brother's death early that afternoon, took charge of the funeral plans. It was he who helped the widow make the major decisions. He had his brother-in-law, Sargent Shriver, take charge of the details. Operating out of a White House office, young Peace Corps director Shriver was constantly in conference or on the telephone, delegating tasks and planning the decorations, invitations, funeral masses, burial site and myriad other details connected with a huge state funeral. He had already decided that the burial would take place on Monday.[11]

Now Robert Kennedy, before retiring for some rest, had to make the decision about an open casket. Even though the body was prepared for public viewing, no decision about it was yet made. Mrs. Kennedy did not want an open casket but left the final decision to her brother-in-law. He had the lid of the coffin opened, looked upon his brother's features and had a few others from the Bethesda party do the same. He then solicited their opinions. As sometimes happens, the application of the undertaker's craft had left JFK's face looking waxen and unnatural, lacking resemblance to the living person. And it was pointed out that FDR's casket had been closed. So Robert Kennedy agreed with his sister-in-law; the coffin would remain closed to the public. Reports that the casket was closed because the president's face was disfigured were untrue.[12]

Saturday, November 23, was a cold, rainy day in Washington, D.C. It fit the mood of the country perfectly. The military honor guard in the White House East Room continued its silent watch at the bier, interrupted only by a change of shifts each half hour. Priests had conducted a prayer vigil at the casket throughout the night. In Dallas, accused assassin Lee Harvey Oswald had been repeatedly questioned about the shooting of the president and Officer Tippit, but consistently denied he had shot anyone or had anything to do with the murders of Kennedy and Tippit.

A private requiem mass was held in the East Room at 10 A.M. for relatives and close friends, with several eminent men attending as personal friends. Mrs. Kennedy and her two children, Caroline and John Jr. attended. Absent from the mass were the late president's parents, who chose to remain in seclusion at their Massachusetts home, and his brother Edward, who had flown there to be with them. He and his mother would attend Monday's funeral, but his father was too ill to travel. JFK was the only president or former president to die before both his parents.

Shortly after the mass ended, government officials began arriving at the White House to pay their respects in the East Room. President Johnson and Congressional leaders were the first to approach the casket, followed by the cabinet. Former presidents Truman and Eisenhower went through, but Herbert Hoover was ill in New York City and could not attend any of the ceremonies. His office issued a statement expressing his grief, and he was represented at the funeral by his two sons.

A basic invitation schedule was followed. The executive branch visited in the early afternoon, the Supreme Court followed, then governors and congressmen. Foreign diplomats went through in the early evening, and finally the press and White House servants.

Throughout the day the White House was surrounded by milling crowds of people drawn there to pay their respects by silently watching the mansion. Most of the nation remained near a television set throughout the day, watching scenes of the White House, reports of reaction to the death, the new president's activities, and repetitions of the stories they now knew all too well.

The grief and sadness continued abroad on Saturday. The extent of the worldwide mourning for an American was unprecedented. To cite just one example, the bell of Westminster Abbey in London tolled every minute for one hour in a tribute usually reserved for British royalty. Invitations to Monday's funeral went out to foreign leaders, and the White House was deluged with acceptances.

President John F. Kennedy's body lies in state in the White House East Room. At the right, a group of reporters and photographers record the scene. To the left, two Roman Catholic priests maintain a prayer vigil at the bier. (John F. Kennedy Presidential Library; Robert Knudsen/White House)

Following the decision to hold the burial on Monday, November 25, President Johnson declared that day a national day of mourning for President Kennedy, closing all federal offices and ordering flags flown at half staff for thirty days. All foreign embassies were officially notified of Kennedy's death and Johnson's assumption of the presidency. The new chief executive spent Saturday meeting with congressional leaders, the cabinet and former president Eisenhower. President Johnson was working out of his vice presidential office in the Executive Office Building across from the White House. He was careful to give the Kennedy family and staff several days to vacate the executive mansion.

Also on Saturday, most of the major funeral decisions were finalized. Mrs. Kennedy chose St. Matthew's Cathedral in Washington for Monday's funeral mass, made decisions concerning bands, music and the funeral procession, and finally decided on a burial site.

It was assumed that JFK would be buried in Massachusetts, either in the family plot in Brookline or on the Boston Common. In fact, a destroyer was on stand-by in case a decision was made to transport the body to Boston by sea. But many people had a strong preference that the late president be buried in Arlington National Cemetery, resting place of American heroes. His widow visited Arlington Saturday afternoon and decided on a site on a slope just below the Custis-Lee mansion overlooking the city of Washington. The beautiful view of the capital city was one about which Kennedy had personally expressed his enjoyment. He would be the second president interred at Arlington, joining William Howard Taft, who rested three hundred yards east of the newly chosen site. There was only one problem with Jacqueline Kennedy's choice. The land was actually part of the Custis-Lee mansion controlled by the Department of the Interior, and not within the borders of the cemetery. Some quick paper work and cutting of red tape had to be performed to transfer the site to the adjacent Arlington National Cemetery. The choice of the burial place was made public later on Saturday.[13]

Sunday dawned clear and cold. In the late morning another mass was celebrated in the East Room for the family and friends, with Jacqueline and Robert Kennedy once again in attendance. Shortly after noon the two of them returned to the room to view the body for the last time. The military guard was marched away and the coffin opened by an aide. The widow and brother of the slain president knelt at the casket. Jackie placed a pair of gold cufflinks and a carving of the presidential seal in the coffin. She then placed three farewell letters inside, one from herself and one from each of her children. Robert left a tie pin and silver rosary. Mrs. Kennedy snipped off a lock of her husband's hair, then they left.[14]

While these events took place in the White House, the country was jolted by another violent shock. In Dallas, shortly after 11 A.M. local time, accused assassin Lee Harvey Oswald was being transferred from Dallas city jail to Dallas county jail in accordance with established procedures. As he was being escorted through the city jail basement to a waiting car for the transfer, he was shot in the abdomen at close range by Jack Ruby, a Dallas nightclub owner. The shooting was broadcast live on national television. Oswald died two hours later at Parkland Memorial Hospital, about the same time John F. Kennedy was being eulogized in the Capitol building.

Kennedy's body left the White House for the Capitol in the early afternoon. The flag-draped coffin was carried outside and placed on a caisson, the same one used to carry President Roosevelt's coffin eighteen years earlier. Six gray horses, three with riders, pulled the carriage away from the north portico of the mansion. The procession moved down Pennsylvania Avenue to the Capitol, led by military troops and followed by the caisson and then the presidential flag and traditional riderless horse, boots reversed in the stirrups. Mrs. Kennedy, her children, and President Johnson followed behind in several limousines that also carried other family members. The sound of muffled drums boomed out a somber marching cadence as the solemn parade moved past large silent crowds in the cold air. After it passed them, thousands of people joined in at the end of the official procession.

Once inside the Capitol Rotunda, the coffin was placed by the military body bearers on the catafalque that had borne the body of Lincoln and other fallen presidents in that hall. The crowd gathered inside consisted mostly of government officials and family, including President and Mrs. Johnson. Eulogies were read by Senator Michael Mansfield, Chief Justice Earl Warren, and House Speaker John McCormack. Wreaths were placed, then Mrs. Kennedy and her six-year-old daughter Caroline knelt at the coffin. It was yet another emotional scene that would remain etched in the minds of the millions who watched both on television and in person. The official crowd filed out and the public began to move in, filing through the Rotunda past the casket. In the next eighteen hours more than a quarter of a million people would pass through to pay their respects.

In the evening family members visited the bier in the Capitol, including the widow, Robert and Edward Kennedy, and their mother Rose, who had arrived from Massachusetts that afternoon. About fifty family members and two hundred friends, as well as many foreign leaders, arrived for Monday's funeral.

At Arlington National Cemetery the grave was dug as hundreds watched. At nearby Fort Meyer, headquarters for state funeral operations, military rehearsals for the next day's funeral were taking place. The armed forces were already somewhat prepared for a state funeral, having recently rehearsed for one. This was because former president Hoover was seriously ill, and the ceremonial troops had to be ready in case of his death.[15]

Late Monday morning, the day of the funeral, the casket was carried out of the Capitol and once again placed on the caisson by the body bearers while a military band played solemn hymns. The funeral procession moved forward toward the White House through the cold, crisp air. Soldiers again led the caisson, with the riderless horse right behind, fitfully tugging at his reins as if to express his outrage at the death of the commander in chief. The Kennedy entourage followed behind in automobiles. Muffled drums pounded out the beat. The marching bands continued to play various hymns as the parade moved, including John Kennedy's favorite, "Onward, Christian Soldiers." Silent crowds, estimated at one million, lined the streets of Washington.

The procession halted in front of the White House where Mrs. Kennedy and other family members left their cars to walk the remainder of the way to the funeral mass at St. Matthew's Cathedral. Here at the White House President and Mrs. Johnson, the cabinet, the Supreme Court, family, friends, and foreign dignitaries joined the procession on foot. The foreigners walked in one large group, with several bodyguards, as threats had been received against some of them.[16] More than ninety countries had sent representatives. Some of the more notable marchers were Prime Minister Alec Douglas-Home and

Prince Philip of the United Kingdom, President Charles de Gaulle of France, Emperor Haile Selassie of Ethiopia, first deputy premier of the USSR Anastas Mikoyan, Soviet ambassador Anatole Dobrynin, United Nations Secretary General U Thant, and the royalty of various European nations.

The Black Watch bagpipers of Scotland joined the somber parade and wailed their music as they marched in kilted uniforms. The procession reached the church shortly after noon, and the mourners filed inside to join others already there. A Roman Catholic funeral mass was celebrated by Richard Cardinal Cushing, a Kennedy family friend.

Memorial services were not confined to the nation's capital that day. Virtually every house of worship in America held a memorial service for the late president. And the nation's streets and highways were all but deserted during the televised funeral mass and burial ceremony. The entire United States of America was close to being shut down. At noon, a minute of silence was observed throughout the country. Most transportation and communications halted, bells tolled, and people stopped to pay tribute. Twenty-one-gun artillery salutes were fired on every U.S. military base in the world.

After the mass in St. Matthew's ended, the coffin was once again carried out by the eight servicemen and lashed to the gun carriage. Mrs. Kennedy stood outside the church, with daughter Caroline and son John Jr. at her side. The band played "Hail to the Chief" for the last time, and the servicemen saluted. In the most poignant scene of these mournful days, little John F. Kennedy, Jr., raised his hand and also saluted his father goodbye. This very day was his third birthday.

The family, clergy and other churchgoers filed into limousines, and the procession for the cemetery got underway. The muffled drums once again provided a doleful beat as the cortege proceeded along the three-mile route, past the White House and Lincoln Memorial, then across the Potomac River and into the cemetery. The procession came to a halt at the bottom of the slope where the empty grave awaited, surrounded by a platoon of men from each of the armed services, Air Force bagpipers, and Irish cadets. Nearby lay a mass of flowers sent by the bereaved from throughout the world.

The mourners left their cars and made their way up the hill to surround the grave site. There stood Mrs. Kennedy, clad in black and veiled. The Kennedy men wore formal tails, while many of the foreigners sported colorful uniforms. Near them were President and Mrs. Johnson, former presidents Truman and Eisenhower, future president Richard M. Nixon, future presidential candidates Barry Goldwater and Hubert H. Humphrey, former candidate Adlai Stevenson, and dozens of others.

After the national anthem was played, the coffin was taken from the caisson and carried up the slope by the military casket team. It was escorted by an honor guard of Green Beret soldiers and followed by the honorary pallbearers, made up of the joint chiefs of staff and three presidential military aides. The coffin was placed over the grave, then fifty Air Force jets roared overhead in tribute, followed by the president's airplane, Air Force One, which dipped its wing in salute.

At the head of the grave Cardinal Cushing recited his incantations, then a twenty-one-gun artillery salute sounded. This was followed by three rifle volleys and the playing of "Taps," with an appropriate missed note. The Marine Band played a slow, funereal version of "Anchors Aweigh," a navy hymn for navy veteran Kennedy. Then the flag draping the coffin was folded and presented to Jacqueline Kennedy.

Throughout the ordeal of those four days in November, the widow had maintained her public composure, and at this most moving point of the funeral service for any veteran's widow, she remained strong and steadfast. Now she stepped forward and lit a torch set in the ground, an eternal flame, which was her idea of a lasting tribute to her husband.

Burial ceremony of President Kennedy at Arlington National Cemetery. The veiled widow Jacqueline Kennedy stands to the right. Dozens of foreign dignitaries look on, dominated by the figure of French president Charles de Gaulle in the light-colored uniform. (John F. Kennedy Presidential Library; Abbie Rowe/White House)

The ceremonies now concluded, Mrs. Kennedy and the two Kennedy brothers and their mother got into their limousines and were driven away, as were all the other mourners. Fifteen minutes later, at 3:31 P.M., the coffin was lowered into the grave. Four Green Berets were posted as a guard of honor around it. The Green Berets would later add a black mourning band to their berets as a permanent tribute to President Kennedy.

The public was allowed to circle past the grave for a short time. A few hours later it was filled in, a white picket fence erected around it, and flowers blanketed over the five-square-yard plot.

On December 4, 1963, Kennedy's two deceased infant children were removed from their New England graves and buried that night beside their father in a brief private religious ceremony attended by Mrs. Kennedy.[17]

President Kennedy's funeral was the first presidential funeral to be broadcast on television. Through this medium millions of people throughout the nation shared the tragic news and grief through the visual images presented in their own homes, much of it televised live as it happened. America was one, unified in its profound sadness through television. From Friday afternoon through Monday evening the three television networks carried only news of the assassination, funeral and succession to the presidency, as well as related features. At great expense to the networks, no commercials were shown. Many foreign countries also carried extensive television coverage, and even the USSR televised the funeral on Monday.

An interesting sidelight to the funeral was the reconciliation of former presidents Truman and Eisenhower.[18] They were bitter political foes and had not been on speaking terms for years, but they ended their feud during the weekend of mourning for their successor. Also, both former chief executives were said to be appalled at the "circus atmosphere" of the Kennedy funeral. Eisenhower thought the continuous coverage of the events that weekend was too upsetting to the American people and should only have been reported in brief hourly summaries by radio and television.[19]

Two days after the funeral, President Johnson addressed Congress and assured the nation and the world of America's resolve to pick up the pieces and continue forward. On December 6, Jacqueline Kennedy moved out of the White House. The next month she received a bill from undertaker Vernon Oneal of Dallas for the Dallas casket and services rendered; the family eventually paid him $3,495.[20]

Within a short time after his death, the world began to memorialize John F. Kennedy by naming countless streets, parks and buildings in his honor. Some of the more notable tributes paid to him were the naming of the Kennedy Center for the Performing Arts in Washington, D.C., the renaming of New York's Idlewild International Airport to John F. Kennedy International Airport, and the renaming of Cape Canaveral Space Center in Florida to John F. Kennedy Space Center. His likeness was put on the U.S. fifty cent piece in 1964. Dallas did not see fit to honor JFK in any such way. The city tried to forget the assassination had ever occurred. Eventually, in 1970, private contributions built a Kennedy Memorial structure near the assassination site, a walled fifty-by-fifty-foot enclosure with an empty pedestal at its center. But Dealey Plaza itself remains the real Kennedy Memorial in Dallas, where the city and state have placed historical markers and preserved the buildings, and which has been declared a National Historic Landmark by the federal government. The sixth floor of the Texas School Book Depository houses a Kennedy assassination museum.

Most of the artifacts and evidence connected to the assassination are in the possession of the U.S. National Archives and Records Administration, including the alleged murder weapon rifle, bullet fragments, the president's clothes, autopsy photographs and x-rays, the Zapruder camera and original film, and the windshield of the car in which the president was riding. The collection includes five million documents, photographs and recordings. The car in which president Kennedy was riding when he was shot was cleaned, remanufactured and put back into service at the White House for a few years. It is now at the Henry Ford Museum in Dearborn, Michigan, and bears little resemblance to its appearance on November 22, 1963.

Lee Harvey Oswald's clothes are in the possession of Dallas County, Texas. The Dallas casket was sunk 131 miles off the Delaware coast by the Air Force in 1966 at the request of the Kennedy family. It was dropped from a plane into 9,000 feet of water.[21] The Air Force One airplane that returned Kennedy's body to Washington and on which President Johnson took the oath of office was retired as the presidential aircraft in 1972 and is now housed at the U.S. Air Force Museum at Wright-Patterson Air Force Base in Ohio.

Americans seemed to blame Texas and Dallas for Kennedy's death. The city's reputation was devastated by the events that had happened there. During the weekend of the assassination the city received scores of vituperative and threatening messages. The mayor's life was threatened, and so was the life of U.S. senator John Tower of Texas. The *Dallas Morning News* also received threats. Subscribers dropped the paper, and many advertisers cancelled contracts due to the paper's anti–Kennedy policy. The conduct of Dallas officials that weekend was severely criticized and the state of Texas berated.[22] Any Texan who drove his car out of state in the following months was liable to become a target of derision and scorn as soon as his Lone Star license plate was spotted.

In 1967 President Kennedy's body was moved to a permanent grave twenty feet below the original site. During the night of March 14, without public announcement, the coffins of Kennedy and his two children were lifted by crane to the new location, a plaza of marble and granite ringed by low marble walls, with the president's grave in the center. The next morning members of the Kennedy family, President Johnson and an army band attended a short, private, religious ceremony to dedicate the new gravesite.[23]

The president's widow, Jacqueline Lee Bouvier Kennedy Onassis, died on May 19, 1994, of lymphatic cancer at the age of sixty-four. She lived in New York City and had remarried in 1968 to Greek tycoon Aristotle Onassis; she was widowed a second time in 1975. She then took a job as a book editor. Four days after her death, she was buried next to President Kennedy in Arlington National Cemetery. Under the law, Mrs. Kennedy had received Secret Service protection for life as the widow of a president, but a new law was passed after President Kennedy's death that extended protection to a former president's children up to age sixteen, and that applied to her two children. She also received a presidential widow's pension.

John F. Kennedy was worth approximately ten million dollars at the time of his death. His wife inherited all his personal property plus $25,000. The remainder was equally divided into two trust funds, one for the widow and one for the two children.[24]

No one was ever brought to trial for the murder of John F. Kennedy, save a group of men tried in 1969 by the New Orleans district attorney in a highly controversial and dubious proceeding, after which all defendants were quickly acquitted. Dozens of different theories have been advanced over the years in an effort to identify the killer or killers of the president. They range from a lone gunman to elaborate international conspiracies. Some theories claim fabrication of evidence or tampering with Kennedy's body prior to autopsy. The position of the victim's wounds seems to have changed between Dealey Plaza, the hospital and the post mortem. Suspects include, but are not limited to, Lee Harvey Oswald, the Central Intelligence Agency, organized crime, rightists, Fidel Castro, the Secret Service, Lyndon B. Johnson, or some combination of these. The U.S. government conducted two official investigations into the assassination.

One week after the murder, President Johnson appointed a group of seven men to investigate it. Officially called the President's Commission on the Assassination of President Kennedy, its chairman was Chief Justice Earl Warren and included six other prominent government officials, including future president and then representative Gerald R. Ford.

The Warren Commission's report was released in September 1964. It concluded that President Kennedy was killed by Lee Harvey Oswald firing from the sixth floor of the Texas School Book Depository. He fired three shots, the first striking Kennedy in the back of the neck and passing through to strike Governor Connally. A second shot missed the motorcade and a third shattered the right side of Kennedy's skull. Oswald acted alone and was not part of any conspiracy. He and his killer Jack Ruby did not know each other, nor was Ruby a hired killer sent to silence Oswald.[25]

The Warren Report was bombarded with criticism almost from the start. The critics contended that the Commission's work was slipshod, inept, hurried for political reasons and had preconceived conclusions. Some claimed the Commission was concealing facts because the crime involved government officials, and they feared the public reaction to this fact. It is a fact that the Commission failed to interview several witnesses. It failed to examine the autopsy photographs and x-rays, yet its conclusions relied heavily on the autopsy results. There were twenty-five people facing the grassy knoll in Dealey Plaza who were not called before the Warren Commission. Some of them saw smoke rising from the knoll, and others had heard shots fired from its direction. Some noticed people standing there immediately before the shots were fired. Photographs supposedly showed human-like images in the area.

In 1976 the House of Representatives formed the House Select Committee on Assassinations. Its purpose was to investigate the political assassinations and attempts of the 1960s and 1970s, but its main work concerned the JFK murder. In 1979 its report was released. The committee dealt with topics brought up by Warren Report critics and attempted to cover all the omissions and inconsistencies noticeable in that report. The autopsy x-rays and photographs were studied, and witnesses not called before the Warren Commission were interviewed. A suggestion that President Kennedy's body be exhumed and reexamined was rejected as unnecessary. With the help of a previously undiscovered tape recording of Dallas police radio transmissions on November 22, 1963, the committee determined that four shots were fired in Dealey Plaza, and that the fourth shot came from the area of the grassy knoll, but missed. The conclusions of the House Select

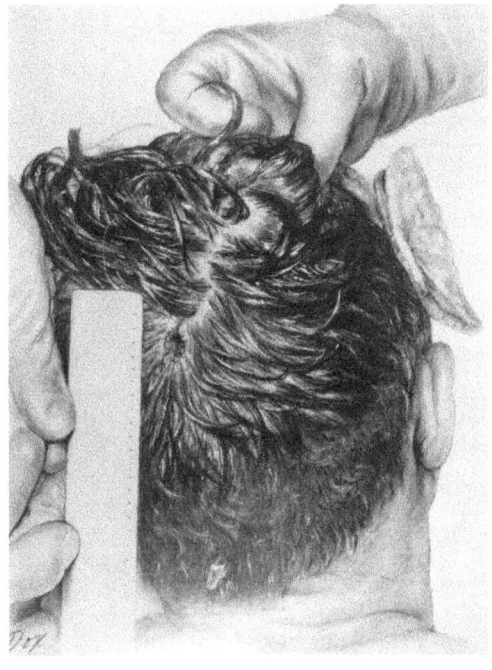

An exact copy of one of the JFK autopsy photographs, drawn by an artist for the House Assassinations Committee in 1978. (National Archives)

Committee's investigation: four shots were fired at Kennedy; Oswald shot at and killed him, but one shot came from the grassy knoll; it probably was a conspiracy, though who was behind the conspiracy could not be determined.[26]

The committee was criticized from all sides as having been a waste of time and money that solved nothing. It had not reached any concrete conclusions and did not really satisfy any of the doubts surrounding the crime. It perhaps was inherently deficient from the start, coming more than fifteen years after the event. And the authenticity of the Dealey Plaza police tape recording was later disputed.

In 1992, the Assassination Records Review Board was created by law to release documents associated with the crime to the public by the year 2017, but even that law makes exceptions for certain materials. Perhaps new evidence will one day resolve the controversy surrounding the murder of the thirty-fifth president of the United States. Or, more likely, the case will continue to be one of the greatest unresolved mysteries in the annals of American history.

Lee Harvey Oswald

Lee Harvey Oswald was an ex–Marine, self-styled Marxist and defector to the USSR for two years. He had at different times professed a desire to kill President Eisenhower and Vice President Johnson. In Dallas on April 10, 1963, he attempted to kill right wing advocate General Edwin A. Walker, but his rifle shot missed.

Oswald will always be called the alleged assassin of President Kennedy because he died before he was tried for the crime. After his capture in a Dallas movie theater on the day of the assassination he was taken to the city jail where he was charged with the murders of Kennedy and police officer J.D. Tippit. He remained in custody at the jail until the following Sunday morning, November 24, when he was scheduled to be transferred to the Dallas County Jail (a normal procedure in such cases).

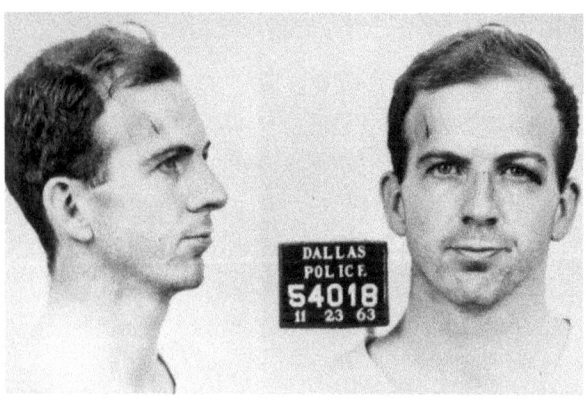

Dallas police mug shot of Lee Harvey Oswald. (**National Archives**)

As Oswald was led through the city jail basement to a waiting car for the transfer, he was shot once in the abdomen by Jack Ruby, a local nightclub owner.

Rushed to a heavily guarded Parkland Memorial Hospital, Oswald was wheeled into an emergency room just ten feet from where President Kennedy had died. He was moved to surgery and died about two hours after being shot. The bullet had caused massive internal bleeding and organ injuries, and had cut through a major artery.

Oswald's family was allowed to view the body before it was autopsied. The post mortem was conducted at Parkland Hospital by Dr. Earl Rose. The body was then transported to Miller Funeral Home in Fort Worth where it was embalmed and prepared for burial. During the night Federal Bureau of Investigation agents took hand prints and photographs of the body. Oswald's mother expressed a desire to have her son interred at Arlington National Cemetery because she believed he was a government agent and entitled to a hero's burial.[27] Her wish was not seriously considered. After much difficulty, a cemetery was found that would sell a plot for the burial.

On November 25, the day of the funerals of President Kennedy in Washington and police officer Tippit in Dallas, Oswald was buried. His mother, brother, widow and two children were driven to Rose Hill Cemetery in Fort Worth by the Secret Service. The cemetery and grave were protected by a hundred policemen; and about fifty reporters were in attendance. A number of people stood behind a fence outside the cemetery some distance away. The body had arrived earlier and had been put in the cemetery chapel. Fort Worth police chief Cato Hightower entered the chapel and emerged three minutes later, saying, "It is Oswald. He is in the casket. I opened the casket."[28]

Seven reporters carried the wooden casket, covered with gray moleskin, to the freshly dug grave a few minutes before the family arrived. At the last moment a minister was found to conduct a brief service at the graveside. Reporters were kept several feet away from the family. The coffin was opened as the brother, mother and widow each kissed the body. Oswald's widow put two rings on his fingers. The casket was closed, then lowered into in an asphalt-concrete vault reinforced with steel bars, and covered as the family left the cemetery.

Eighteen years later Oswald's widow had his body exhumed in order to check a writer's speculations that the body was that of a Soviet spy. On October 4, 1981, the body and coffin were removed to a Dallas medical center. In a four-hour examination of the badly decomposed, skeletonized body in its crumbling coffin, the remains were positively identified as those of Lee Harvey Oswald. Videotapes and photographs of the procedure were taken for the record for the former Mrs. Oswald, but were kept instead by the men who videotaped it. The remains were placed in a new steel casket and promptly returned to the cemetery grave.[29]

Jack Ruby

Jack Ruby (given name Jacob Rubinstein) was convicted in March 1964 of the murder of Lee Harvey Oswald and sentenced to die. He attempted suicide three times. In October 1966 his conviction was reversed on a legal point. But just as Oswald was never convicted of President Kennedy's murder, Ruby was never legally convicted of Oswald's murder because he died before he could be retried. He died in Parkland Memorial Hospital in Dallas, as had Kennedy and Oswald, on January 3, 1967, at the age of fifty-five. He had been undergoing treatment for cancer but died of a blood clot in the lungs. Dr. Earl Rose performed an autopsy at the hospital. Ruby's body was flown to Chicago for burial. On January 6, brief Jewish ceremonies were held at a funeral home and at Westlawn Cemetery in the city. Because he was an army veteran, Ruby's coffin was covered with the American flag. About twenty relatives stood near the grave as burial services were conducted.[30]

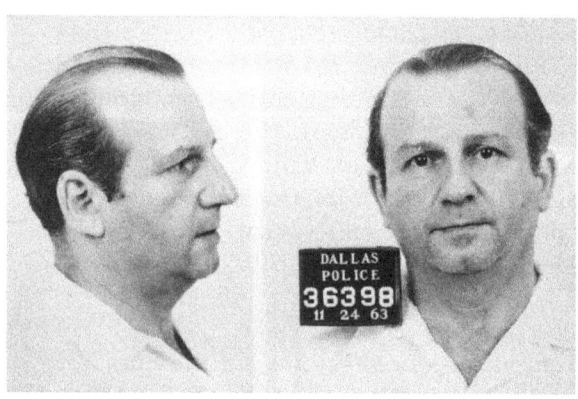

Dallas police mug shot of Jack Ruby. (National Archives)

Appendix: Laws and Regulations

The Unites States Code of the federal government enumerates the federal laws of the United States of America. Title 18, Part I, Chapter 84, Section 1751 deals with the assault, kidnapping and murder of the president.

Section 1751. Presidential and Presidential staff assassination, kidnapping, and assault; penalties
(a) Whoever kills (1) any individual who is the president of the United States, the president-elect, the vice president, or, if there is no vice president, the officer next in the order of succession to the office of the president of the United States, the vice president–elect, or any person who is acting as president under the Constitution and laws of the United States, or (2) any person appointed under section 105(a)(2)(A) of title 3 employed in the executive office of the president or appointed under section 106(a)(1)(A) of title 3 employed in the office of the vice president, shall be punished as provided by sections 1111 and 1112 of this title.
(b) Whoever kidnaps any individual designated in subsection (a) of this section shall be punished (1) by imprisonment for any term of years or for life, or (2) by death or imprisonment for any term of years or for life, if death results to such individual.
(c) Whoever attempts to kill or kidnap any individual designated in subsection (a) of this section shall be punished by imprisonment for any term of years or for life.
(d) If two or more persons conspire to kill or kidnap any individual designated in subsection (a) of this section and one or more of such persons do any act to effect the object of the conspiracy, each shall be punished (1) by imprisonment for any term of years or for life, or (2) by death or imprisonment for any term of years or for life, if death results to such individual.
(e) Whoever assaults any person designated in subsection (a)(1) shall be fined under this title, or imprisoned not more than ten years, or both. Whoever assaults any person designated in subsection (a)(2) shall be fined under this title, or imprisoned not more than one year, or both; and if the assault involved

the use of a dangerous weapon, or personal injury results, shall be fined under this title, or imprisoned not more than ten years, or both.

(f) The terms "president-elect" and "vice president–elect" as used in this section shall mean such persons as are the apparent successful candidates for the offices of president and vice president, respectively, as ascertained from the results of the general elections held to determine the electors of president and vice president in accordance with title 3, United States Code, sections 1 and 2.

(g) The attorney general of the United States, in his discretion is authorized to pay an amount not to exceed $100,000 for information and services concerning a violation of subsection (a)(1). Any officer or employee of the United States or of any State or local government who furnishes information or renders service in the performance of his official duties shall not be eligible for payment under this subsection.

(h) If Federal investigative or prosecutive jurisdiction is asserted for a violation of this section, such assertion shall suspend the exercise of jurisdiction by a State or local authority, under any applicable State or local law, until Federal action is terminated.

(i) Violations of this section shall be investigated by the Federal Bureau of Investigation. Assistance may be requested from any Federal, State, or local agency, including the Army, Navy, and Air Force, any statute, rule, or regulation to the contrary notwithstanding.

(j) In a prosecution for an offense under this section the government need not prove that the defendant knew that the victim of the offense was an official protected by this section.

(k) There is extraterritorial jurisdiction over the conduct prohibited by this section.

Title 18, Part I, Chapter 41, Section 871 of the United States Code deals with threats against the president.

Section 871. Threats against president and successors to the presidency

1.
   (a) Whoever knowingly and willfully deposits for conveyance in the mail or for a delivery from any post office or by any letter carrier any letter, paper, writing, print, missive, or document containing any threat to take the life of, to kidnap, or to inflict bodily harm upon the president of the United States, the president-elect, the vice president or other officer next in the order of succession to the office of president of the United States, or the vice president–elect, or knowingly and willfully otherwise makes any such threat against the president, president-elect, vice president or other officer next in the order of succession to the office of president, or vice president–elect, shall be fined under this title or imprisoned not more than five years, or both.

   (b) The terms "president-elect" and "vice president–elect" as used in this section shall mean such persons as are the apparent successful candidates for the offices of president and vice president, respectively, as ascertained from the results of the general elections held to determine the electors of president and vice president in accordance with title 3, United States Code, sections 1 and 2. The phrase "other officer next in the order of succession to the office of president" as used in this section shall mean the person next in the order of succession to act as president in accordance with title 3, United States Code, sections 19 and 20.

Title 18, Part II, Chapter 203, Section 3056 of the United States Code enumerates the role of the Secret Service.

Section 3056. Powers, authorities, and duties of United States Secret Service
(a) Under the direction of the Secretary of Homeland Security, the United States Secret Service is authorized to protect the following persons:
   (1) The president, the vice president (or other officer next in the order of succession to the office of president), the president-elect, and the vice president–elect.
   (2) The immediate families of those individuals listed in paragraph (1).
   (3) Former presidents and their spouses for their lifetimes, except that protection of a spouse shall terminate in the event of remarriage unless the former president did not serve as president prior to January 1, 1997, in which case, former presidents and their spouses for a period of not more than ten years from the date a former president leaves office, except that —
      (A) protection of a spouse shall terminate in the event of remarriage or the divorce from, or death of a former president;
      and
      (B) should the death of a president occur while in office or within one year after leaving office, the spouse shall receive protection for one year from the time of such death:
      Provided, that the secretary of Homeland Security shall have the authority to direct the Secret Service to provide temporary protection for any of these individuals at any time if the secretary of Homeland Security or designee determines that information or conditions warrant such protection.
   (4) Children of a former president who are under 16 years of age for a period not to exceed ten years or upon the child becoming 16 years of age, whichever comes first.
   (5) Visiting heads of foreign states or foreign governments.
   (6) Other distinguished foreign visitors to the United States and official representatives of the United States performing special missions abroad when the president directs that such protection be provided.
   (7) Major presidential and vice presidential candidates and, within 120 days of the general presidential election, the spouses of such candidates. As used in this paragraph, the term "major presidential and vice presidential candidates" means those individuals identified as such by the secretary of Homeland Security after consultation with an advisory committee consisting of the speaker of the House of Representatives, the minority leader of the House of Representatives, the majority and minority leaders of the Senate, and one additional member selected by the other members of the committee.
   The protection authorized in paragraphs (2) through (7) may be declined.

(b) Under the direction of the secretary of Homeland Security, the Secret Service is authorized to detect and arrest any person who violates—
  (1) section 508, 509, 510, 871, or 879 of this title or, with respect to the Federal Deposit Insurance Corporation, Federal land banks, and Federal land bank associations, section 213, 216,(!1) 433, 493, 657, 709, 1006, 1007, 1011, 1013, 1014, 1907, or 1909 of this title;
  (2) any of the laws of the United States relating to coins, obligations, and securities of the United States and of foreign governments; or
  (3) any of the laws of the United States relating to electronic fund transfer frauds, access device frauds, false identification documents or devices, and any fraud or other criminal or unlawful activity in or against any federally insured financial institution; except that the authority conferred by this paragraph shall be exercised subject to the agreement of the attorney general and the secretary of Homeland Security and shall not affect the authority of any other Federal law enforcement agency with respect to those laws.
(c)(1) Under the direction of the secretary of Homeland Security, officers and agents of the Secret Service are authorized to—
  (A) execute warrants issued under the laws of the United States;
  (B) carry firearms;
  (C) make arrests without warrant for any offense against the United States committed in their presence, or for any felony cognizable under the laws of the United States if they have reasonable grounds to believe that the person to be arrested has committed or is committing such felony;
  (D) offer and pay rewards for services and information leading to the apprehension of persons involved in the violation or potential violation of those provisions of law which the Secret Service is authorized to enforce;
  (E) pay expenses for unforeseen emergencies of a confidential nature under the direction of the secretary of Homeland Security and accounted for solely on the secretary's certificate; and
  (F) perform such other functions and duties as are authorized by law.
  (2) Funds expended from appropriations available to the Secret Service for the purchase of counterfeits and subsequently recovered shall be reimbursed to the appropriations available to the Secret Service at the time of the reimbursement.
(d) Whoever knowingly and willfully obstructs, resists, or interferes with a Federal law enforcement agent engaged in the performance of the protective functions authorized by this section or by section 1752 of this title shall be fined not more than $1,000 or imprisoned not more than one year, or both.
(e)(1) When directed by the president, the United States Secret Service is authorized to participate, under the direction of the secretary of Homeland Security, in the planning, coordination, and implementation of security operations at special events of national significance, as determined by the president.
  (2) At the end of each fiscal year, the president through such agency or office as the president may designate, shall report to the Congress—

(A) what events, if any, were designated special events of national significance for security purposes under paragraph (1); and

(B) the criteria and information used in making each designation.

(f) Under the direction of the secretary of Homeland Security, officers and agents of the Secret Service are authorized, at the request of any State or local law enforcement agency, or at the request of the National Center for Missing and Exploited Children, to provide forensic and investigative assistance in support of any investigation involving missing or exploited children.

State Funeral Policy

Presidents of the United States are entitled to a state funeral. Rules pertaining to such ceremonies are encoded in the regulations of the armed forces of the United States, and are as follows.

Section I: GENERAL

1. Persons entitled to State Funeral.
    a. The president of the United States.
    b. An ex-president of the United States.
    c. The president-elect of the United States.
    d. Any other person specifically designated by the president of the United States.
2. Eligibility for burial in national cemetery.
    a. Eligibility for a State Funeral does not in itself entitle the deceased to burial in Arlington National Cemetery or any other national cemetery. (Reference: Act of 14 May 1948 [62 Stat. 234; 24 U.S.C. 281]).
    b. Paragraph not used.
3. Responsibilities.
    a. The president notifies the Congress that he has directed that a State Funeral be conducted. The Congress, which has sole authority for use of the U.S. Capitol, makes the Rotunda available for the State Ceremony through its own procedures.
    b. The secretary of Defense is the designated representative of the president of the United States. The secretary of the Army is the designated representative of the secretary of Defense for the purpose of making all arrangements for State Funerals in Washington, D.C. This includes participation of all Armed Forces and coordination with the State Department for participation of all branches of the Government and the Diplomatic Corps.
    c. The commanding general, Military District of Washington, U.S. Army as the designated representative of the secretary of the Army, will make all ceremonial arrangements for State Funerals in Washington, D.C. and will be responsible for the planning and arranging of State Funerals throughout the continental United States.
    d. The Department of the Army (secretary of the General Staff) will —

(1) Upon the demise obtain the president's desires as to type of funeral to be offered.
(2) Furnish a liaison officer to Headquarters, Military District of Washington, U.S. Army, (MDW), to coordinate activities and participation of the Department of Defense.
(3) Designate an appropriate officer aide to the next of kin.
(4) In coordination with the other military services and governmental departments, determine the distinguished persons to attend all phases of the funeral, and forward the names to the adjutant general for preparation of announcements. An information copy will be forwarded to HQ, MDW.
(5) Designate a time and place for briefing of all military distinguished persons and inform HQ, MDW.
e. The Department of the Army (the adjutant general) will —
(1) Formulate the list of honorary pallbearers consonant with desires of the next of kin and notify persons selected.
(2) Issue announcements to distinguished persons, family, and friends to attend the funeral service and certain other phases of the funeral ceremony to include:
(a) Reply as to acceptance, if time will permit.
(b) Time and place of participation.
(c) Seating and parking permits as appropriate.
(3) Furnish field grade officer guides beyond the capability of HQ, MDW to provide.
f. Department of the Navy, Department of the Air Force, and the U.S. Coast Guard will furnish liaison officers to HQ, MDW to coordinate participation of the Marine Corps, Navy, Air Force, and Coast Guard.
g. Each agency, headquarters, or unit, which incurs costs incident to these funerals will pay the costs from available funds and forward data as to payments through their normal command funding channels.
4. Procedure.
a. Movement to repose.
(1) If the demise occurs in Washington, D.C., the remains will be moved to a selected place of repose (Room of Repose: Amphitheater, Arlington National Cemetery; local funeral home; Washington Cathedral or other site of repose; the White House) where it will be attended by a guard of honor composed of representatives of all the Armed Forces.
(2) If the demise occurs outside Washington, D.C., the remains will be met at the point of arrival in Washington, D.C., by a reception group and escorted to the place of repose.
b. Burial in Washington, D.C.
(1) Lying in state. Following approximately one day of repose, the remains will be moved to the Rotunda of the U.S. Capitol where the body will lie in state for a period of approximately 24 hours.
(2) Funeral service. Following the lying in state, the remains will be escorted by motor to the place of the funeral service. Following the

funeral service, the remains will be escorted to the Capitol to join the main funeral procession.
- (3) The main funeral procession. The procession will be conducted from the Capitol to Arlington National Cemetery if the funeral service or interment is to be conducted there.

c. Burial outside Washington, D.C.
- (1) The main funeral procession will commence from 15th Street and Constitution Avenue, NW, following the day of repose when interment is outside Washington, D.C.
- (2) The funeral service, if conducted in Washington, D.C., will follow the period of lying in state.
- (3) Following the funeral service, or following the lying in state period if no funeral service is conducted in (4) Washington, D.C., the remains will be escorted to the point of departure.

d. Lying in state.
- (1) The remains will normally lie in state in the Capitol Rotunda for approximately 24 hours, depending on the ceremonial requirements and desires of the president and the next of kin.
- (2) Public viewing of the remains lying in state in the Capitol Rotunda will be continued throughout the entire period of lying in state, to end two hours prior to the removal of the remains from the Capitol, unless the family of the deceased expressly state a desire to the contrary. If desired the family will be permitted a short period for private services.

Section II: DEMISE AND MOVEMENT TO WASHINGTON, D.C.

5. Demise outside continental United States.
   If demise occurs outside continental United States—
   a. The senior U.S. Armed Forces commander in the area of demise will—
   - (1) Immediately form a guard of honor to attend remains until departure for the United States.
   - (2) Coordinate arrangements for—
     - *(a)* Return of remains to the United States.
     - *(b)* Designation of a suitable escort to accompany remains to the United States.
     - *(c)* Appropriate local ceremonies.

   b. The appropriate Army commander will coordinate, utilizing the facilities of all Armed Forces as required, the reception and transportation of the remains to Washington, D.C., including appropriate escort.

6. Demise within continental United States.
   If demise occurs within the continental United States but outside the Washington, D.C. area appropriate Army commander will—
   a. Immediately form a guard of honor composed of representatives of all Armed Forces, if practicable, to attend the remains.
   b. Coordinate arrangements, utilizing the facilities of all Armed Forces as required, for transportation of the remains to Washington, D.C., including appropriate escort and local ceremonies.

7. Demise in Washington, D.C. area.
    If demise occurs in the Washington, D.C. area the CG, MDW will—
    a. Arrange for the remains to be moved to the place of repose with appropriate ceremony.
    b. Immediately form a guard of honor composed of representatives of all Armed Forces to attend the remains while lying in repose.
    c. Proceed as indicated in paragraph 11 through 13 (Burial Outside the Washington, D.C. area) or paragraphs 14 through 17 (Burial in the Washington, D.C. area).

Section III: DEMISE OUTSIDE WASHINGTON D.C. AREA, ARRIVAL OF REMAINS AND MOVEMENT TO THE PLACE OF REPOSE

8. Arrival.
    The CG, MDW will—
    a. Coordinate the arrangements for the reception of the remains to include an appropriate ceremony.
    b. Ascertain place and time of arrival of the remains by coordination with the secretary of the General Staff, Department of the Army, and arrange for the attendance of:
        (1) Special honor guard.
        (2) Family.
        (3) Honorary pallbearers.
        (4) Clergy.
        (5) Other official mourners.
        (6) Troops.
            (a) Selected body bearers composed of enlisted personnel from each of the Armed Forces.
            (b) National Color detail and personal flag bearer, as appropriate.
            (c) Joint honor cordon.
            (d) Security cordon.
            (e) Band.
            (f) Saluting battery.
            (g) Medical support.
9. Movement to place of repose.
    The CG, MDW will—
    a. Arrange for military escort for motorized funeral cortege from point of arrival of the remains to the place of repose to consist of the following:
        (1) Police escort.
        (2) Escort commander (CG, MDW).
        (3) Special honor guard.
        (4) Clergy.
        (5) Hearse.
        (6) Body bearers, National Color detail, and personal flag bearer, as appropriate.
        (7) Family.

Appendix: Laws and Regulations 221

      (8) Honorary pallbearers.
      (9) Other official mourners.
   b. Coordinate with the chief of Metropolitan and/or U.S. Park Police to determine route of cortege from point of arrival to the place of repose.
10. Arrival at place of repose.
   The CG, MDW will arrange for:
   a. Band.
   b. Joint honor cordon.
   c. Security cordon.
   d. Guard of honor.
   e. Medical support.
   f. Appropriate ceremony to include personnel in attendance at the point of arrival.

Section IV: BURIAL OUTSIDE WASHINGTON, D.C. AREA

11. Period of repose and lying in state at the Capitol.
   a. When demise occurs in the Washington, D.C. area, the remains will lie in repose for approximately 24 hours. Repose will begin at 1100 hours the day following the day of demise. When demise occurs outside the Washington area, repose will begin at the time of arrival in Washington, D.C. Repose will end at 1100 hours, the day following the beginning of repose.
   b. The remains will be removed from the place of repose and will lie in state in the Rotunda of the Capitol for a period of approximately 24 hours beginning at 1300 hours one day prior to the day of departure until 1300 hours on the day of departure. The period from 1030 to 1230 hours on the day of departure will be reserved for the family group. At 1300 hours, the remains will be removed from the Rotunda of the Capitol, unless religious faith of the deceased and time of funeral service dictate another time.
12. Departure of remains from place of repose and movement to the Capitol.
   The CG, MDW will arrange for the following:
   a. Appropriate ceremony at place of repose to consist of following personnel:
      (1) The president of the United States.
      (2) Chiefs of State and heads of Government.
      (3) The vice president of the United States.
      (4) Speaker of the U.S. House of Representatives.
      (5) Chief justice and associate justices (active and retired), marshal, clerk, (U.S. Supreme Court).
      (6) Dean of the Diplomatic Corps.
      (7) Members of the Cabinet.
      (8) State and Territorial governors.
      (9) Family.
      (10) Honorary pallbearers.
      (11) Clergy.
      (12) Other official mourners.
      (13) Special honor guard (para 31b[1]).
      (14) Escort commander. (CG, MDW).

(15) Band.
(16) Joint honor cordon.
(17) Security cordon.
(18) Selected body bearers composed of enlisted personnel from each of the Armed Forces.
(19) National Color detail and personal flag bearer, as appropriate.
(20) Medical support.

b. Military escort for motorized funeral cortege from place of repose to the main funeral procession formation area (15th Street and Constitution Avenue, NW).

c. Main funeral procession.
(1) Participants to consist of the following as desired and appropriate.
   (a) Police escort.
   (b) Escort commander (CG, MDW).
   (c) Troops. Troop commander and staff.
       FIRST MARCH UNIT
           Commander and Staff
           Band
           Company of Cadets, USMA*
           Company of Midshipmen, USNA
           Squadron of Cadets, USAFA
           Company of Cadets, USCGA
           Company, U.S. Army*
           Company, U.S. Marine Corps*
           Company, U.S. Navy*
           Squadron, U.S. Air Forces*
           Company, U.S. Coast Guard*
           Composite Company, U.S. Service Women* (Minus U.S. Coast Guard)
       SECOND MARCH UNIT
           Troop Commander and Staff Band
           Company, Army National Guard
           Company, U.S. Army Reserve
           Company, U.S. Marine Corps Reserve
           Company, U.S. Naval Reserve
           Squadron, Air National Guard
           Squadron, U.S. Air Force Reserve
           Company, U.S. Coast Guard Reserve
       THIRD MARCH UNIT
           National Host of Veterans Day Committee
           Band
           National commanders of the 14 veterans organizations chartered by Congress
   (d) Special honor guard (para 31b[1]).
   (e) Honorary pallbearers.
   (f) National Color.

Appendix: Laws and Regulations

      (g) Clergy.
      (h) Hearse or caisson.
      (i) Body bearers.
      (j) Personal flag (if appropriate).
      (k) Caparisoned horse (if appropriate).
      (l) Family.**
      (m) President of the United States and party.
      (n) Chiefs of State and heads of Government.
      (o) Vice president of the United States and party.
      (p) Speaker of the U.S. House of Representatives.
      (q) Chief justice and associate justices (active and retired), marshal, clerk, (U.S. Supreme Court).
      (r) Dean of the Diplomatic Corps.
      (s) Cabinet members.
      (t) State and Territorial governors.
      (u) Other official mourners.
      (v) Police escort.
    (2) Coordination with the chief of Metropolitan and/or U.S. Park Police to determine the route of the cortege from the place of repose to the location where the cortege will join the main funeral procession and the route of the procession.
    (3) Cars for all participants in motorized cortege.
    (4) Suitable flights of aircraft to fly over procession, if appropriate.
  d. Appropriate ceremony at Capitol to consist of following additional personnel:
    (1) Band.
    (2) Joint honor cordon.
    (3) Saluting battery.
    (4) Guard of honor.
    (5) Security cordon.
13. Departure of remains from Capitol.
  The CG, MDW will arrange for —
  a. Appropriate ceremony at the Capitol to consist of following personnel:
    (1) Family.
    (2) Honorary pallbearers.
    (3) Clergy.
    (4) Special honor guard (para 31b[1]).
    (5) Band.
    (6) Joint honor cordon.
    (7) Selected body bearers composed of enlisted personnel from each of the Armed Forces.
    (8) National Color detail and personal flag bearer, as appropriate.
    (9) Other official mourners.
  b. Movement of motorized cortege to the funeral service.
  c. Appropriate arrangements at place of funeral service, to include:
    (1) Joint honor cordon.
    (2) General seating and parking plan.

(3) Usher detail.
  (4) Medical support.
  (5) Security cordon.
 d. Movement of motorized funeral cortege to point of departure.
 e. Appropriate ceremony at point of departure to consist of the following additional participating personnel:
  (1) Band.
  (2) Joint honor cordon.
  (3) Joint street honor cordon (departure).
  (4) Security cordon.
  (5) Saluting battery.
 f. Escort to accompany remains to final resting place.
 g. Rail, air, or motor transportation to move remains and accompany party to final resting place.

Section V: BURIAL IN THE WASHINGTON, D.C. AREA

14. Period of repose and lying in state at the Capitol.
 a. The remains will lie in repose in the White House or other designated place from 1200 hours of day following day of demise in Washington, D.C., until 1100 hours one day prior to the day of the burial.
 b. The remains will lie in state in the Rotunda of the Capitol for a period of approximately 24 hours beginning at 1300 hours one day prior to the day of burial until 1200 hours on the day of burial. The public will be permitted to file past the bier from 1300 hours one day prior to the day of burial until 1030 hours on the day of burial at which time the family group may pay their final respects. At 1200 hours, the remains will be removed from the Rotunda of the Capitol, unless the religion of the deceased and time of funeral service dictate another time.
15. Departure of remains from place of repose and movement to the Capitol. The CG, MDW will arrange the following:
 a. Appropriate ceremony at the place of repose to consist of the following personnel:
  (1) Clergy.
  (2) Honorary pallbearers.
  (3) Family.
  (4) Special honor guard (para 31b[1]).
  (5) Escort commander (CG, MDW).
  (6) Band.
  (7) Joint honor cordon.
  (8) Security cordon.
  (9) Body bearers, National Color detail, and personal flag bearer, as appropriate.
  (10) Other official mourners.
 b. Military escort for motorized funeral cortege from the place of repose to the Capitol to consist of:
  (1) Police escort.

(2) Escort commander (CG, MDW).
(3) Special honor guard (para 31b[1]).
(4) Honorary pallbearers.
(5) Clergy.
(6) Hearse.
(7) Body bearers, National Color detail, and personal flag bearer, as appropriate.
(8) Family.
(9) Police.
(10) Medical support.
  c. Coordination with the chief of the Metropolitan and/or U.S. Park Police to determine route of cortege to the east steps of the Capitol from the place of repose.
  d. Reception committee at the Capitol to await the arrival of the remains to consist of following personnel:
(1) The president of the United States.
(2) Chiefs of State and heads of Government.
(3) The vice president of the United States.
(4) Speaker of the U.S. House of Representatives.
(5) Chief justice and associate justices (active and retired), marshal, clerk, (U.S. Supreme Court).
(6) Dean of the Diplomatic Corps and Diplomatic Corps.
(7) Members of Congress.
(8) State and Territorial governors.
(9) Deputy secretary of Defense, service secretaries, and assistant secretary of Treasury.
  e. Appropriate ceremony upon arrival of the remains at the Capitol to consist of:
(1) Band.
(2) Joint honor cordon.
(3) Security cordon.
(4) Saluting battery.
(5) Body bearers, National Color detail, and personal flag bearer, as appropriate.
(6) Guard of honor.
(7) Escort commander (CG, MDW).
(8) Special honor guard (para 31b[1]).
(9) Clergy.
(10) Family.
(11) Honorary pallbearers.
(12) Other official mourners.
(13) Medical support.
16. Departure of remains from Capitol and movement to the funeral site for funeral services and return to transfer point.
The CG, MDW will arrange for —
  a. Appropriate ceremony at the Capitol to consist of following personnel:

(1) The president of the United States.
(2) Chiefs of State and heads of Government.
(3) The vice president of the United States.
(4) Speaker of the U.S. House of Representatives.
(5) Chief justice and associate justices (active and retired), marshal, clerk, (U.S. Supreme Court).
(6) Dean of the Diplomatic Corps.
(7) Members of the Cabinet.
(8) State and Territorial governors.
(9) Family.
(10) Honorary pallbearers.
(11) Other official mourners.
(12) Clergy.
(13) Special honor guard (para 31b[1]).
(14) Escort commander (CG, MDW).
(15) Band.
(16) Honor cordon.
(17) Security cordon.
(18) Selected body bearers composed of enlisted personnel from each of the Armed Forces.
(19) National Color detail and personal flag bearer, as appropriate.
(20) Medical support.

b. Motorized funeral cortege to the place of funeral service and return to the transfer point (New Jersey and Constitution Avenues) if the funeral service is not in the Amphitheater, Arlington National Cemetery.

c. Appropriate arrangements at place of funeral service to include:
(1) Joint honor cordon.
(2) General seating and parking plan.
(3) Usher detail.
(4) Medical support.
(5) Security cordon.

17. Main funeral procession to Arlington National Cemetery for funeral service and/or interment.

The CG, MDW will arrange for —

a. Main funeral procession from the transfer point (New Jersey and Constitution Avenues) to Arlington National Cemetery (composed as shown in para 12c).

b. Appropriate ceremony at the Amphitheater and gravesite to include the following additional personnel:
(1) Saluting battery.
(2) Firing party.
(3) Security cordon.
(4) Usher detail.
(5) Parking detail.
(6) Band.
(7) Medical support.

c. General seating plan for Amphitheater.

Section VI: ARRIVAL AND FUNERAL SERVICES AT FINAL RESTING PLACE
18. Responsibilities.

The Army commander, within whose area interment will take place, is the designated representative of the president of the United States for the purpose of making arrangements for participation of all Armed Forces and coordination with State and local authorities. He is responsible for the reception and funeral service at the place of interment as follows:

a. Carry out the above responsibilities in accordance with the wishes of the immediate family.

b. Utilize the services of local agencies insofar as practicable.

c. Employ local units of Reserve and National Guard components as practicable.

d. Participation of veterans and patriotic organizations as appropriate.

e. Provide medical support.

Notes

Introduction

1. John M. Potter, *Plots Against Presidents* (New York: Astor-Honor, 1968), 286.
2. Ibid., 286–9.
3. Ibid., 292–8.
4. Report of the President's Commission on the Assassination of President Kennedy, hereafter referred to as the Warren Report, after its chairman, Chief Justice Earl Warren (New York: Bantam Books, 1964), 477.
5. Report of the Select Committee on Assassinations of the U.S. House of Representatives (Washington, D.C.: U.S. Government Printing Office, 1979).
6. Article II, Section 1 of the Constitution contains the original clause regarding succession to the presidency. The Twenty-fifth Amendment, ratified February 10, 1967, changed the clause in an attempt to clarify succession.
7. Barbara Mikkelson, "The Curse of Tecumseh," http://www.snopes.com/history/american/curse.asp (accessed June 2009); Robert Ripley, *Ripley's Big Book of Believe It Or Not!* (New York: Simon & Schuster, 1934), 296.
8. Mikkelson.
9. Nicholas Whyte, "The Curse of the Presidents," http://www.nicholaswhyte.info/curse.htm (accessed June 2009).

Chapter 1

1. Bradley H. Patterson, *To Serve the President: Continuity and Innovation in the White House Staff* (Washington, D.C.: Brooking Institution Press, 2008), 78.

2. The source for much of the information concerning protection of the president is the *Warren Report*, Appendix VII; the U.S. Secret Service website, http://www.secretservice.gov/history.shtml; and the White House Security Review of May 1995 as it appears on the website http://prop1.org/park/pave/rev9.htm.
3. "President Assassination Attempts," http://www.usatrivia.com/pasnatt.html (accessed January 2008).
4. John R. Bumgarner, *The Health of the Presidents: The Forty-One U.S. Presidents Through 1993 from a Physician's Point of View* (Jefferson, NC: McFarland, 1994), 6.
5. Ibid., 29.
6. Warren G. Harding, II, and J. Mark Stewart, *Mere Mortals: The Lives and Health Histories of American Presidents* (Worthington, OH: Renaissance Publications, 1992), 28.
7. Bumgarner, 74.
8. *Warren Report*, 477.
9. Ibid.
10. Ibid., 479.
11. White House Security Review of May 1995, http://prop1.org/park/pave/rev9.htm (accessed January 2008).
12. Interview with Joe Petro, former Secret Service agent, by Paul Harris of KMOX radio of St. Louis, January 10, 2005. Petro is the co-author, with Jeffrey Robinson, of *Standing Next to History: An Agent's Life in the Secret Service* (New York: Macmillan, 2005).
13. Ibid.
14. Carl S. Anthony, *America's First Families* (New York: Simon & Schuster, 2000), 200.
15. Ludwig M. Deppisch, *The White House Physician* (Jefferson, NC: McFarland, 2007), 41. The Deppisch book is undoubtedly the

best source for information about the health care provided to the presidents, its history and current status.
  16. *Ibid.*, 45.
  17. *Ibid.*, 63, 75.
  18. *Ibid.*, 75.

Chapter 2

  1. John Quincy Adams, *Diary of John Quincy Adams, 1794–1845* (New York: Longmans, Green, 1929), 522.
  2. Norma L. Peterson, *The Presidencies of William Henry Harrison and John Tyler* (Lawrence: University Press of Kansas, 1989), 18.
  3. Rudolph Marx, *The Health of the Presidents* (New York: Putnam, 1960), 129.
  4. *Ibid.*, 127–8.
  5. Claude G. Bowers, *Party Battles of the Jackson Period* (Boston: Houghton Mifflin, 1922), 14.
  6. An excellent account of Harrison's last illness and death may be found in Henry Montgomery, *The Life of Major General William Henry Harrison* (Chicago: John C. Winston, 1852), 371–7, 441–65.
  7. *New York Herald*, April 7, 1841.
  8. Marx, 131.
  9. Allan Nevins, ed., *Diary of Philip Hone* (New York: Dodd, Mead, 1927), 534.
  10. *Niles National Register*, April 10, 1841.
  11. *New York Herald*, April 7, 1841.
  12. *National Intelligencer*, April 7, 1841.
  13. Robert Seager II, *And Tyler Too: A Biography of John and Julia Gardiner Tyler* (New York: McGraw-Hill, 1963), 147–8.
  14. Nevins, 536.
  15. Robert V. Remini, *The Life of Andrew Jackson* (New York: HarperCollins, 2001), 346.
  16. "State Funerals Bound by Rules, History, Judgment," Associated Press story of June 8, 2004, http://www.msnbc.msn.com/id 5151474/ (accessed March 2005).
  17. House Document Number 5, 1st Session, 27th Congress, Serial 392, May 31–September 13, 1841.
  18. Bernard C. Steiner, *Life of Roger Brooke Taney* (Baltimore: Williams and Wilkins, 1922), 257–8.
  19. Montgomery, 446; *New York Herald*, April 8, 1841.
  20. Montgomery, 459.
  21. Nevins, 539–40.
  22. James A. Green, *William Henry Harrison: His Life and Times* (Richmond: Garrett and Massie, 1941), 403.
  23. *Niles National Register*, May 22, 1841.
  24. Charles Francis Adams, ed., *Memoirs of John Quincy Adams, Vol. 10* (Freeport, NY: Books for Libraries Press, 1969), 488.
  25. Green, 406.
  26. "Neglected Graves of American Presidents," *Harper's Weekly*, no. 43, May 30, 1899, p. 497.
  27. John S. Dye, *History of the Plots and Crimes of the Great Conspiracy to Overthrow Liberty in America* (New York: John S. Dye, 1866), 45–47.
  28. John M. Potter, *Plots Against Presidents* (New York: Astor-Honor, 1968), 286–9.
  29. Herbert R. Collins and David B. Weaver, *Wills of the U.S. Presidents* (Atlanta: Communication Channels, 1976), 80–84.

Chapter 3

  1. Rudolph Marx, *The Health of the Presidents* (New York: Putnam, 1960), 150.
  2. Holman Hamilton, *Zachary Taylor: Soldier in the White House* (Indianapolis: Bobbs-Merrill, 1951), 388.
  3. Hamilton, 389; Henry Montgomery, *The Life of Major General Zachary Taylor* (Buffalo: Derby and Hewson Publishers, 1847), 425; *New York Tribune*, July 12, 1850, from reports of the *Philadelphia Bulletin*.
  4. Hamilton, 389; *New York Tribune*, July 12, 1850, from reports of the *Philadelphia Bulletin*.
  5. Hamilton, 387, 389.
  6. Brainerd Dyer, *Zachary Taylor* (Baton Rouge: Louisiana State University Press, 1946), 402.
  7. *New York Tribune*, July 12, 1850, from reports of the *Philadelphia Bulletin*.
  8. Montgomery, 432.
  9. *Ibid.*, 440–1.
  10. Hamilton, 396.
  11. *New York Tribune*, July 12, 1850.
  12. Montgomery, 434.
  13. *New York Tribune*, July 12, 1850.
  14. Allan Nevins, ed., *Diary of Philip Hone* (New York: Dodd, Mead, 1927), 900.
  15. K. Jack Bauer, *Zachary Taylor* (Baton Rouge: Louisiana State University Press, 1993), 319.

16. *Louisville Journal*, October 26 and 31, and November 1 and 2, 1850.
17. *Louisville Journal*, November 2, 1850.
18. Bauer, 319.
19. "Cemeteries—Zachary Taylor National Cemetery—Burial and Memorials," http://www.cem.va.gov/CEM/cems/nchp/zacharytaylor.asp (accessed May 2008).
20. *Louisville Times*, May 6 and 31, 1926.
21. John M. Potter, *Plots Against Presidents* (New York: Astor-Honor, 1968), 287–9.
22. *Louisville Courier-Journal*, June 18, 1991; *New York Times*, June 18, 1991.
23. Ibid.
24. *New York Times*, June 27, 1991.
25. Michael Parenti, *History as Mystery* (San Francisco: City Lights Books, 1999), 209–39.
26. Herbert R. Collins and David B. Weaver, *Wills of the U.S. Presidents* (Atlanta: Communication Channels, 1976), 98–101.

Chapter 4

1. "President Abraham Lincoln: Health and Medical History," http://www.doctorzebra.com/prez/g16.htm (accessed January 2007).
2. James McPherson, *The Most Fearful Ordeal: Original Coverage of the Civil War* (New York: St. Martin's Press, 2004), 329.
3. "How Wilkes Booth's Friend Described His Crime," *Literary Digest*, no. 88, March 6, 1936, p. 59.
4. Victor Searcher, *The Farewell to Lincoln* (New York: Abingdon Press, 1965), 18.
5. Harold Holzer, "Ford's Theater," *American History Illustrated*, no. 20, February 1986, 18.
6. Searcher, 21.
7. Ibid., 32.
8. Ibid., 261.
9. John S. Goff, *Robert Todd Lincoln: A Man in His Own Right* (Norman: University of Oklahoma Press, 1969), 70.
10. Charles A. Leale, "Lincoln's Last Hours," 11, as cited in Goff, p. 70. The room in which Lincoln died was so small that a dozen persons would have had difficulty squeezing in.
11. McPherson, 332.
12. Searcher, 145–9.
13. McPherson, 346.
14. Ibid., 347.
15. Searcher, 39.
16. Ibid., 41, as reported in the *Buffalo Commercial Advertiser* and *Buffalo Morning Express* of April 29, 1865, and the *Concord Patriot* of April 19, 1865, excerpted from the *New York Times* of April 26, 1865.
17. Searcher, 37.
18. T. Roscoe, "The Abraham Lincoln Murder Case," *Reader's Digest*, no. 76, February 1960, p. 272–3.
19. "How Wilkes Booth's Friend Described His Crime," *Literary Digest*, no. 88, March 6, 1936, p. 59.
20. Searcher, 54.
21. Ibid., 53.
22. Thomas J. Craughwell, *Stealing Lincoln's Body* (Cambridge, MA: Belknap Press of Harvard University Press, 2007), 8.
23. Searcher, 53.
24. Dorothy M. Kunhardt and Philip B. Kunhardt, Jr., *Twenty Days* (New York: Castle Books, 1965), 95.
25. Searcher, 290.
26. Kunhardt, 120.
27. McPherson, 343.
28. Searcher, 265.
29. Ibid., 57.
30. Ibid.
31. Kunhardt, 247–9.
32. Searcher, 63.
33. Ibid., 66–67.
34. Ibid., 76.
35. Kunhardt, 141–3.
36. Ibid., 143.
37. Ibid., 144.
38. Searcher, 113.
39. Ibid., 119.
40. Kunhardt, 166.
41. Searcher, 277.
42. Kunhardt, 162.
43. Searcher, 131.
44. Ibid., 186.
45. Ibid., 187.
46. Kunhardt, 219.
47. Ibid., 230–1.
48. Kunhardt, 235.
49. Ibid., 240.
50. Searcher, 240.
51. Kunhardt, 256.
52. Gary Lederman, *The Sacred Remains: American Attitudes Toward Death, 1799–1883* (New Haven: Yale University Press, 1999), 158–9.
53. Kunhardt, 284.
54. Ibid., 249.
55. Searcher, 247–8.

56. *Ibid.*, 290.
57. Holzer, 12–19.
58. Craughwell, 140.
59. Herbert R. Collins and Avid B. Weaver, *Wills of the U.S. Presidents* (Atlanta: Communication Channels, 1976), 124.
60. D. Robertson and P. Robertson, "Journey's End," *American Heritage*, no. 33, April/May 1982, p. 82.
61. Goff, 81.
62. The most complete story of the attempted theft can be found in the book by Thomas J. Craughwell, *Stealing Lincoln's Body* (Cambridge, MA: Belknap Press of Harvard University Press, 2007).
63. "Strange History Brought to Life," *Life*, no. 54, February 15, 1963, p. 87.
64. Craughwell, 185.
65. "Strange History Brought to Life," *Life*, no. 54, February 15, 1963, pp. 83–88.
66. John S. Goff, *Robert Todd Lincoln: A Man in His Own Right* (Norman: University of Oklahoma Press, 1969), 71.
67. *Ibid.*, 68–69.
68. *Ibid.*, 119–22.
69. Shirley Samuels, *Facing America: Iconography and the Civil War* (New York: Oxford University Press, 2004), 150.
70. Goff, 234.
71. *Ibid.*, 260.
72. *Ibid.*, 264.
73. Robert J. Donovan, *The Assassins* (New York: Popular Library, 1964), 248–9.
74. Philip Van Doren Stern, *The Man Who Killed Lincoln* (Garden City, NY: Doubleday, 1965), 270.
75. For an excellent account of Booth's escape, see C. Wyatt Evans, *The Legend of John Wilkes Booth* (Lawrence: University of Kansas Press, 2004).

Chapter 5

1. Margaret Leech and Harry J. Brown, *The Garfield Orbit* (New York: Harper & Row, 1978), 18.
2. Allan Peskin, *Garfield: A Biography* (Kent, OH: Kent State University Press, 1978), 12–13.
3. Leech, 115.
4. Accounts differ as to whether it was the first or second shot that hit Garfield in the back. The author has come to the conclusion stated here based upon a review of those accounts. An excellent detailing of the entire Garfield case is James C. Clark, *The Murder of James A. Garfield: The President's Last Days and the Trial and Execution of His Assassin* (Jefferson, NC: McFarland, 1993).
5. *The Attempted Assassination of President Garfield* (Philadelphia: Barclay, 1881), 41.
6. See Chapter 4, "Robert Todd Lincoln."
7. Ludwig M. Deppisch, *The White House Physician* (Jefferson, NC: McFarland, 2007), 49.
8. Peskin, 605.
9. *Ibid.*, 606.
10. *Ibid.*, 607.
11. *New York Times*, September 21, 1881; *Frank Leslie's Illustrated Newspaper*, October 8, 1881, p. 86.
12. *Washington Post*, September 20, 1881.
13. *New York Times*, September 20, 1881.
14. *New York Times*, September 21, 1881; *Washington Post*, September 21, 1881.
15. *New York Times*, September 21, 1881.
16. *Ibid.*; Russell H. Conwell, *The Life, Speeches and Public Services of James A. Garfield* (Portland, ME: George Stinson, 1881), 361–2.
17. *New York Times*, September 21, 1881.
18. *The Nation*, September 20, 1881.
19. George F. Howe, *Chester A. Arthur: A Quarter-Century of Machine Politics* (New York: Dodd, Mead, 1934), 154–5.
20. *New York Times*, April 27, 1886.
21. *Ibid.*, September 28, 1881.
22. Stewart M. Brooks, *Our Assassinated Presidents: The True Medical Stories* (New York: Bell Publishing, 1985), 123–5.
23. *Decisions of the First Comptroller in the Department of the Treasury*, Vol. 3 (Washington, D.C.: U.S. Government Printing Office, 1882), 394.
24. David Ovason, *The Secret Architecture of Our Nation's Capital* (New York: HarperCollins, 2002), 285–6.
25. "Life and Death in the White House, James A. Garfield," http://americanhistory.si.edu/presidency/3d1d.html (accessed June 2009).
26. Michael G. Rhode, "Foreword to Photographic Atlas of Civil War Injuries," by Brad P. Bengston and Julia E. Kuz. http://nmhm.washingtondcmuseum/collection/archival/a products/aatlas/ (accessed February 2005).
27. *New York Times*, October 6, 1881.
28. *Ibid.*, October 23, 1881.
29. *Ibid.*, June 17, 1882.
30. *Ibid.*, February 7, 1886.

31. *Ibid.*, May 21, 1890.
32. *Ibid.*, May 31, 1890.
33. Herbert R. Collins and David B. Weaver, *Wills of the U.S. Presidents* (Atlanta: Communication Channels, 1976), 135.
34. http://nmhm.washingtondcmuseum/collections/archives/aproducts/aatlas/ (accessed February 2005); http://www.findagrave.com/php/famous.php?page+name & firstname=Charles&lastname-GUITEAU (accessed February 2005).

Chapter 6

1. Robert J. Donovan, *The Assassins* (New York: Popular Library, 1964), 102.
2. Margaret Leech, *In the Days of McKinley* (New York: Harper and Brothers, 1959), 595.
3. *Ibid.*, 595–6.
4. *Ibid.*, 596–7.
5. Carry Nation, *The Use and Need of the Life of Carry Nation* (Topeka: F.M. Steves and Sons, 1908), 238.
6. Leech, 599; Stewart M. Brooks, *Our Assassinated Presidents: The True Medical Stories* (New York: Bell Publishing, 1985), 155, 158–9; Selig Adler, "The Operation on President McKinley," *Scientific American*, no. 208, March 1963, pp. 126–7.
7. H. Wayne Morgan, *William McKinley and His America* (Syracuse, NY: Syracuse University Press, 1963), 524.
8. Charles G. Dawes, *A Journal of the McKinley Years* (Chicago: Lakeside Press, 1950), 281.
9. *New York Times*, September 15, 1901.
10. B.O. Fowler, "The Assassination of the President and the Aftermath," *Arena*, no. 26, November 1901, pp. 533–4.
11. Editorial, *The Literary Digest*, September 21, 1901, p. 335.
12. Editorial, *The Nation*, September 12, 1901; Fowler, 534.
13. Leech, 602.
14. Jack C. Fisher, *Stolen Glory: The McKinley Assassination* (La Jolla, CA: Alamar Books, 2001), 114; A. Wesley Johns, *The Man Who Shot McKinley* (Cranbury, NJ: A.S. Barnes, 1970), 167.
15. *Buffalo Evening News*, September 24, 1901; *New York Times*, September 15, 1901.
16. *Buffalo News*, July 22, 1990.
17. *New York Times*, September 16, 1901.
18. *Ibid.*, September 18, 1901.
19. *Ibid.*
20. *Ibid.*
21. *Ibid.*, September 19, 1901.
22. *Ibid.*
23. *Ibid.*, September 20, 1901.
24. Roger Daniels, *Coming to America* (New York: HarperCollins, 2002), 279.
25. Donovan, 121–9.
26. An excellent review of the controversy surrounding the treatment given to the president may be found in an article entitled "The Operation on President McKinley," by Selig Adler, in the March 1963 issue of *Scientific American*, pp. 118–30.
27. Adler, 130; Brooks, 173–4.
28. *New York Times*, September 19, 1907.
29. *Ibid.*, September 20,1907.
30. *Ibid.*, October 1, 1907.
31. Herbert R. Collins and David B. Weaver, *Wills of the U.S. Presidents* (Atlanta: Communication Channels, 1976), 159–60.
32. Donovan, 105–6; Fisher, 132.
33. Jeffrey W. Seibert, *I Done My Duty* (Westminster, MD: Heritage Books, 2002), 312.
34. Jean Arbeiter and Linda Cirino, *Permanent Addresses* (New York: M. Evans, 1983), 199.
35. Johns, 39; Walter Channing, "The Mental Status of Czolgosz, the Assassin of President McKinley," *American Journal of Insanity*, no. 59, October 1902, pp. 23–46.

Chapter 7

1. Samuel Hopkins Adams, *Incredible Era: The Life and Times of Warren G. Harding* (New York: Houghton Mifflin, 1939), 100; Francis Russell, *The Shadow of Blooming Grove* (New York: McGraw-Hill, 1968), 353–4.
2. Rudolph Marx, *The Health of the Presidents* (New York: Putnam, 1960), 330–1; Robert K. Murray, *The Harding Era* (Minneapolis: University of Minnesota Press, 1969), 438–9.
3. Andrew Sinclair, *The Available Man: The Life Behind the Mask of Warren G. Harding* (New York: Macmillan, 1965), 286.
4. Russell, 588.
5. *Ibid.*, 589.
6. *Ibid.*, 590.
7. Samuel G. Blythe, "A Calm Review of

a Calm Man," *Saturday Evening Post*, no. 196, July 28, 1923, pp. 3–4.
  8. Edmund W. Starling and Thomas Sugrue, *Starling of the White House* (New York: Simon & Schuster, 1946), 201, cited in Murray, 450.
  9. *New York Times*, August 3, 1921.
  10. *Ibid*.
  11. *Ibid*.
  12. Claude M. Fuess, *Calvin Coolidge: The Man from Vermont* (Boston: Little, Brown, 1940), 310.
  13. *Ibid*., 315.
  14. Murray, 451; Russell, 591; Sinclair, 286.
  15. "David Kalakaua," http://www.hawaiihistory.com/index.cfm?fuseaction=ig.page&pageID=404 (accessed February 2009).
  16. *New York Times*, August 9, 1923; Murray, 452; Russell, 597.
  17. *New York Times*, August 9, 1923; Russell, 597.
  18. *New York Times*, August 9, 1923.
  19. *Ibid*., August 10, 1923; Russell, 600.
  20. Russell, 600.
  21. *New York Times*, August 11, 1923.
  22. *Ibid*.
  23. *Ibid*.
  24. Gaston B. Means and May Dixon Thacker, *The Strange Death of President Harding* (New York: Guild Publishing, 1930).
  25. *New York Times*, June 25, 1924.
  26. *Ibid*., July 21, 1925, May 5, 1926.
  27. *Ibid*., May 30, 1926.
  28. *Ibid*., December 21, 1927.
  29. *Ibid*., December 22, 1927.
  30. *New York Times*, June 17, 1931, as cited in Murray, 493; Russell, 640.
  31. E-mail interview conducted with Renee Roberts of the Palace Hotel of San Francisco, August 19, 2008.
  32. Herbert R. Collins and David B. Weaver, *Wills of the U.S. Presidents* (Atlanta: Communication Channels, 1976), 98–101.

Chapter 8

  1. Rudolph Marx, *The Health of the Presidents* (New York: Putnam, 1960), 353.
  2. Jim Bishop, *FDR's Last Year* (New York: William Morrow, 1975), 4–10, 18; Hugh G. Gallagher, *FDR's Splendid Deception: The Moving Story of Roosevelt's Massive Disability* (New York: Dodd, Mead, 1985), 180–1.
  3. Jean Edward Smith, *FDR* (New York: Random House, 2007), 620, 629.
  4. Geoffrey C. Ward, ed., *Closest Companion: The Unknown Story of the Intimate Friendship Between Franklin D. Roosevelt and Margaret Suckley* (Boston: Houghton Mifflin, 1995), 418.
  5. Bishop, 605–6, 616; Conrad Black, *Franklin Delano Roosevelt: Champion of Freedom* (New York: Public Affairs, 2003), 1119.
  6. Bishop, 615.
  7. Bishop, 653–4; Grace Tully, *FDR, My Boss* (New York: Scribner's, 1949), 367–8.
  8. Elliott Roosevelt, "Why Stalin Never Forgave Eleanor Roosevelt," *Parade*, February 9, 1986, pp. 14–17.
  9. Bishop, 653.
  10. Elliott Roosevelt, 14–17.
  11. Herbert R. Collins and David B. Weaver, *Wills of the U.S. Presidents* (Atlanta: Communication Channels, 1976), 200–10.

Chapter 9

  1. Charles C. Kenney, *John F. Kennedy: The Presidential Portfolio* (New York: Public Affairs, 2000), 30.
  2. Herbert S. Parmet, *Jack: The Struggles of John F. Kennedy* (New York: Dial Press, 1980), 116–7.
  3. *Dallas Morning News*, November 22, 1963; William Manchester, *The Death of a President* (New York: Harper & Row, 1967), 109.
  4. *Hearings Before the President's Commission on the Assassination of President John F. Kennedy, Vol. III* (Washington, D.C.: U.S. Government Printing Office, 1964), 93.
  5. *Hearings Before the President's Commission on the Assassination of President John F. Kennedy, Vol. IV* (Washington, D.C.: U.S. Government Printing Office, 1964), 133, 144, 147.
  6. *Ibid*., 134, 148.
  7. Jim Bishop, *The Day Kennedy Was Shot* (New York: Bantam Books, 1969), 328; Manchester, 293–4; Kenneth P. O'Donnell and David F. Powers, *Johnny, We Hardly Knew Ye* (Boston: Little, Brown, 1970), 33.
  8. Manchester, 250.
  9. David Lifton, *Best Evidence* (New York: Dell Publishing, 1982), 663, 828.
  10. Josiah Thompson, *Six Seconds in Dallas* (New York: Berkley Publishing, 1967), 130.

11. Bishop, 379.
12. Manchester, 442–3.
13. *Fort Worth Star-Telegram*, November 24, 1963; Manchester, 490–7.
14. Manchester, 242.
15. Bishop, 242.
16. Manchester, 573.
17. *New York Times*, December 5, 1963.
18. Manchester, 567.
19. *Ibid.*, 394.
20. *Ibid.*, 634.
21. "Coffin Used to Transport Kennedy's Body Sunk at Sea," http://www.cnn.com/ALLPOLITICS/stories/1999/06/01/kennedy.papers/ (accessed February 2009).
22. *Dallas Morning News*, November 24 and 25, 1963; Craig Flournoy, "All Eyes Turn to Dallas," *Dallas Morning News* supplement entitled "Twenty Years Later," November 20, 1983, pp. 30–34; *Forth Worth Star-Telegram*, November 24, 1963.
23. *Time*, March 24, 1967.
24. Herbert R. Collins and David B. Weaver, *Wills of the U.S. Presidents* (Atlanta: Communication Channels, 1976), 249–58.
25. Final conclusions from the *Report of the Select Committee on Assassinations of the U.S. House of Representatives* (Washington, D.C.: U.S. Government Printing Office, 1979).
26. *Ibid.*
27. *Dallas Morning News*, November 26, 1963.
28. *Fort Worth Press*, November 26, 1963.
29. *Fort Worth Star-Telegram*, October 5 and 6, 1981.
30. *New York Times*, January 4 and 7, 1967.

Bibliography

Books

Adams, Charles Francis (ed.). *Memoirs of John Quincy Adams, Vol. 10*. Freeport, NY: Books for Libraries Press, 1969.

Adams, John Quincy, and Allan Nevins (ed.). *The Diary of John Quincy Adams, 1794–1845*. New York: Longmans, Green, 1929.

Adams, Samuel Hopkins. *Incredible Era: The Life and Times of Warren G. Harding*. New York: Houghton Mifflin, 1939.

Alexander, Henry H. *The Life of Guiteau and the Official History of the Most Exciting Case on Record*. Cleveland: N.G. Hamilton, 1882.

Anthony, Carl S. *America's First Families*. New York: Simon & Schuster, 2000.

Arbeiter, Jean, and Linda Cirino. *Permanent Addresses: A Guide to the Resting Places of Famous Americans*. New York: M. Evans, 1983.

Asbell, Bernard. *When FDR Died*. New York: Holt, Rinehart and Winston, 1961.

The Attempted Assassination of President Garfield. Philadelphia: Barclay, 1881.

Bauer, K. Jack. *Zachary Taylor*. Baton Rouge: Louisiana State University Press, 1993.

Bishop, Jim. *The Day Kennedy Was Shot*. New York: Bantam Books, 1969.

_____. *The Day Lincoln Was Shot*. New York: Harper & Row, 1955.

_____. *FDR's Last Year*. New York: William Morrow, 1974.

Black, Conrad. *Franklin Delano Roosevelt: Champion of Freedom*. New York: Public Affairs, 2003.

Bonney, Catharina V.R. *A Legacy of Historical Gleanings*. Albany, NY: J. Munsell, 1875.

Bowers, Claude G. *Party Battles of the Jackson Period*. Boston and New York: Houghton Mifflin, 1922.

Brooks, Stewart M. *Our Assassinated Presidents: The True Medical Stories*. New York: Bell Publishing, 1985.

Bumgarner, John R. *The Health of the Presidents: The Forty-one U.S. Presidents Through 1993 from a Physician's Point of View*. Jefferson, NC: McFarland, 1994.

Chitwood, Oliver P. *John Tyler: Champion of the Old South*. New York: D. Appleton–Century, 1939.

Clark, James C. *The Murder of James A. Garfield*. Jefferson, NC: McFarland, 1993.

Cleaves, Freeman. *Old Tippecanoe*. Port Washington, NY: Kennikat Press, 1939.

Coggeshall, William T. *Lincoln Memorial: The Journeys of Abraham Lincoln*. Columbus: Ohio State Journal, 1865.

Collins, Herbert Ridgeway, and David B. Weaver. *Wills of the U.S. Presidents*. Atlanta: Communication Channels, 1976.

Conwell, Russell H. *The Life, Speeches, and Public Services of James A. Garfield*. Portland, ME: George Stinson, 1881.

Craughwell, Thomas J. *Stealing Lincoln's Body*. Cambridge, MA: Belknap Press of Harvard University Press, 2007.

Daniels, Roger. *Coming to America: A History of Immigration and Ethnicity in American Life*. New York: HarperCollins, 1990.

Dawes, Charles G. *A Journal of the McKinley Years*. Chicago: Lakeside Press, 1950.

DeGregorio, William A. *The Complete Book of U.S. Presidents*. New York: Dembner Books, 1984.

Dehler, Gregory J. *Chester Alan Arthur*. Hauppauge, NY: Nova Publishers, 2006.

Deppisch, Ludwig M. *The White House Physician*. Jefferson, NC: McFarland, 2007.

Donovan, Robert J. *The Assassins*. New York: Popular Library, 1964.

Dye, John S. *History of the Plots and Crimes of the Great Conspiracy to Overthrow Liberty in America.* New York: John S. Dye, 1866.

Eddowes, Michael. *The Oswald File.* New York: C.N. Potter, 1977.

Eisenschiml, Otto. *In the Shadow of Lincoln's Death.* New York: W. Funk, 1940.

Evans, C. Wyatt. *The Legend of John Wilkes Booth.* Lawrence: University of Kansas Press, 2004.

Ferrell, Robert H. *Ill-Advised: Presidential Health and Public Trust.* Columbia: University of Missouri Press, 1992.

Fisher, Jack C. *Stolen Glory: The McKinley Assassination.* LaJolla, CA: Alamar Books, 2001.

Fuess, Claude M. *Calvin Coolidge: The Man from Vermont.* Boston: Little, Brown, 1940.

Gallagher, Hugh G. *FDR's Splendid Deception: The Moving Story of Roosevelt's Massive Disability.* New York: Dodd, Mead, 1985.

Goebel, Dorothy Burne. *William Henry Harrison: A Political Biography.* Philadelphia: Porcupine Press, 1926.

Goff, John S. *Robert Todd Lincoln.* Norman: University of Oklahoma Press, 1969.

Goldhurst, Richard. *Many Are the Hearts: The Agony and the Triumph of Ulysses S. Grant.* New York: Reader's Digest Press, 1975.

Green, James A. *William Henry Harrison: His Life and Times.* Richmond, VA: Garrett and Massie, 1941.

Hale, Edward Everett, Jr. *William H. Seward.* Philadelphia: G.W. Jacobs, 1910.

Halstead, Murat. *The Illustrious Life of William McKinley, Our Martyred President.* Chicago: Murat Halstead, 1901.

Hamilton, Charles, and Lloyd Ostendorf. *Lincoln in Photographs.* Norman: University of Oklahoma Press, 1963.

Hamilton, Holman. *Zachary Taylor: Soldier in the White House.* Indianapolis: Bobbs-Merrill, 1951.

Haraven, Tamara K. *Eleanor Roosevelt: An American Conscience.* Chicago: Quadrangle Books, 1968.

Harding, Warren G., II, and J. Mark Stewart. *Mere Mortals: The Lives and Health Histories of American Presidents.* Worthington, OH: Renaissance Publications, 1992.

Hassett, William D. *Off the Record with FDR, 1942-1945.* Piscataway, NJ: Rutgers University Press, 1958.

Howe, George F. *Chester A. Arthur: A Quarter-Century of Machine Politics.* New York: Dodd, Mead, 1934.

Johns, A. Wesley. *The Man Who Shot McKinley.* Cranbury, NJ: A.S. Barnes, 1970.

Kane, Joseph Nathan. *Facts About the Presidents.* New York: H.W. Wilson, 1993.

Kenney, Charles C. *John F. Kennedy: The Presidential Portfolio.* New York: Public Affairs, 2000.

Kunhardt, Dorothy M., and Philip B. Kunhardt, Jr. *Twenty Days.* New York: Castle Books, 1965.

Laderman, Gary. *The Sacred Remains: American Attitudes Toward Death, 1799-1883.* New Haven: Yale University Press, 1999.

Lash, Joseph P. *Eleanor and Franklin.* New York: W.W. Norton, 1971.

Laughlin, Clara E. *The Death of Lincoln: The Story of Booth's Plot, His Deed and the Penalty.* New York: Double, Page, 1909.

Leech, Margaret. *In the Days of McKinley.* New York: Harper and Brothers, 1959.

_____, and Harry J. Brown. *The Garfield Orbit.* New York: Harper & Row, 1978.

Levin, Linda L. *The Making of FDR: The Story of Stephen T. Early, America's First Modern Press Secretary.* Amherst, NY: Prometheus Books, 2007.

Lewis, David A., and Darryl E. Hicks. *The Presidential Zero-Year Mystery.* Plainfield, NJ: Haven Books, 1980.

Lifton, David S. *Best Evidence.* New York: Dell Publishing, 1982.

MacIntire, Ross T. *White House Physician.* New York: Putnam, 1946.

Manchester, William. *The Death of a President.* New York: Harper & Row, 1967.

Marx, Rudolph. *The Health of the Presidents.* New York: Putnam, 1960.

McKinley, Silas B. *Old Rough and Ready: The Life and Times of Zachary Taylor.* New York: Vanguard Press, 1946.

McPherson, James. *The Most Fearful Ordeal: Original Coverage of the Civil War.* New York: St. Martin's Press, 2004.

Means, Gaston B., and Mary Dixon Thacker. *The Strange Death of President Harding.* New York: Guild Publishing, 1930.

Miller, Nathan. *FDR: An Intimate History.* Garden City, NY: Doubleday, 1983.

Montgomery, Henry. *The Life of Major General William Henry Harrison.* Chicago: John C. Winston, 1852.

_____. *The Life of Major General Zachary Taylor.* Buffalo: Derby and Hewson Publishers, 1847.

Morgan, H. Wayne. *William McKinley and*

His America. Syracuse, NY: Syracuse University Press, 1963.
Murray, Robert K. *The Harding Era*. Minneapolis: University of Minnesota Press, 1969.
Nation, Carry Amelia. *The Use and Need of the Life of Carry A. Nation*. Topeka: F.M. Steves and Sons, 1908.
Nevins, Allan (ed.). *Diary of Philip Hone*. New York: Dodd, Mead, 1927.
O'Donnell, Kenneth P., and David F. Powers. *Johnny, We Hardly Knew Ye*. Boston: Little, Brown, 1970.
Olcott, Charles S. *The Life of William McKinley*. Boston: Houghton Mifflin, 1916.
Oswald, Robert L. *Lee: A Portrait of Lee Harvey Oswald*. New York: Coward-McCann, 1967.
Ovason, David. *The Secret Architecture of Our Nation's Capital*. New York: HarperCollins, 2002.
Paletta, Lu Ann, and Fred L. Worth. *The World Almanac of Presidential Facts*. New York: World Almanac, 1988.
Parenti, Michael. *History as Mystery*. San Francisco: City Lights Books, 1999.
Parmet, Herbert S. *Jack: The Struggles of John F. Kennedy*. New York: Dial Press, 1980.
Peskin, Allan. *Garfield: A Biography*. Kent, OH: Kent State University Press, 1978.
Peterson, Norma L. *The Presidencies of William Henry Harrison and John Tyler*. Lawrence: University Press of Kansas, 1989.
Poore, Benjamin Perley. *Perley's Reminiscences*. Philadelphia: Hubbard Brothers, 1886.
Popkin, Richard H. *The Second Oswald*. New York: Avon Books, 1966.
Potter, John M. *Plots Against Presidents*. New York: Astor-Honor, 1968.
Reilly, Michael F. *Reilly of the White House*. New York: Simon & Schuster, 1947.
Remini, Robert V. *The Life of Andrew Jackson*. New York: HarperCollins, 2001.
Ripley, Robert. *Ripley's Big Book of Believe It or Not*. New York: Simon & Schuster, 1934.
Roosevelt, Eleanor. *On My Own*. New York: Harper Brothers, 1958.
_____. *This I Remember*. New York: Harper Brothers, 1949.
Rosenberg, Charles E. *The Trial of the Assassin Guiteau: Psychiatry and Law in the Gilded Age*. Chicago: University of Chicago Press, 1995.
Russell, Francis. *The Shadow of Blooming Grove*. New York: McGraw-Hill, 1968.
Samuels, Shirley. *Facing America: Iconography and the Civil War*. New York: Oxford University Press, 2004.
Scharf, Lois. *Eleanor Roosevelt: First Lady of American Liberalism*. Boston: Twayne Publishers, 1987.
Schlesinger, Arthur. *A Thousand Days*. Boston: Houghton Mifflin, 1965.
Seager, Robert II. *And Tyler Too: A Biography of John and Julia Gardiner Tyler*. New York: McGraw-Hill, 1963.
Searcher, Victor. *The Farewell to Lincoln*. New York: Abingdon Press, 1965.
Seibert, Jeffrey W. *I Done My Duty: The Complete Story of the Assassination of President McKinley*. Westminster, MD: Heritage Books, 2002.
Sinclair, Andrew. *The Available Man: The Life Behind the Mask of Warren G. Harding*. New York: Macmillan, 1965.
Smith, Jean Edward. *FDR*. New York: Random House, 2007.
Smith, Theodore C. *The Life and Letters of James Abram Garfield*. New Haven: Yale University Press, 1925.
Stafford, Jean. *A Mother in History: Three Incredible Days with Lee Harvey Oswald's Mother*. New York: Bantam, 1966.
Steiner, Bernard C. *Life of Roger Brooke Taney*. Baltimore: Williams and Wilkins, 1922.
Stern, Philip Van Doren. *The Man Who Killed Lincoln*. Garden City, NY: Doubleday, 1955.
Swanson, James L. *Manhunt: The 18-Day Chase for Abraham Lincoln's Killer*. New York: William Morrow, 2006.
Taylor, Tim. *The Book of Presidents*. New York: Arno Press, 1972.
Thompson, Josiah. *Six Seconds in Dallas*. New York: Berkley Publishing, 1967.
Tully, Grace. *FDR, My Boss*. New York: Scribner's, 1949.
Ward, Geoffrey C. (ed.). *Closest Companion: The Unknown Story of the Intimate Friendship Between Franklin Roosevelt and Margaret Suckley*. Boston: Houghton Mifflin, 1995.
Williamson, David B. *Illustrated Life, Services, Martyrdom and Funeral of Abraham Lincoln*. Philadelphia: T.B. Peterson and Brothers, 1865.
Wills, Gary, and Ovid DeMaris. *Jack Ruby*. New York: Da Capo Press, 1994.
Wilson, Francis. *John Wilkes Booth*. Boston: Houghton Mifflin, 1929.

Periodical Articles

Adler, Selig. "The Operation on President McKinley," *Scientific American*, no. 208, March 1963, pp. 118–30.

"At Rest," *Newsweek*, no. 69, March 27, 1963, p. 38.

"Be at Peace, Dear Jack," *Time*, no. 89, March 24, 1967, p. 19.

Blair, Joan, and Clay Blair, Jr. "The Great Kennedy Coverup," *Saturday Evening Post*, no. 249, January/February 1977, pp. 10+.

Blake, Richard A. "Two Moments of Grief," *America*, no. 129, November 24, 1973, pp. 402–4.

Bliss, D.W. "The Story of President Garfield's Illness," *Century*, no. 23, December 1881, pp. 300–5.

Blythe, Samuel G. "A Calm Review of a Calm Man," *Saturday Evening Post*, no. 196, July 28, 1923, pp. 3–4.

Channing, Walter. "The Mental Status of Czolgosz, the Assassin of President McKinley," *American Journal of Insanity*, no. 59, October 1902, pp. 23–46.

"Dallas: Living with History," *Newsweek*, no. 67, April 18, 1966, p. 48.

David, Paul T. "The TV Image," *The Nation*, no. 197, December 14, 1963, pp. 413–4.

"Death of a President," *Newsweek*, no. 28, November 4, 1946, p. 62.

"The Death of President Harding," *Outlook*, no. 134, August 15, 1923, p. 570–80.

Eisenschiml, Otto. "Could Today's Doctors Have Saved Lincoln?" *Today's Health*, no. 38, April 1960, pp. 32–5+.

"The Empty Room," *Time*, no. 86, December 24, 1965, p. 38.

"Everybody Knew It but the People," *Saturday Evening Post*, no. 217, May 19, 1945, p. 108.

"FDR: How He Died," *Newsweek*, no. 60, December 3, 1962, pp. 29–30.

Fowler, B.O. "The Assassination of the President and the Aftermath," *Arena*, no. 26, November 1901, pp. 532–8.

Frost, Stanley. "Washington Correspondence," *Outlook*, no. 134, August 22, 1923, pp. 622–4.

Gilder, Richard W. "Edwin Booth and Lincoln," *Century*, no. 77, April 1909, pp. 950–3.

Goldman, Emma. "The Assassination of McKinley," *American Mercury*, no. 24, September 1931, pp. 53–67.

Halstead, James A. "FDR's Little Strokes: A Medical Myth," *Today's Health*, no. 40, December 1962, pp. 53+.

Havinghurst, Walter. "Journey's End: 1865," *American Heritage*, no. 13, February 1962, pp. 32–35+.

Holzer, Harold. "Ford's Theater," *American History Illustrated*, no. 20, February 1986, 12–19+.

"How Wilkes Booth's Friend Described His Crime," *Literary Digest*, no. 88, March 6, 1926, pp. 58–60.

"The JFK Assassination," *Gallery*, no. 7, July 1979, 57–88.

"The Last Hours," *Newsweek*, no. 52, December 29, 1958, p. 19.

Lewis, Edward S. "The Death and Funeral of William Henry Harrison," *Ohio History*, no. 37(4), October 1928, pp. 605–12.

"Lincoln's Doctor Used Closed Chest Massage," *Science News Letter*, no. 84, September 21, 1963, p. 185.

"Little D," *Time*, no. 87, April 15, 1966, p. 25.

Lovett, Robert M. "A Strange Story," *New Republic*, no. 64, August 27, 1930, pp. 51–52.

MacCulloch, Campbell. "This Man Saw Lincoln Shot," *Good Housekeeping*, no. 84, February 1927, pp. 20–21.

Meriam, Arthur L. "Final Interment of President Abraham Lincoln's Remains," *Illinois State Historical Society Journal*, no. 23(1), April 1930, pp. 171–4.

Munroe, Seaton. "Recollections of Lincoln's Assassination," *North American Review*, no. 162, April 1896, pp. 224–32.

"Neglected Graves of American Presidents," *Harper's Weekly*, no. 43, May 20, 1899, p. 497.

Palmer, Francis M. "The Tombs of Our Presidents," *Munsey's Magazine*, no. 26, November 1901, pp. 224–32.

Palmer, Mrs. John M. "The Illinois State Capitol Grounds," *Illinois State Historical Society Journal*, no. 15 (3–4), October 1922–January 1923, pp. 601–3.

"A Primer of Assassination Theories," *Esquire*, no. 66, December 1966, pp. 205–10+.

"The Progress of the World: The President's Illness and Death," *American Review of Reviews*, no. 68, September 1923, pp. 226–32.

Robertson, D., and P. Robertson. "Journey's End," *American Heritage*, no. 33, April/May 1982, p. 82.

Roosevelt, Elliott. "Why Stalin Never Forgave Eleanor Roosevelt," *Parade*, February 9, 1986, pp. 14–17.

Roscoe, T. "The Abraham Lincoln Murder

Case," *Reader's Digest*, no. 76, February 1960, pp. 248–50+.
Rosenbaum, Ron. "Still on the Case," *Texas Monthly*, no. 11, November 1983, pp. 152–7+.
Russell, Francis. "The Four Mysteries of Warren Harding," *American Heritage*, no. 14, April 1963, pp. 4–9+.
Smith, A. Merriman. "Death of a Leader," *Coronet*, no. 27, April 1950, pp. 58–61.
Stiles, Lela. "The Day FDR Died," *Saturday Evening Post*, no. 227, April 16, 1955, pp. 22–23+.
"Strange History Brought to Life," *Life*, no. 54, February 15, 1963, pp. 83–85+.
Taft, Charles Sabin. "Abraham Lincoln's Last Hours," *Century*, no. 45, February 1893, pp. 634–6.
"Undedicated Memorial," *Outlook and Independent*, no. 156, October 22, 1930, pp. 289–90.
"U.S. Closes Ranks Under Truman After Shock of Roosevelt's Death," *Newsweek*, no. 25, April 23, 1945, pp. 26–33.
Van Ark, Dorothy H. "New Light on Lincoln's Death," *Saturday Evening Post*, no. 216, February 12, 1944, p. 82.
Weik, Jess W. "A New Story of Lincoln's Assassination," *Century*, no. 77, April 1909, pp. 917–8.
Wilbur, Ray Lyman. "The Last Illness of a Calm Man," *Saturday Evening Post*, no. 196, October 13, 1923, p. 64.

Newspapers and News Magazines

Buffalo Courier
Buffalo Evening News
Buffalo Express
Buffalo News
Dallas Morning News
Dallas Times Herald
Fort Worth Press
Fort Worth Star Telegram
Frank Leslie's Illustrated Newspaper
Harper's Weekly
The Independent
The Literary Digest
Louisville Courier-Journal
Louisville Daily Journal
Louisville Journal
Louisville Times
The Nation
National Intelligencer
New York Herald
New York Times
New York Tribune
Niles National Register
The Outlook
Review of Reviews

Government Publications

Army Pamphlet 1-1. State, Official and Special Military Funerals.
Decisions of the First Comptroller in the Department of the Treasury, Washington, D.C.: U.S. Government Printing Office, 1882.
Hearings Before the President's Commission on the Assassination of President Kennedy, Washington, D.C.: U.S. Government Printing Office, 1964.
House Document Numbers 5, 21 and 55, First Session, 27th Congress, Serial 392, May 31–September 13, 1841.
Lincoln Tomb State Historic Site. Illinois Historic Preservation Agency, State of Illinois, 1993.
Report of the President's Commission on the Assassination of President Kennedy, Washington, D.C.: U.S. Government Printing Office, 1964.
Report of the Select Committee on Assassinations of the U.S. House of Representatives, Washington, D.C.: U.S. Government Printing Office, 1979.
The Story of Franklin D. Roosevelt, Warm Springs and the Little White House. Georgia Department of Natural Resources, 1987.
United States Code, Title 18, Part I, Chapter 41, Section 871.
United States Code, Title 18, Part I, Chapter 84, Section 1751.
United States Code, Title 18, Part II, Chapter 203, Section 3056.

Internet Sources

Barbian, Jonas T., and Paul S. Sledzik. "From Privates to Presidents: Past and Present Memoirs." <http://nmhm.washingtondc museum/collection/archives/aproducts/a atlas>
"Boxes of Kennedy Documents Found in Dallas Courthouse." <http://nydailynews.

com/news/us world/2008/02/18/2008-02-18>

"The Case of the Failed Hand Grenade Attack." <http://www.fbi.gov/page2/jan06/grenadeattack011106.htm>

"Cemeteries—Zachary Taylor National Cemetery—Burial and Memorials." <http://www.cem.va.gov/CEM/cems/nchp/zacharytaylor.asp>

"Charge and Specification Against David T. Herold et al." <http://www.surratt.org/documents/dcharges.html>

"Coffin Used to Transport Kennedy's Body Sunk at Sea." <http://www.cnn.com/ALLPOLITICS/stories/1999/06/01/kennedy.papers/index.html>

"David Kalakaua." http://www.hawaiihistory.com/index.cfm?fuseaction=ig.page&pageID=404

Find a Grave. <http://www.findagrave.com/php/famous>

"Guiteau's Assassination of President Garfield." <http://www.click2biography.com/charles guiteau>

Haines, D.E. "Spitzka and Spitzka on the Brains of the Assassins of Presidents." <http://www.ncbi.nlm.nih.gov/entrez/query>

"How Alexander Graham Bell Helped Kill the President." <http://home.nycap.rr.com/useless/garfiled.html>

"Kennedy Presidential Limousine." <http://www.thehenryford.org/research/kennedylimo.aspx>

"Life and Death in the White House, James A. Garfield." <http://americanhistory.si.edu/presidency/3d1d.html>

Mikkelson, Barbara. "The Curse of Tecumseh." <http://www.snopes.com/history/american/curse.asp>

"The President John F. Kennedy Assassination Records Collection." <http://www.archives.gov/research/jfk/>

"Protection of the White House Complex in the Twentieth Century." <http://prop1.org/park/pave/rev9.htm>

Rhode, Michael G. "Foreword to *Photographic Atlas of Civil War* Injuries, by Bradley P. Bengston and Julia E. Kuz." <http://nmhm.washingtondcmuseum/collection/archival/aproducts/aatlas>

"Secret Service History." <http://secretservice.gov/history.shtml>

"State Funerals Bound by Rules, History, Judgment," Associated Press article of June 8, 2004. <http://www.msnbc.msn.com/id/5151474/>

"United States Secret Service: Protective Mission." <http://www.treas.gov/usss/protection.shtml>

Whyte, Nicholas. "The Curse of the Presidents." <http://www.nicholaswhyte.info/curse.htm>

"Zachary Taylor: Action of Congress Following the Death of President Taylor"; "Zachary Taylor: Announcement to the Vice-President of the Death of President Taylor." <http://www.presidency.ucsb.edu/ws/index.php?pid>

Index

Numbers in ***bold italics*** indicate pages with photographs.

Adams, John Quincy 17, 29, 36, 37, 38, 40, 42, 54
Alaska 150
Albany, NY 79–80
anarchy 125, 129, 131
Arlington National Cemetery 12, 93, 201–2, 203–5, ***205***, 208, 211
Arthur, Chester A. 9, 21, 96, 99, 102–4, 106–10, ***107***, 118, 131
assassination attempts 16, 17, 19, 23–5, 58
assassins: Booth, John Wilkes 93–4; Czolgosz, Leon F. 147–8; Guiteau, Charles J. 121; Oswald, Lee Harvey 210–1
Atzerodt, George 64, 87, 93
autopsies: Booth 94; Garfield 103, ***103***, 104, 116; Harding 154, 166; Harrison 36; Kennedy 196, 197–8, 208, 209, ***209***; Lincoln 68; McKinley 132–3, 141; Oswald 211; Roosevelt 177–8, 187

Baltimore, MD 19, 35, 37, 40, 42, 55, 75, 94, 106, 110, 139, 163, 184
Baltimore and Potomac Railroad Station 96, ***97***, 106, 110, ***117***, 118
Blaine, James G. 96–7, ***97***, 102, 106, ***107***, 108, 115, 121
Bliss, Dr. D.W. 98, 99, 100, 102, ***117***
Boone, Dr. Joel T. 26, 151, 152, 160
Booth, John Wilkes 5–6, 19–20, 60–2, ***61***, 64, 80, 86, 91, 93–4, ***93***, 121
Brady, John F. 102, 108
Buchanan, James 26, 40, 76
Buffalo, NY 12, 48, 67, 80, 123–36, ***124***, ***135***, 144–5
burial *see* funerals; reburial
Bush, George W. 13, 17, 24–5

Calhoun, John C. 43
Canton, OH 12, 132, 134, 140–4, ***141***, 163
Capitol, U.S. 12, 17, 31, 40, 41, 52, 69, 73–4, 105, 106–10, 132, 137–9, 159–62, 166, 171, 176, 202–3
Cermak, Anton 23
Charles City, VA 35
Chicago, IL 70, 81–2, 156, 157–8, 162, 212
Churchill, Winston 176, 171, 187
Cincinnati, OH 41, 42, 43, 55, 67, 75, 81, 109
Cleveland, Grover 21, 27, 80, 135, 137, 138, 144
Cleveland, OH 12, 21–2, 95, 105, 108, 111–5, ***115***, ***119***
Clinton, William J. (Bill) 24
Columbus, OH 80–1
communism 11, 125, 196
Compromise of 1850 4, 9, 56
Confederacy 5, 8, 19, 67, 86, 87, 93
Congressional Burial Ground 36, 40, 41, 51, 53–4, 55, 69
Connally, John 190, 191, 192, 208
conspiracy theories 4–7; Harding death 166–7; Harrison death 43–5; Kennedy death 194, 208–10; Lincoln death 67–8, 86–7; McKinley death 125, 129, 145; Roosevelt death 187; Taylor death 56–7
Constitution, U.S. 7, 8, 15, 29–30, 70, 87, 108
Coolidge, Calvin 10, 153–4, 155, 157, 158, 160, 161, 162, 165, 166, 168
Coolidge, John 153
Cortelyou, George 123, 124–5, 126, 129, 130
Cranch, William 37, 50
Cuba, Cuban 6, 11
Czolgosz, Leon F. 6, 22, 125–7, ***126***, 128, 131, 145, 147–8, ***147***

Dallas, TX 24, 189, 190–6, ***191***, ***192***, ***193***, 198, 202, 207, 209–12
Davis, Jefferson 48, 52
Dealey Plaza 190–2, ***191***, ***192***, 198, 207, 209–10

243

deaths: Booth 94; Czolgosz 148; Garfield 100, *101*; Guiteau 121; Harding 152; Harrison 34, *35*; Kennedy 194; Lincoln 65–6, *66*; McKinley 130; Oswald 202, 211; Roosevelt 173–5; Ruby 212; Taylor 49, *49*
Dye, John S. 43

Early, Stephen T. 152, 175–8
East Room of White House 12, 38, 51–2, 69, 70–2, 137, 158–60, *159*, 180, 182–3, *184*, 199–200, *201*, 202
Edison, Thomas A. 164, 165
Eisenhower, Dwight D. 21, 26, 177, 200, 201, 204, 206, 210
Elberon, NJ 99–106, 118; *see also* Long Branch, NJ
embalming 83; Garfield 104; Harding 154; Kennedy 198–9; Lincoln 68–9; McKinley 133; Roosevelt 177–8, 183, 187
Erie, PA 18, 48
exhumation: Oswald 211; Taylor 56–7

Federal Bureau of Investigation (FBI) 25, 211
Fillmore, Millard 4, 8–9, 49–54, *49*, 56, 67, 80
Firestone, Harvey 164, 165
Ford, Gerald R. 14, 24, 208
Ford, Henry 164, 165
Ford's Theater 19, 59–64, *61*, *63*, 68, 87–8, 91, 93–4
Fort Worth, TX 211
funerals: Garfield 114–5, *115*; Harding 165–6; Harrison 40; Kennedy 204–5, *205*; Lincoln 84–6; Lincoln's cross-country ceremonies 20, 74–86; McKinley 143–4; Oswald 211; Roosevelt 185–7 *186*; Ruby 212; state funeral policy 217–27; Taylor 53–4; *see also* reburial

Garfield, Eliza 112, 113–4
Garfield, Harry 96, 98, 106, 109, 112–4, *115*
Garfield, James Abram 5, 9, 12, 13, 18, 20, 27, 92, 95–121, *117*, 131, 138, 148, 155, *159*; artifacts related to assassination 118; autopsy *103*, 104, 116; burial 114, *115*; cause of death 116; controversy over doctors' treatment 115–6; death 100, *101*; early career 95; embalming 104; final illness 99–100; gravesite 118–20, *119*, *120*; illnesses 95; lying in state 105, *107*, *117*, 108–10, 112–14; shooting of 96–8, *97*; will 120
Garfield, James R. (son) 96, 98, 112–4, *115*, 118
Garfield, Lucretia Rudolph (wife of the president) 96, 98, 100, *101*, 105, 106, 109, 112–4, *115*, 120; death 120
Garfield, Mollie 96, 98, 100, *101*, 109, 110
Goldman, Emma 145
Gore, Albert 13

Granbury, TX 94
Grant, Ulysses S. 59, 71, 72, 73, 74, 86, 105, 106, *107*, 108, 109, 155
graves: Booth 94; Czolgosz 148; Garfield 118–20; Harding *167*, 168; Harrison 43, *44*; Kennedy *205*, 207–8; Lincoln *85*, *90*, 91; McKinley *146*, 147; Oswald 211; Roosevelt *186*, 187, *188*; Ruby 212; Taylor 55–6, *56*
Guiteau, Charles J. 5, 20, 95–8, *97*, 103, 104, *117*, 121, 148

Hall, Dr. James C. 33. 8, 66
Harding, Florence Mabel Kling DeWolfe (wife of the president) 149, 152, 154–68, 180; death 167–8
Harding, George T. 153, 157, 163, 165, 166, 168
Harding, Warren Gamaliel 4, 5, 10, 12, 13, 18, 23, *92*, 93, 149–68, 175, 180; alleged poisoning 152, 166–7; autopsy not performed 154, 166; burial 165–6; cause of death 152, 154; controversy over doctors' treatment 151; death 152; early career 149; embalming 154; final illness 150–2; funeral in Marion, OH 165–6; funeral in San Francisco 155–6; gravesite *167*, 168; illnesses 150; lying in state 154–5, 158–60, *159*, 161–2, 163–5; reburial 168; scandals 149–50, 166; will 168
Harris, Clara 59, 60, *61*, 62, 64
Harrisburg, PA 55, 75–6, 110, 139
Harrison, Anna Tuthill Symmes (wife of the president) 34, 35, 41, 45; death 43
Harrison, Benjamin 30, 43, 91, 120
Harrison, John Scott 30, 41
Harrison, William Henry 4, 7, 8, 11, 12–3, 18, 29–45, *32*, 46, 54, 56, 58, 66; alleged poisoning of 43–5; autopsy 36; burial 40; cause of death 43–5; death 34, *35*; early career 31; final illness 31–4; funeral 38–40; gravesite 43, *44*; illnesses 31; lying in state 37; reburial 42–3; will 45
Hayes, Rutherford B. *107*, 108, 109, 111, 113, 120, 122, 130, 155
Hazel, John R. 131–2
health care of presidents *see* medical care
Herold, David 64, 87, 93, 94
Hoehling, A.A. 154
Hoover, Herbert 26, 150, 151, 152, 153, 155, 168, 200, 203
House Select Committee on Assassinations 209–10
Hughes, Sarah T. 196
Hyde Park, NY 180, 185–8, *186*

Indianapolis, IN 81

Jackson, Andrew 17, 21, 36, 58, 68, 95
Jefferson, Thomas 17

Index

Johnson, Andrew 9, 54, 65, 67, 72, 74, 86, 87, 93, 94
Johnson, Lyndon B. 11, 190, 192, 195–7, 200, 201, 203, 204, 206, 208, 210

Kalakaua, King David 155
Kennedy, Edward M. 200, 203, 206
Kennedy, Jacqueline Lee Bouvier (wife of the president) 189–206, *205*; death 208
Kennedy, John Fitzgerald 5, 6–7, 10–11, 12, 13, 18, 21, 23, 24, 27, 93, 189–212; artifacts related to assassination 207; autopsy 196, 197–8, 209, *209*; burial *205*, 206; cause of death 198; conspiracy theories 194, 208–10; death 194; embalming 198–9; gravesite 204–6, *205*, 207–8; illnesses 189–90; lying in state 199–200, *201*, 202; reburial 207–8; shooting of 190–2, *192*; will 208
Kennedy, John F., Jr. 200, 204
Kennedy, Robert F. 13, 23, 197, 198, 199, 202, 203, 206
Kennedy, Rose 200, 203, 206
King, Rev. Dr. Martin Luther, Jr. 13
Ku Klux Klan (KKK) 165

Lancaster, PA 40, 76
Lawrence, Richard 17
laws: presidential assassination, assault 213–4; Secret Service 215–7; threats against the president 214–5
Leale, Dr. Charles A. 62–4
Lennon, John 14
Lincoln, Abraham 5–6, 9, 13, 18, 19–20, 21 44, 50, 58–94, 96, 107, 111, 116, 155, 138, 159, 199, 203; artifacts related to assassination 87–8; attempt to steal body of 12, 89, 121; attempted assassinations 58; autopsy 68; body transported and displayed in different cities 75–83; burial, initial 85–6; cause of death 62, 68; death 65–6, *66*; early career 58–9; embalming 68–9; gravesite *85*, *90*, 88–91; illnesses 58–9; lying in state in Capitol 74; lying in state in White House 72; photo in death 77, *78*; reburials 89–91; shooting of 61, *61*; will 88
Lincoln, Mary Todd (wife of the president) 59, 61, *61*, 64–6, 68, 69–70, 71, 73, 77, 84, 88; death 89
Lincoln, Robert Todd 65–6, 72, 73, 75, 84, 85, 86, 88, 90–3, *92*, 102
Lincoln, Tad 71, 73, 84, 85–6, 88, 89
Lincoln, Willie 59, 74, 85, 89
Little White House *see* Warm Springs, GA
Long Branch, NJ 96, 99, 100, 104, 106, 118; *see also* Elberon, NJ
Louisville, KY 42, 55–7, *56*

Madison, James 7, 18, 21, 30
Malcolm X 13
Marion, OH 12, 153, 154, 157, 162–8, *164*, *167*
McIntire, Dr. Ross 170–1, 174–8
McKinley, Ida Saxton (wife of the president) 123, 128, 129, 130, 131, 134, 136–7, 139, 140, 141, 142, 147; death 146–7
McKinley, William 5, 6, 10, 12, 13, 17, 18, 22, 27, 91, 92, 120, 122–48, *124*, 155, 159, 163; artifacts related to assassination 144; autopsy 132–3, 141; burial 143; cause of death 133, 146; controversy over doctors' treatment 145–6; death 130; early career 122; embalming 133; final illness 129–30; funeral 142–3; gravesite *146*, 147; illnesses 122, 146; lying in state 135–9, *138*, 140–1; reburial 147; shooting of 125–6, *126*; surgery 127–8; will 147
medical care 16, 25–8; Garfield 97–100, 115–8; Harding 151–2; Harrison 32–3, 43; Kennedy 192–4; Lincoln 62–6; McKinley 127–8, 129, 145–6; Roosevelt 170–1, 174–5; Taylor 47–9
memorials 43, *44*, 55, 89–91, 112, 118–20, *119*, *120*, 147, *167*, 168, 187, 206–7
Miami, FL 23
Michigan City, IN 81
Milburn, John 123, 124–5, *124*, 145
Miller, Dr. Thomas 26, 32–3
Monroe, James 18, 26
monuments *see* memorials
murder *see* shooting

Nation, Carry 129
National Gallery of Art 118
New York, NY 26, 35, 40, 54, *54*, 66, 67, 77–9, *78*, *79*, 96, 99, 102, 104, 106, 153, 162, 184–5, 208
Niagara Falls, NY 48, 125, 127
Nixon, Richard 204
North Bend, OH 34, 41, 42–45, *44*

oath of office: Arthur 102, 108; Coolidge 153–4; Fillmore 50; Johnson, A. 67; Johnson, L. 195, 196; Roosevelt, T. 131–2; Truman 176; Tyler 37–8
Obama, Barack 27
Onassis, Jacqueline Lee Bouvier Kennedy *see* Kennedy, Jacqueline Lee Bouvier
Oswald, Lee Harvey 6–7, 194–5, 196, 200, 202, 207, 208–12, *210*

Paine, Lewis *see* Powell, Lewis
Palace Hotel, San Francisco 151–6, 168
Pan American Exposition 22, 92, 123–8, *124*, 131, 133, 136, 144
Parkland Memorial Hospital 192–6, *193*, 202, 211, 212

Pasadena, CA 120
Petersen House 64–5, **66**, 68, 88
Philadelphia, PA 26, 35, 40, 76–7, 106, 184
Pierce, Franklin 21, 67
Pittsburgh, PA 55, 75, 81, 110–1, 139–40, 163
Plymouth Notch, VT 153
poisoning plots, alleged: against Harding 167; against Harrison 43–5; against Roosevelt 187; against Taylor 56–7
Poland 172
Powell, Lewis 64, 87, 93
presidential curse *see* zero-year curse
presidential succession 15–6, 108–9
protection of the president 15–28, 118, 123, 145; *see also* Secret Service

Rathbone, Henry R. 59, 60, 61–2, **61**, 64
Reagan, Ronald 13, 14, 16, 19, 21, 24, 45
reburial 12, 42–3; Booth 94; Garfield 119–20, Harding 168; Harrison 42–3; Kennedy 207–8; Lincoln 88–91; McKinley 147; Oswald 211; Taylor 54–5, 56–7
Rising, Clara 56–7
Rixey, Dr. Presley M. 26, 128, 130, 134, 137, 140
Roosevelt, Anna (daughter) 172, 180, 181, 183
Roosevelt, Anna Eleanor *see* Roosevelt, Eleanor
Roosevelt, Eleanor (wife of the president) 169, 172, 175, 176, 177–87, **186**, **187**; death 187
Roosevelt, Elliott 187
Roosevelt, Franklin Delano 5, 10, 12, 18, 23, 27, 152, 169–88, **174**, 198; autopsy not performed 177–8, 187; burial 185–7, **186**; cause of death 177; controversy over doctors' treatment 170–1; death 173–5; early career 169–70; embalming 177–8, 183, 187; final illness 170–5; gravesite **186**, 187, **188**; illnesses 170–1; love affair 169, 172, 180; lying in state 182–4, **184**, will 188
Roosevelt, James 171, 180
Roosevelt, Theodore 10, 22, 23, 79, 93, 128, 130–2, 134–40, 142, 143, 145, 147
Root, Elihu 102, 131–2
Rotunda, U.S. Capitol 12, 41, 73, 107–10, **107**, **117**, 138–9, **138**, 159–62, 203; *see also* Capitol, U.S.
Rubinstein, Jacob *see* Ruby, Jack
Ruby, Jack 202, 209, 211, 212, **212**
Russia 11, 176; *see also* USSR
Rutherford, Lucy Mercer 172, 173, **174**, 180

St. John Paul the Great 14
San Francisco, CA 14, 151–6, 162, 165
Sawyer, Dr. Charles 151, 152, 153, 154, 158, 160, 167
Seattle, WA 150
Secret Service 21–5, 96, 123, 124–5, 145, 160, 171, 173, 175, 177, 178, 185, 190, 192, 194, 195, 196, 208; laws pertaining to 215–7
Seward, William 64, 65, 67, 87, 93
shooting: of Booth 94; of Garfield 97, **97**; of Kennedy 190–2, **192**; of Lincoln 61–2; **61**; of McKinley 125–6, **126**; of Oswald 202, 210–1; of prominent persons 13–4
slavery 4, 8, 9, 50, 56, 59
Sousa, John Philip 106
Soviet Union *see* USSR
Springfield, IL 12, 59, 69–70, 72, 74, 81, 82–6, **85**, 93
Stalin, Josef 171–2, 176, 187
Stanton, Edwin M. 6, 59, 65, 67, 68–9, 77, 86, 93
stock exchanges 66, 104, 113, 144, 166
Stone, Harlan F. 176
succession, presidential *see* presidential succession
Surratt, John 87
Surratt, Mary 87
Swaim, David 100

Taft, William Howard 22, **92**, 153, 158, 160, 161, 165, 166, 202
Taney, Roger B. 37
Taylor, Margaret Mackall Smith (wife of the president) 49, **49**, 50–1, 52, 54; death 55
Taylor, Zachary 4–5, 8, 12, 13, 18, 45, 46–57, **47**, 58, 66; alleged poisoning 56–7; burial 54; cause of death 49, 56–7; death 49, **49**; early career 46; exhumation 56–7; final illness 47–9; funeral 53–4; gravesite 55–6, **56**; illnesses 46; lying in state 51–2; reburial 55; will 57
Tbilisi, Republic of Georgia 24–5
Tecumseh 12–3; *see also* zero-year curse
Texas School Book Depository **191**, 194–5, 207, 208
Tippecanoe 12–3, 31; *see also* zero-year curse
Tippitt, J.D. 194, 200, 210, 211
tomb *see* grave
Truman, Harry S 10, 15, 23–4, 171, 175–6, 181–6, **188**, 200, 204, 206
twenty-year curse *see* zero-year curse
Tyler, John 7–9, 17, 29–30, 34–43, 50
Tyler, Julia 67

undertakers 36, 50–1, 72, 75, 77, 83, 104, 105, 109, 113, 120, 132, 133, 141, 154, 177–8, 179, 183, 196, 198–9, 204, 206, 210
USSR 6, 176, 187, 192; *see also* Russia

Van Buren, Martin 17, 26, 31, 40

Waite, Morrison K. 106, 108, 113
Wallace, George 14, 23

Warm Springs, GA 18, 172–9, *173*, *174*, 188
Warren, Earl 208; *see also* Warren Report
Warren Report 7, 208–9
Washington, George 18, 25–6, 41, 43, 60, 69
White House Medical Unit (WHMU) 27
wills: Garfield 120; Harding 168; Harrison 45; Kennedy 208; Lincoln 88; McKinley 147; Roosevelt 188; Taylor 57
Wilson, Woodrow 144, 150, 155, 160

Yalta Conference 171–2

zero-year curse 12–3, 45

www.ingramcontent.com/pod-product-compliance
Ingram Content Group UK Ltd.
Pitfield, Milton Keynes, MK11 3LW, UK
UKHW041937140426
5217IPUK00014B/525